FENG
SHUI

ANGEL THOMPSON

Photographs by Angel Thompson
Illustrations by Gabriel Jorge Ruspini
and Karen McCauley

FENG
SHUI

HOW TO ACHIEVE THE MOST
HARMONIOUS ARRANGEMENT OF
YOUR HOME AND OFFICE

ST. MARTIN'S GRIFFIN / NEW YORK

Design by Pei Loi Koay

Illustrations on pages 22, 183 copyright © 1996 by Gabriel Jorge Ruspini.
Illustrations on pages 46, 53, 64, 66, 175, 176, 177, 178 copyright © 1996 by Karen McCauley.

Library of Congress Cataloging-in-Publication Data
Thompson, Angel.
      Feng shui : how to achieve the most harmonious arrangement
   of your home and office   /   by Angel Thompson.
            p. cm.
         ISBN 0-312-14333-8
         1. Feng shui. I. Title
BF1779.F4T43   1996
133.3'33—dc20   96-4357
                                                          CIP

First St. Martin's Griffin Edition: August 1996

10   9   8   7   6

*This book is dedicated to all those
who seek the truth and who choose
to emulate, imitate, and reflect
the exquisite everlasting balance and harmony
of Mother Nature.*

I wish to convey my special thanks to the following:

- my mother, Theresa, and my father, Frank, for doing their part in the life cycle and bringing me into this world
- my son, Seth, whose inquiring mind and infinite patience with the fish pond led me to a realization of how nature works
- my daughter, Lily, and her ability to scrutinize and synthesize
- Karen McCauley, for her Herculean editing skills and common sense
- Mikey, whose wisdom and advice put me on the right track
- Tad, Noel, and Marion, who believed in me
- my family—Jo, Frankie, Shane, Herman, Beth, Kate, Jill, Kelly, and Paul—for their unconditional love and support
- all my students, clients, and friends for their enthusiasm and encouragement
- Barbara Anderson, editor, and Joy Chang, assistant editor, at St. Martin's Press, for their support and patience.

Your space is your kingdom. How you arrange that space and what is included in it determine whether energy flows freely around you. Free-flowing energy is like a river, stocked with Mother Nature's gifts of health, prosperity, and well-being. Feng shui is the guest, bringing this gift of life into your home, your office, everywhere you are, all the time.

Everybody wants prosperity. That's obvious. How to achieve it is the tricky part. What would you think if someone said you could improve your life by buying just a few goldfish or a houseplant, or by simply changing the month on the calendar hanging on the kitchen wall? Would you think that the advice was crazy? Surprisingly, such simple acts as these can produce very powerful effects. Consider the following scenarios:

- Mary has been out of work for months. A few days after hanging a small mirror behind her stove, she gets a new job.
- Thomas has been widowed for five years. He's ready to meet someone and start a new life, but for some reason it's just not happening. He plants some red flowers near his front door. In a matter of hours, an interesting neighbor stops by to give him a freshly baked pie.
- Cindy and Steve are frustrated. They have been trying to sell their house for more than a year, but potential buyers have shown no interest. They fix the broken front gate, and within days the house is sold.

Coincidence? Not to students of feng shui (pronounced *fung-shway*). Feng shui, which translates as "wind and water," is an ancient Chinese practice that considers the environment to be a metaphor for everything that occurs in your life. Are you feeling depressed? Maybe the bushes framing the windows have grown so tall that they block the sun. Do you feel that your purse or pocket has a mysterious hole in it through which money just disappears? Check the plumbing for leaks or dripping faucets. Does your life seem complicated, jumbled, or messy? Perhaps it's time to clean your car or house.

Feng shui is based on the idea that the energy, or *chi* (pronounced *chee*), in every space has its own personality. Those who occupy the space reflect the personality of the *chi* in it. When the space you live or work in is arranged in harmony with nature, life can be good.

Feng shui has long been used in the Orient. It is a belief that the auspicious placement of buildings, doors, and furniture can ensure a happy life. Now this ancient art is helping people throughout the world change their luck and improve their lives. Feng shui can effect immediate change, something no other philosophy, traditional discipline, or practice can claim to do. Anyone who's tried to make a major change in his or her life or behavior knows what a long, slow, and difficult process it can be. Feng shui helps you change—easily, simply, quickly, and, best of all, painlessly. It's a fast-acting method for getting the results you desire.

For centuries, the Chinese have known that when you are willing to change the outside, inner change is already beginning to occur. Change your surroundings and you change your life. How can this be, when we have been taught to believe that what is inside of us creates both our destiny and the quality of our lives? We have spent decades investigating the inner self, thousands of dollars on therapies to cure childhood traumas, and endless hours confessing our addictive behavioral patterns to anyone who will listen. We've blamed our problems on the government, karma, past lives, our horoscopes, Mom's cooking, and even God. Why is it, though, that we haven't considered the space we call home or the place where we work as contributing to the cause of our problems?

Many people say, "I hate my job," when in fact it may not be the job or boss that is bothering them but the workplace. We talk about the environment as if it were something far removed from our day-to-day lives. We pledge to save the rain forest and quit killing trees, but what do we do about our own space? Doesn't that need saving? By wisely choosing where your home or business is located, and thoughtfully organizing its interior design, you can bring good fortune and happiness into your life. Good feng shui keeps the good energy flowing freely through a building, creating harmony and facilitating communication among those who live or work there.

The feng shui masters in Hong Kong, Taiwan, Singapore, and other places with large Chinese populations can measure a building's ability to attract riches and prosperity based on its shape, direction, and location. Despite high fees, feng shui masters are in great demand, because when their advice is followed, prosperity and success are the typical results.

Traditional feng shui has its roots in the Tao, which means the "way of nature." By watching the many cycles of the physical universe, including those of the heavens and stars, the visible and the invisible, the shadow and the light, Chinese philosophers perceived a rhythm connecting humanity with nature and confirming that the laws of nature were also the laws of life. In rural China five thousand years ago, a system was developed to enhance that connection. Elements within the landscape—specifically Water, Earth, Metal, Wood, and Fire—helped them to describe the basic nature or personality of a specific place and provided them with signs and symbols to interpret. Life imitated nature. Mountains were like dragons; the rivers were their blood. This was a simple way to understand and cooperate with the powerful forces of nature.

Growing towns and cities destroyed the natural features of the landscape, and as the people migrated to the flat, central plains of China, the feng shui School of the Compass emerged. Instead of using natural features in the landscape to define a location's personality, the School of the Compass used directions (north, south, east, and west) to locate and describe a specific place. The compass directions were derived from watching the sun's daily travels through the sky from the east, where it rose each day; through the south, which received its light; to the west, where it set at twilight; and to the north, where it was invisible at night. Each direction then became associated with a specific type of energy. As life became more complicated, intermediate directions (southeast, northeast, southwest, and northwest) were added to give more specific orientation and detail.

Since 1975, the Tantric Buddhist Black Sect has contributed to traditional feng shui by the use of religious, spiritual, and magical practices, prayers and chants to break bad spells, chase away ghosts, or purify and bless surroundings. The sect has been very sympathetic to the need of Westerners to interpret traditional Chinese concepts through contemporary thought and practice.

Feng shui is a quasi-scientific technique that analyzes the environment and interprets natural earth forms through a mix of geomancy and architectural fortune-telling. Although it is mystical and creative, it is also consummately practical. The goal is to have our personal environments imitate the harmony and balance of the natural environment. The texts are ancient, the classroom is the world of nature and the space you're in, here and now, the knowledge is based on universal truth and can be experienced by everyone. It is open, reliable, available, and applicable. Aesthetics, energy flow, and common sense are the basis for the advice offered by feng shui practitioners.

Anyone can easily improve the quality of his or her life by paying attention to the subtle influences in the environment. A dripping faucet not only wastes water but also correlates with resources dripping away. The desk chair with the broken leg may keep you and your work off balance. A mirror hung too low can reflect the fact that you are "losing your head" or don't have a clear picture of yourself. Many of the little things we take for granted, ignore or overlook can explain the problems in our lives. We step over boxes in the doorway, sit in the dark, and adapt to most conditions as fast as we can. We are skilled in our ability to deny what is happening and not to see what is right in front of our noses. We can adjust to the worst circumstances, get comfy, and call it home because we have been trained to expect and accept, ignore and adapt to, all the obstacles in our environment. But should we?

Sensitive people respond to energy all the time whether they realize it or not. Doctors advise a change of scenery to a distressed patient; a friend suggests a change in hairstyle or the purchase of a luxury item to make you feel better. Flowers brighten up the sickroom; fans circulate stale air; doorbells announce the presence of visitors.

Most intuitive people recognize feng shui as something they have naturally practiced and report that they can tell good space from bad. To those, feng shui gives a language for describing what they intuit; to others, it provides a conscious way to embrace nature and improve the quality of life.

We live at a time of planetary and environmental crisis, when knowledge of feng shui, the ultimate authority on the environment, can contribute greatly to global healing. For the past five hundred years, we have looked away from nature, turning our gaze instead toward industrial and electronic progress and claiming to be unique and superior. Although our efforts to control nature have created the modern world, control is an illusion, often shattered by devastating floods, earthquakes, tornadoes, and other devices Mother Nature uses to maintain balance and harmony.

We can't turn back the clock of progress, nor would we want to. Modern life with all its conveniences is great. What we can do, however, is acknowledge and respect the natural laws that establish balance and harmony. As we accept and embrace our connection to Mother Nature, we become eligible to receive the gifts she bestows on all her children—the treasure of a long, prosperous, and peaceful life. This book can help you do that. Use it as a guide to develop a relationship with Nature, yourself, and the space you inhabit. In the long run, this is the only relationship in life that is eternal.

There is infinitely more to feng shui than the simple practices outlined in this book. Feng shui is a lifetime study. It has been my experience, though, that people can profit from the basics without having to delve into the underlying complicated and esoteric philosophy. The system I have developed—a blend of ancient principles and contemporary realities—works without costly renovations. In this book you will find information you can use today. Right now. This minute. Maybe you won't win the lottery or marry a billionaire, but if you regularly use these methods, your life will get better and better. Good luck!

Part 1

FENG SHUI BASICS

Understanding

the Elements

and Directions

USING COLORS, SHAPES, AND DIRECTIONS TO IMITATE NATURE

Where do you go when you want to relax and enjoy yourself? Is it the beach, the mountains, the desert? Some people like the open skies or camping in the woods. Others like the lights of the city or the thrill of amusement parks. Maybe you like to stay home and relax as you're washing dishes, watering your plants, or just taking a walk. Wherever you go to regroup, one thing is certain: Being in this space makes you feel good. It's where you can unwind, relax, and let go of everyday worries and concerns. For now, let's call this special place your private paradise.

What if I told you that you could create the good feelings of this magical space wherever you are? Would you be willing to learn a way of seeing if it would help you do this? If you answered yes, then you are ready for the first step of feng shui—the five elements. The elements hold the answer to why some spaces are good and others are not. As you understand how they work, you can use them to create your private paradise.

The five elements—Wood, Fire, Earth, Metal, and Water—represent everything in the visible and invisible universe, including the directions of the compass. In nature, we see the five elements in their natural forms. Trees and flowers represent Wood, the sun represents Fire, and so on. Landscapes are classified by their predominant element. If you live next to a lake, yours is a Water environment. In the desert, you live in a Fire environment. Buildings and interior rooms are also classified by their predominant element.

In the realm of humanmade objects and spaces, the elements are represented by colors, shapes, and directions. For example, all of the following are classified as Wood element: a building constructed of wood; a tall or rectangular building; a building whose entry faces east; a place where plants are grown or sold; a green-painted building. This means that we can re-create nature indoors, using colors, shapes, and everyday materials.

Let's say your private paradise is the beach. What makes a beach special? Untamed nature and open space, sunlight, palm trees swaying in the breeze, the salty sea, crashing waves, fluffy white clouds, crimson sunsets, gray seagulls, bright striped umbrellas. All of these things contribute to "beach." You may not be able to bring the ocean to your door, but by using colors, shapes, and directions that represent the natural elements of the beach, you can easily re-create its atmosphere.

At the beach, the Wood element provides palm trees, straw mats, and wooden poles supporting cotton umbrellas. Inside, the the color green, organic fabrics, wood furniture, and miniature palm trees can re-create the Wood element. At the beach, the Fire element is seen through the sun, light, heat, crimson sunsets and red sails dotting the landscape, plus all the critters that live in the sea. Inside, lights and heat take the place of the sun, seashells can be used as ornamentation, and pictures of sunsets or red accessories brighten the home and office. At the beach, the sand represents the element Earth. You can use the colors of sand or miniature sand gardens on your desk. To re-create the sparkling sea, use shiny stones and reflective surfaces that twinkle and glitter. You certainly wouldn't want the ocean in the living room, but how about a wave machine, pictures of the crashing surf, or environmental sounds of the sea as background music? By understanding all the correspondences that accompany the elements, it is easy to re-create any atmosphere you desire.

THE FIVE ELEMENTS

There is a rhythm in the universe. Those who live close to nature follow this rhythm consciously. Farmers plant in the spring, grow in the summer, harvest in the fall, and let the land lie dormant all winter. Sailors and fishermen are acutely aware of the movement of the moon, sun, and stars and of how they affect the tides and movement of fish. City dwellers, who live far removed from nature in buildings of steel and glass, are also affected by this rhythm but not on a conscious level. As a result, it is easy for urbanites to be out of step with nature. When this happens, inner rhythms are disrupted, and life can turn discordant and unpleasant.

The Chinese analyzed the rhythm of the universe by observing the movement of the sun and discovered that nature and life also followed this rhythm. Life begins in the morning when the sun rises in the east. During the day, the sun grows in power until it sinks in the west and finally disappears. Clearly, the passage from light to darkness and back to light consists of four stages: a beginning, a middle, a decline, and an end. In nature, the Chinese saw this rhythm expressed through the five elements.

Wood: The Element of Spring

Life is awakened from the deep sleep of winter when the sun announces the arrival of spring. The element WOOD sends out tender green shoots to reach for the light. This energy is similar to the energy at dawn, when the sun rises in the east, announcing the arrival of a new day. It is from these events that the Wood element came to be represented by early morning; spring; everything that grows; the color green; tall, rectangular, treelike shapes; the direction east; and the principle of growth or beginnings.

A Wood landscape is characterized by forests and jungles, many tall trees, and plants or foliage, cultivated or growing organically. A profusion of poles, pillars, posts, or columns also is indicative of a Wood site. Houses constructed primarily of wood (or a picket fence or a forest, for example) belong to the Wood element.

If there is too much Wood in the environment, trim it, cut it down, or remove it. A saw, hatchet, or axe (all Metal items) in the hands of an able-bodied gardener can remove excess plant growth. If you don't want to remove it, the addition of Fire reduces Wood and makes it manageable. Symbolically, you can add Fire with burning incense, lighted candles, decorative swords or knives, electric lights, red flowers, or the color red. If nothing else, you can turn on the lights and turn up the heat.

When there is not enough Wood in the environment, there's nothing to believe in. You might become fearful and anxious, not only of change but also of commitment. With no strong opinions, you might get along with others for a while but end up with an inability to speak out or stand up for yourself. If there is not enough Wood, it is a simple matter to add flowers, plants, bonsai trees, aquatic plants in a bowl of water, a green filing cabinet, or pictures of plants. If living plants are not available, use fruits and vegetables, or dried or artificial plants.

This house looks like it emerged from its Wood environment and is in perfect harmony with it.

This humble wooden fence (top) evokes the sames feeling as the columns from a Greek temple (bottom). Both are Wood-element shapes.

Wood corresponds to the following:

QUALITIES: *Creation, nourishment, upward growth, primal anger*
VIRTUES: *Love of humanity, benevolence, balance between roots and branches/family and career, flexible thinking*
SYMBOL: *Mythical green dragon*
SEASON: *Spring*
DIRECTION: *East*
COLOR: *Green*
TIME: *Early morning, youth*
PLANET: *Jupiter*

Seen from Hong Kong Harbor, these tall buildings are reminiscent of trees in a forest. The Wood-shaped buildings are in harmony with the overall Water landscape (above left). The pagoda of the Temple of the Six Banyan Trees (ca. 537) in Canton, China (above right), is a Wood-shaped building (tall) with balancing details of Water (the curved balconies) and Fire (the spire on the top).

MATERIAL:	*All types of wood; organic natural fibers and fabrics (silk, cotton, linen); vegetables, fruits, herbs, flowers, plants (alive, artificial, or represented in photos or art)*
INTERIORS:	*Dining rooms, children's rooms, bedrooms*
SHAPES AND TYPES:	*Tall, oblong, rectangular, columnar, shapes often used for memorial or religious structures, skyscrapers, high towers*
IDEAL USES:	*All matters related to creativity, nourishment, and growth: nurseries and buildings where plants are grown, such as hothouses; hospitals, nursing homes, healing centers; restaurants, cafés, and catering businesses; manufacturers or retailers of wooden goods; artists' ateliers*

Fire: The Element of Summer

The element FIRE is represented by the sun at its zenith—the middle of the day when the sun is high and hot and bright. This is similar to the energy expressed during the summer, a season of promise and full growth. The sun travels through the southern part of the sky so south came to be known as the direction of Fire. Flames give Fire its red color and triangular, pointed shape.

Landscapes that feature sharply peaked mountains, or buildings with peaked, angled, or sloping roofs, are considered to be Fire sites. The Great Pyramids at Giza, near Cairo, Egypt, are classic Fire-shaped structures. Their closeness to the

The three pyramids at Giza set the standard for the classic Fire shape. Even today, pyramids are believed to have magical properties, including the ability to channel wisdom from heaven to mere mortals on Earth.

Nile created a perfect Fire-Water matrix for life to emerge, and, indeed the Nile flowed through a lush valley.

Fire is the element of understanding, courtesy, and ceremony. A Fire-dominated individual is usually reasonable and able to communicate feelings appropriately. This person holds no grudge and has compassion for others. There is an imbalance in Fire, however, which can manifest as an inability to project oneself forward with passion or spirit. A person working in a kitchen or bakery or other hot, enclosed space, or someone living in the desert or in the shadow of a triangular (Fire)-shaped mountain, would manifest extremes of emotion—from passive and lifeless to manic and overactive.

With lack of Fire, we suffer from stiff joints, dry skin, bad eyes, poor circulation. We may be tired, lack passion, and find it difficult to participate in sex or come to orgasm. We may feel panic and anxiety and fear about the future. If your environment needs Fire, add fish, a birdfeeder or birdhouse, or dogs, cats, or other animals. Or build a fire in the fireplace, have a barbecue, light candles and incense, place red flowers on the desk, bed, or table. Paint the front door red. If you feel you need Fire in your life, go outside during the day and breathe in the light of the sun, an easy way to increase your internal fires.

On the other hand, too much Fire might manifest as a volatile, critical, loud, and obnoxious individual who angrily incites disputes and arguments. If you want to reduce the Fire, add ceramic pots, clay tiles, and other earthy substances or colors. Think of a Mexican hacienda with its tile floors and roofs. There is a good reason tropical places often use tile as a primary building material. Earth materials provide good insulation from the heat of the sun. They make a house cool in summer and warm in winter.

The addition of water will also cool off a hot condition, which is why those same Mexican haciendas always feature a fountain or pool by the front entry. Use water in its many forms—fountains, bowls of water, glass items, or pictures of

The Fire-shaped spires of the castle (top left) reach for heaven, as do the Fire-shaped sails on these boats sailing the Nile (top right). The pinnacles and spires of the west front of the Mormon Temple in Salt Lake City, Utah (bottom left), reach heavenward. The Fire-shaped smokestacks (bottom right) are a modern attempt to connect the god of industry to the gods of the sky.

oceans and lakes. If you feel you have too much Fire, go outside during the night and breathe in the light of the moon. Breathing outside at night is a sure way to calm down. This is an old folk remedy.

Remember, Fire is the element of life and light. Without it, we perish. With it, we blossom and grow. Fire corresponds to the following:

QUALITIES:	*Intelligence, spirit, human and animal life*
VIRTUES:	*Wisdom, reason, etiquette*
SYMBOL:	*Red phoenix*
SEASON:	*Summer*
DIRECTION:	*South*
COLOR:	*Red (any shade, hue, intensity)*
TIME:	*High noon: young adulthood*
PLANET:	*Mars*
MATERIAL:	*Animal products, including leather and wool; anything that generates light or heat; shiny fabrics that reflect light and heat*
INTERIORS:	*Kitchens and other places where cooking takes places; stoves, fireplaces*
SHAPES AND TYPES:	*Pointed, slanted, sharp angles; buildings with sloping roofs; buildings where animals are housed (Fire is associated with animals)*
IDEAL USES:	*Fire-type buildings are suitable for libraries, religious schools, and other places of learning, as well as for businesses involved in design and fashion; manufacturing processes involving fire or furnaces or chemicals; veterinary clinics because of Fire's association with animal life*

Earth: The Element of Indian Summer

Between summer and fall comes Indian summer, a period of calm and stability when the hours of darkness equal the hours of daylight, and when life seems balanced and easy. To the Chinese, this phase was most like EARTH itself—enduring, unchanging, forever supportive of life. It had no direction because it was the center around which we all belonged.

The energy of Earth is reliable, dependable, calm, and centering. The planet Saturn rules Earth and is represented by solidity and security. The color associated with Earth is yellow, probably derived from the yellow soil of China.

The time for the element Earth is the middle of the afternoon, when the high energy of the morning has peaked and is beginning to decline. Earth represents the middle time of life, when experience has, we hope, created wisdom, and the impetuous fires of youth have calmed to a warm glow. All the materials that come from the earth—clay, bricks, concrete, ceramic tile, marble, sand, and rocks—are associated with Earth. The shapes that represent the Earth element are square, box-like, or flat. Landscapes that feature plateaus or flat, featureless areas are Earth land-

Earth landscapes (top) are flat and appear to go on forever. Earth-shaped buildings in an Earth landscape (center) are hardly noticeable. This Japanese temple (below) is a good example of an Earth-shaped building.

Earth-shaped buildings are square with flat tops. A tenement building in Manaus, Brazil (right), is similar in shape to an ancient adobe village in Santa Fe, New Mexico (left).

Blocks of Earth-shaped
buildings march across
the landscape.

scapes, as are flat, low, unadorned, square-shaped, humble structures. Remember the story of the three little pigs? The first pig built his house out of straw, the second out of wood, and the third one built his house of bricks. Of course, the house of bricks lasted the longest. If you want to have a solid and reliable life, live in an Earth-type house.

Earth is represented by sympathy, trust, integrity, and a well-balanced person who is reliable and sincere and handles material resources appropriately. An imbalance in Earth results in either an opportunistic cheapskate or a generous fool who gives away everything. The person with too little Earth will disappear when the check comes. The individual with balanced Earth will divide the check into who ate what, and the individual with too much Earth will offer to pick up the entire check but will have to borrow money from the others to do so.

Living very high up in a tall building or living underground may cause an imbalance in Earth. With too much Earth, we become too stable. We may feel stuck and unable to change. With too little Earth, we may have difficulty attracting money or resources. To create a more balanced environment, add any kind of Metal, such as silver, brass, copper, mirrored or other reflective surfaces, or the color white. The addition of plants or the color green also reduces the imbalance in Earth.

If you feel lethargic or off-balance (like a feather in the wind), or suffer from low self-esteem, lack of direction, and an inability to set goals, there may be too little Earth in your environment. Add Earth in the way of sand and rock gardens, bonsai trees in ceramic bowls, rocks, stone jars, pottery, marble, statuary, or earthy colors of gold, orange, ocher, yellow. Fire increases Earth, so add animal products such as leather, cotton, and wool; or pottery oil lamps; incense; candles; or the color red.

Remember that the element Earth is calm and stable. Without it, we drift. With it, we are able to stand tall. Who could ask for anything better?

Earth is represented by the following:

QUALITIES:	*Sympathy, honesty, faith*
VIRTUES:	*Reliability, responsible handling of material resources*
SYMBOLS:	*Earth, the center*
SEASON:	*Indian summer*
DIRECTION:	*The center or southwest*
COLORS:	*Yellow, earth tones*
TIME:	*Middle of the afternoon; middle of life*
PLANET:	*Saturn*
MATERIALS:	*Clay, bricks, concrete, tile, marble, porcelain, crystal, sand, anything that comes from the earth*
INTERIORS:	*Storage areas, seldom-used lounges, garages, conservatories (when combined with Wood), inner courtyards*
SHAPES AND TYPES:	*Flat, low, unadorned, boxy, or square; appearing to be humble and constructed of bricks, concrete, clay, or other earth materials (even a steep-roofed brick building is still classified as an Earth building)*
IDEAL USES:	*Hospitals, jails, government buildings, or businesses that need to be perceived as solid and enduring; tombs, mausoleums, vaults, and storage buildings; businesses that involve mining or tunneling, the production or sale of ceramics, agriculture, farming, or civil engineering; banks and financial institutions*

Metal: The Element of Fall

At the end of summer, the leaves turn color and frost glistens like diamonds on the grass, announcing the arrival of fall, a season to match the fading light of the sun in the west. The principles of contraction and reduction are at work. Pressure reduced and compressed minerals in the earth, creating metals, which could be extracted, melted, and formed into spades, shovels, and scythes to assist in the harvest. Coins were minted out of silver and gold, so the element METAL became associated with the west, the color silver, and round, coin-like shapes.

A Metal landscape features gently rounded hilltops, like those in Italy's Tuscany region, and is characterized by arches, domes, curves, and buildings made of or trimmed in ferroconcrete, iron, steel, or copper. Rounded and reflective surfaces as well as the underpasses of roadways and building areas, which are usually made of metal, curved or round, are also ruled by the element Metal.

The virtues of Metal are morals, ethics, righteousness, and precise thinking. The element of Metal represents righteousness and purity. Individuals ruled by Metal are able to communicate well and can speak up or be silent when appropriate. There is precise thinking as well as new thoughts and ideas.

Too little Metal makes a person quiet, cautious, and careful. This person is as difficult to get along with as one with too much Metal, who might be talkative, righteous, overly enthusiastic, and unthinking in speech and behavior. Emotional grief is a symptom of a Metal imbalance. There may be an inability to organize thoughts and resources; objects may be lost due to scattered attention and lack of focus. To add Metal to any environment, use the colors white, gray, or black-and-white patterns. Silver trays, metal cookware, brass pots, gold jewelry, wrought-iron railings, steel furniture, metal sculptures—anything made of any kind of metal—can be used. Real or fake money, gold coins, or military or athletic medals can be placed strategically to attract more resources.

Metal represents letting go, withdrawal, and reversal. When you hold on to the past, there might be an excess of Metal with its subsequent problems of constipation, inhibition, or breathing disorders (in acupuncture, Metal is associated with the lungs). Trouble accepting reality manifests as stiff joints and poor circulation. There may be an emphasis on money and the material world. When there is an excess of Metal, make it more manageable by adding a hearth with a blazing fire (or watch a videotape of a fire burning), candles, incense, decorative axes or swords, a red porcelain vase, gold or brass candlesticks, a steel filing cabinet, or an electric stove. Another way to reduce Metal is to add Water in the form of water gardens, fountains or bowls of water, or a glass water dispenser. You could also add the element Earth in the form of sand, rocks, tile, and so on to create a more balanced environment.

Metal enables us to focus and concentrate. If you want to emphasize Metal in your life, wear a metal ring on the finger that represents the activity you desire. Place the ring on your left hand if you're male, the right hand if you're female.

THUMB:	*Personal power*
INDEX FINGER:	*Scholarly success*
THIRD FINGER:	*Stability*
RING FINGER:	*Love*
SMALL FINGER:	*Creativity*

Metal is an important element in our lives because it represents sharp thinking, intense focus, and the ability to come to a conclusion. Endings are just as important as beginnings.

Metal-shaped buildings are round, curved, arched, and domed. Because of Metal's connection with coins, Metal-shaped buildings are ideal for businesses associated with finance and money. One example is the Casino in Avalon, California (bottom), which is a Metal building in a Water environment (very auspicious if the water is clean).

Metal is represented by the following:

QUALITIES: *Reversal and withdrawal*

VIRTUES: *Morality, ethics, righteousness, and precise thinking*

SYMBOL: *The white tiger*

SEASON: *Autumn*

DIRECTION: *West*

COLORS: *White, gray, silver*

TIME: *Sunset*

PLANET: *Venus*

MATERIALS: *Aluminum, ferroconcrete, iron, steel, copper, tin—all types of metal; mirrors made of glass and coated with silver or aluminum; wires that transmit sound, light, or heat; transparent film covered with silver*

INTERIORS: *Workshops or places where tools and knives are used, kitchens, stoves, metal sinks. Be sure to separate your stove and sink with ceramic tile (Earth) because Fire and Metal are competitive.*

SHAPES AND TYPES: *The gently rounded hilltops of the Tuscan countryside, as well as the underpasses of roads and highways; round, curved, and domed roofs; arches; arcades; and semicircles; castles, mansions, and other expensive real estate*

IDEAL USES: *All businesses that deal with financial or civic concerns, as well as for manufacturers of metal jewelry, hardware, knives, and swords. Today, many buildings are made of a combination of Earth and Metal elements. Because Earth and Metal sequence into each other (see page 182), this is regarded as fortunate and produces wealth and financial success. The Metal element, however, is more suitable to commercial and manufacturing buildings than to domestic ones. Metal promises monetary gain, but it is not conducive to simple, everyday life.*

Water: The Element of Winter

The cycle appears to be concluded. All is dark like deep WATER, the final element. It is winter. No sun shines in the far north. Life is hidden beneath the frozen waters of the lake, waiting for spring and the warmth of the sun to give new life. The color associated with Water is black, and its shape is curved, like the flow of a river or the shape of a wave.

Water is the blood of life. Nothing can live without water. The element is represented by communication, the transmission of ideas, wisdom, and social interaction. If there is an imbalance of water, the individual may be lonely and isolated, forgetful, infertile, or impotent. He or she may suffer from rigid joints, dull vision, lack of clarity, insomnia, disturbed dreams, or feelings of inferiority.

A Water-shaped mountain (above) resembles incoming waves. Water-shaped buildings, such as the Sea Ranch Condominium complex north of San Francisco, California (below), have irregular rooflines and appear to sprout from the landscape. Water-shaped building in a Water environment is harmonious.

A Wave-shaped roof in Tahiti (above). A Wave-shaped roof on Bali Way in Marina del Rey, California (below).

When there is too much active Water, the individual is like an ocean—unconfined, overwhelmed, and overpowering. If there is too much water, such as when the roof is leaking, place your plants to catch the water. Wood and Water are harmonious, and Wood will reduce the effect of Water without destroying it. Adding ceramic pots or other items from the earth will sop up extra water. Think of how sandbags hold back the ocean and river floods.

Too little moving water and an individual is like water dripping off rocks, or like a fountain that bubbles constantly yet goes nowhere. Water rules social interaction, and if you want to activate the Water element in your life to be more popular, call someone you haven't talked to in six months. Or make a point to introduce yourself to one new person every time you go out. Make no complaints or requests.

Nonmoving or still water, like lakes, ponds, and pools, represents clarity gained through calmness. Too much still water makes for someone who cannot resolve anything—someone who is always reading deeper meaning into everything and forever pondering the best solution. Too little nonactive water and we become like a muddy pond with narrow vision and poor judgment. An imbalance in Water often coincides with confused thinking. For clarity, place a bowl of clean water next to your bed at night. Visualize your mind being as clear as the water. In the morning, replace the water. Do this until you have attained the clarity you desire. All life needs water to live. It is the essence that feeds and renews the life force. The addition of clean water can improve any environment. It is quite simple to add the Water element to any environment by introducing bowls of clean water, fountains, water coolers, or glass objects such as vases and jars. Adding any kind of object or color from the Metal category encourages the Water to be more present. Remember when you were a kid and ran singing through the rain? There is wisdom in this childlike behavior.

Water is represented by the following:

QUALITIES:	*Communication, transmission of ideas, socialization*
VIRTUES:	*Wisdom, social activity*
SYMBOL:	*Black tortoise*
SEASON:	*Winter*
DIRECTION:	*North*
COLOR:	*Black*
TIME:	*Midnight*
PLANET:	*Mercury*
MATERIALS:	*Glass. Buildings that are distinguished by a major use of glass are considered Water buildings, but since glass cannot be used strictly on its own for construction purposes, it must combine with another element. Water and Earth are competitive, and buildings with a great expanse of glass do not do well with brick or concrete supports. However, Wood and Metal are both in sequence*

	with water (see page 183) and are considered much more favorable (as most skyscrapers demonstrate).
INTERIORS:	Bathrooms, laundries, kitchens, wine cellars, swimming pools, spas, ponds, and fountains
SHAPES AND TYPES:	Irregular shapes and construction features that seem to be "thrown together" rather than designed
IDEAL USES:	Water-style buildings are ideally suited for businesses involved in the transmission of ideas—publishers, art galleries, museums, concert halls, ad agencies, broadcasting, media conglomerates. The AT&T building in New York has a crownlike detail at its top, making it a Water-type building. What says communication more than the telephone company? Also suitable are businesses involved in word processing, computer terminology, and electrical engineering, as well as enterprises involving liquids and fluids, such as oil refineries, breweries, and bottling companies. Businesses involved in seagoing affairs, sailing, boats, and so on also are suitable.

A church in Santa Fe, New Mexico (left), built from Earth materials, is in harmony with its environment because it exhibits all five elemental shapes: Wood (tall shape of the bell towers); Fire (pointed detail of the crosses); Earth (square shape of main entry); Metal (bells in the towers); and Water (roofline that looks like falling water). All five elements make this a perfect day at the beach (right): Wood (wooden walkway); Fire (people and sun); Earth (sandy beach); Metal (trash cans and sign); and Water (ocean).

Each element has a specific role in creating balance and harmony. Green growing things infuse the earth with oxygen, Fire from the sun lights and heats the way, Earth provides the womb where all things are supported, Metal provides gravity, which keeps things from flying into space, and Water nourishes everything that lives.

The perfect environment, exterior or interior space, contains all five elements working together to create balance and harmony. When one element dominates the space or the landscape, other elements will be excluded or diminished and balance will be disrupted. For example, when there is too much rain, water floods the land, drowning plants and animals, eroding foundations and supports, corroding and dissolving the strongest metal.

Interiors also suffer from an excess or deficiency of one element or another. A room that is all white (Metal) is sterile and unnatural; a room with too much light and heat (Fire) will have faded drapes and carpets; a room shrouded in heavy fabrics and with few windows (Earth) will have no flow of air or life; a room or garden overgrown with plants (Wood) may make you feel restless and out of control;

The arched metal fence anchored in brick pillars is too small for the tall, two-story wooden building. Metal dominates wood but can't in this instance because the fence is too small. Also, the brick/pillars (Earth) are compatible with Metal but not with Wood. A higher fence constructed of wood would imitate the building and look more balanced.

a space enclosed by brick walls (Earth) might make you feel not so much secure as entombed.

Vito was suffering from a strange, exotic malady. Inside his home, plants proliferated: Vines snaked up the wall and across the ceiling, dead leaves fell on the bed, plants hung from the kitchen cabinets. He was also fond of the color green and had green carpets, walls, and furniture.

It is the balance among all five elements that creates successful spaces. Too much of one element means there will be too little of another. When all five elements are included, space begins to imitate nature. However, the relationships among the five elements must also be considered.

Who among us has not wondered at the caprice of nature as we witnessed the power of wind, water, fire, and earth? Unseen forces seem to lift some of us to dry ground, save us from the flames, and cause our walls to stand fast, while others, less fortunate, watch in horror as their chimneys tumble and roofs blow away. Some buildings survive, some don't. Why?

In times past, the placement of a building was determined after analyzing the site for energy patterns reflected in the movement of the sun and the flow of wind and water. Today, a building is most often placed in line with other buildings, arranged for convenience of the overall town plan. This means that all the buildings on the same side of the street face the same way regardless of how the wind blows, how the water flows, or who owns the building. Thus, some structures on the same block are damaged by floods and high winds while others, which may be placed a bit differently on the lot or have a different roofline or entry path or face a different direction entirely, are saved. If a building is positioned in such a way that no sun shines on it, it will probably be cold and damp and the occupants will be cut off from life-giving *chi*.

If a building is placed to take advantage of the elements, the occupants feel more comfortable and the building prospers. Furthermore, when the interior design and arrangement of furniture and appliances are considered, the space can be fine-tuned to be in harmony with nature and the cosmos.

Striped pants with bold flower print shirts rarely make a fashion statement. It is the same with houses. Did you ever notice a building that looked out of place with its surroundings? Or a fence that made the building look foolish? How about an expensively furnished room that just looked odd? Or a restaurant that took away your appetite? Maybe you noticed, maybe you didn't. Perhaps you just thought the occupants had horrible taste. Compare this with a natural setting. A mountain is never out of place, a river is never ugly or odd, and it's almost impossible for a tree to look foolish. Nature always emits beauty and grace. Why don't buildings and rooms?

Mother Nature maintains balance and harmony through order and structure, combining the five elements—Wood, Fire, Earth, Metal, and Water—in a predetermined sequence that is much like the nurturing relationship between a mother and child. Each element nurtures the next element in sequence: Water feeds Wood;

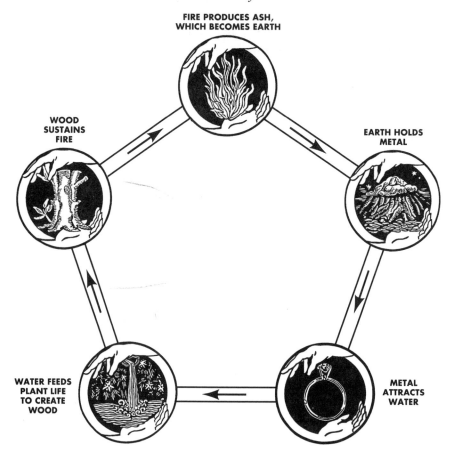

Wood makes Fire burn; Fire leaves ash, adding to the surface of the Earth, which presses down on particles to create Metal. Metal attracts Water through condensation. Try to start a fire using pieces of Metal and you'll be left in the cold. Water your plants with sand and they will shrivel and die.

When the predominant element of the environment and the predominant element of the building are the same or next to each other in sequence, the combination is creative and growth oriented. Egypt's pyramids, a Fire-Earth combination, have endured for centuries. A wood house combines nicely with the Fire of sunny California and is also suitable at the beach because Water, Wood, and Fire are all in sequence. A metal building in sunny California is not as suitable, because Metal and Fire are not in sequence. The diagram above shows the creation sequence of the Elements.

When Charles opened his restaurant, he expected it to be a success. Made of steel and glass, it stood out like a sore thumb on a gently rolling hillside of a farming community. Metal is used to chop down Wood. The building sliced through the landscape and irritated the neighbors, who thought the restaurant was in bad taste and that its owner was an "upstart." Locals continued to frequent Aunt Emma's KitchenKorner, a homespun eatery housed in a wooden shack. The giant apple tree outside welcomed customers, as did window boxes whose flowers bloomed even in the winter.

Aunt Emma's restaurant was in harmony with the environment and was supported by it. Charles's restaurant was not in harmony, and he continued to struggle. When the elements are combined out of sequence, the result can be strange or bizarre. For example, a tall wooden house perched on a mountain cliff combines Wood and Earth, which are not in sequence. The house looks odd and is impractical and unsafe. A house built of concrete or bricks, combining Earth and Earth, would be more suitable for the cliff. Even more beneficial would be a house built of metal, because Earth and Metal are next to each other in sequence. Earth nourishes or leads to Metal. The two elements are in sequence, and thus are also in harmony. New York City, an island surrounded by water, is largely built of steel (Metal) and glass (Water). Metal and Water are next to each other in sequence; such skyscrapers usually prosper. On the contrary, Earth and Water are not in sequence and not in harmony; only a fool would build a sixty-story building out of bricks and glass.

Problems can also arise when the prevailing element of the building makes a different impression from what you had desired. A bank located in a square brick building will be successful because it appears to be solid and enduring; brick is an Earth element, and Earth corresponds to safety and security. A bank located in a building with an irregular shape will not be as successful. According to feng shui principles, an irregular shape is a Water-element shape, which gives the impression of movement or flow and transmits the idea that what is here today will be gone tomorrow. When you match the element of the building shape to the intended business, you have a better chance of success. Refer to pages 147–157 to determine what element would be best for your business.

It is easy to see why the elements play such an important role in feng shui. Knowledge of the five elements helps us to do the following:

1. Compare the building with the landscape to determine whether there is harmony or discord between the occupants and the world.
2. Choose environments that support our work and lifestyles.
3. Imitate Mother Nature's recipe for life in every space we occupy, by showing us how nature includes all five elements in their proper sequence.
4. Provide appropriate accessories in the way of color, shape, and material to fix imbalances caused by conflicting elements.

The elements contribute much to the magic of feng shui. An understanding of their essence and their relationship to one another is essential in creating harmony and balance in every space.

We've all heard the terms "the mysterious East" and "the wild, wild West." We may have had the good fortune to be in the company of a gracious "Southerner" or to hunt elk with "men of the north." Directions have unique characteristics and associations, which are the same as the associations of the five elements. In feng shui, the elements and the directions are synonymous. If you understand the symbolism of five elements, you already know the symbolism of the basic directions.

Directions are basic to life. Our consciousness is in tune with directions whether we realize it or not. Directions are derived from the apparent movement of the sun, as it moves across the sky each day. Watching the movement of the sun gave definition to directions. It was instinct that turned our face to the rising sun in the eastern part of the sky every morning. Thus, east became associated with beginnings. The sun gave us light and warmth throughout the day. Its passage reached its zenith in the southern portion of the sky. Thus, south became associated with achievement and reaching for warmth or success in the world. From these two primary directions, designated by the sun, all other directions were found. North was a place of darkness, far away from the path of the sun. North became associated with life hidden in the darkness. West became a place of death and dying because it is where the sun disappeared each day. From this solar cycle, directions developed personalities.

In feng shui there is a belief that as you align yourself and your environment to the directions, you can stimulate or activate the energy of that direction. For example, if you want to begin a new venture, put yourself in the place of the rising sun, the east. If you want to begin a family, do it in a place where you can see the setting sun, which symbolizes family and children (because they carry on after you are gone). To emphasize achievement and reputation, put yourself in the place of the sun at high noon, which is the south, the place of fame. When you want to get down to business, put yourself away from the sun, in the north, the place of business.

Elements and directions are synonymous, and problems can arise when the directional element of the entry conflicts with the primary element of the neighborhood.

Mary Jane and Susie lived near the beach, across the street from each other. Their age and background were similar, but their social lives were completely different. Mary Jane had many friends and a good, solid relationship. Susie was always on the outs with somebody. Mary Jane's house faced north, the direction associated with the element Water. Her Water house was compatible with the Water environment and was always filled with friendly neighbors stopping by to chat. Susie's house across the street faced south, the direction of Fire. Fire and Water combined make steam. She wanted to be popular, but her critical nature seemed to incite those who stopped by. She had the knack of making others "steaming mad." Was it Susie or the direction her house faced?

The direction the front door faces marks the interaction between the individual and the world. When the direction of the front door is compatible with the surrounding elements, the occupant and the world are in harmony. Conversely, when the direction the house faces is competitive with the environment, the occupant struggles for authority in the world and has problems with those who live nearby.

How can directions be competitive? Directions are associated with the elements, and just as the elements have a creative or controlling relationship with one another, so do directions. For example, a house facing east is regarded as a Wood-type house because Wood and east are synonymous. An east-Wood house in a forest, a Wood environment, is in harmony with its surroundings. An east-Wood house near the beach combines Wood and Water, another harmonious arrangement.

An east-Wood house near a freeway or metal bridge, however, combines Wood and Metal. Metal cuts down Wood, so with this combination, over time the environment would damage the health and well-being of those occupying a Wood house. A Wood house in an Earth environment is not in harmony. Wood takes all the nourishment from the earth; the occupants would eventually deplete the resources available through the environment. For example, they might cut down all the trees to build the house.

In multiunit buildings, the entry to the building can face one direction while the entry to a particular unit faces a different direction. When the directions are compatible, the landlord and the occupant are in harmony. When the direction of the main entry conflicts with the direction of the individual unit, problems between the landlord and the occupant can be ongoing. Mike lived in a beautiful building with an entry that faced east/Wood. His unit was on the second floor, facing west/Metal. East and West conflict, and he was always fighting with the landlord over something.

A problem arises when the element derived from the shape of the roof conflicts with that of the directional element of the front door. Gordon lived in a mountain chalet with a Fire-element peaked roof. His front door faced north/Water. Shortly after moving in, his new bride had a change of heart, decided she didn't want to be married, and left him.

When the roof and the entry conflict by element, whether the element is derived from the shape or the direction, those who live within experience the conflict. Fathers and sons disagree, husbands and wives divorce, and solitary dwellers experience tension within themselves and have many internal, unresolved problems. This is a fairly simple problem to cure: Paint the door a color that is in harmony with the element of the roof or place objects near the entry that harmonize the conflicting elements.

Inside the house or office, the direction in which rooms are placed can cause problems. Sammy's room was in the north part of the house. He always complained that it was cold and dark. He spent a lot of time in bed and lacked ambition or spunk. His sister's room was in the south part of the house. Her room was always bright and sunny, and she did well at school.

The direction of the placement of furniture, particularly beds and desks, can also contribute to failure or success. Mary's bed was situated in the west, the direction of decline and of slowing down. She was always behind in her work, never quite catching up. When she moved her bed to the opposite wall, she was able to take charge of her life by hiring a secretary to help her.

When two people occupy the same room, conflicts can arise when one person feels better sleeping in one direction and the other person prefers another. Many marriages have problems simply because of a conflict in the way the bed is positioned. Once you are aware of this type of problem, it is very easy to correct it by repositioning the furniture or using antidotes from the elements to create harmony and balance.

Julie and John were happy until they moved into their new apartment. For some reason, John started sleeping on the couch in the living room. He said he was more comfortable there. Julie, sure that a divorce was imminent if this situation continued, moved the bed into a different corner of the room. John felt more comfortable and returned to the bedroom. The marriage took a turn for the better.

Directions are important in feng shui. We will be using the directions to determine:

- The relationship between the building and the world based on the direction of the entry compared to the landscape.
- The relationship between the direction of the entry to the shape of the roof. (There are five basic shapes for roofs.)
- Auspicious locations for ourselves and our lives.
- Placement for the rooms within a building.
- Placement of furniture, appliances and accessories, mirrors, and plants.

In conclusion, remember that the directions are synonymous with the elements and activities of life. When you think of health, think of Wood and east. When you think of business, think Water and north. When you think of family, think Metal and west, and when you think of achievement and success, think Fire and south. When you want to bring a particular quality into your life, use an accessory from the corresponding element, almost as if it were a lucky charm for you to attract what you seek. Remember that you can use a color, a shape, a material, or the element itself.

Directions, like the elements, contribute much to the magic of feng shui. Understanding their relationships and the way they interact is essential to understanding the power of placement.

To determine the influence of the directions, in feng shui we use an eight-sided figure called *ba gua* (pronounced *bah-gwa*). Each of the eight sides of the *ba gua* symbolizes one activity of life—family, health, children, love, friendship, travel, business, and money. Each activity is connected to one of eight directions.

Whether you are analyzing an entire shopping center, a lot with a building on it, or a single room in the building, just imagine there are eight different sections within each space, each with its own energy field. Each energy field represents one part of life.

Benefactors

East	Health	Wood
Southeast	Money	Wood
South	Fame	Fire
Southwest	Love	Earth
West	Family	Metal
Northwest	Travel *Journey*	Metal
North *Career* Business		Water
Northeast	Knowledge	Earth

The practice/philosophy of using the *ba gua* is based on the idea that when the space is a regular shape, it will contain all eight sides of the *ba gua,* and the occupants will have the opportunity to participate in all eight areas of life. If the space is not perfectly square or rectangular (and most places are not), there might be some parts of the *ba gua* that are missing entirely, while other parts of the building or room may dangle outside the *ba gua* shape.

Everything was fine at the Smiths' home until they added a family room. The house was a square shape, but the family room addition stuck out of one side like a cowlick that won't stay down. Shortly after adding the family room, Mr. and Mrs. Smith divorced, one child ran away, and the other joined a religious cult.

The Smiths built the family room outside of the square house. No wonder the family ceased to function harmoniously. They experienced what happens when parts of life are missing, or dangling, from the *ba gua.* When a house is missing a function, usually a different function becomes overemphasized. Mr. Smith spent so much time on business that his family life suffered. Mrs. Smith traveled all the time. The children spent much of their time on nonfamily pursuits.

As you align yourself and your environment to a direction, you stimulate and/or activate the energy of that direction. When parts of the space are excluded or dangling from the *ba gua,* you can correct the situation with a variety of simple solutions and antidotes drawn from mirrors, trinkets, and furnishings.

When you can't align your furniture to a particular direction, you can still activate the direction by using shapes, colors, or materials that correspond to the desired direction. For example, north is associated with business. To increase business, put your desk in the north. If you can't do that, add north-type accessories—

black fabric and furniture, irregular shapes, glass, or water—to wherever the desk is. There is more information about the *ba gua* in the Appendix. All you need to know now is that regular shapes (squares and rectangles) are able to contain all parts of the *ba gua* and all activities in life, and that irregular shapes cannot contain an eight-sided figure and, as a result, some areas of the lifestyle will be overemphasized while others will be diminished.

CHAPTER 2

The Power of Chi

YANG AND YIN ENERGY

We loved visiting Grandma. Her house always smelled like golden crusty rolls, fresh from the oven. And the wisteria, a leafy canopy of green and lavender flowers, gracefully sheltered the patio where we used to sit and sip lemonade and gossip about old man Johnson's house next door. It was quite a sight! Overgrown with bushes and vines, broken machines littering the yard like skeletons escaped from the grave, and the wind whistling through the trees, blocking the light and making an eerie sound that frightened our young and tender hearts.

Everyone can tell good energy from bad. Look around you. What do you see? More important, how do you feel? Good energy is light and energized, not heavy or dense. In good energy, you feel calm yet alert and ready for life.

Energy, called *chi*, can be seen everywhere. Where a violet breaks through the rocks, or a hidden garden grows lush with greenery, *chi* is on the surface, accessible and available. Places covered in concrete or that lack water are not so fortunate. Where the land is sterile, barren, parched, and cracked, where plants won't grow and creepy crawly things have to burrow deep within the earth for food and water, the *chi* is deep or distant.

Chi, the breath that fills the lungs, the force that beats the heart, can assume any form. A gentle breeze, thundering rain, swirling tornadoes, snowflakes, dewdrops, sunlight, and moonshine all bring *chi* to the earth. This *chi* merges with the gushing, bubbling *chi* spouting out of natural springs and geysers, flowing endlessly through countless rivers, streaming out of volcanoes, and rising, like a mythical dragon gathering steam, to shake and break the earth's crust.

A total eclipse of the sun (Java, 1983) is nature's most dramatic representation of the marriage between yin and yang, consummated in the diamond ring of light.

Have you ever experienced a headache from being around bad smells, glaring lights, or loud, irritating noises? Do you feel like taking a bath after shopping in a crowded department store? That's from experiencing bad energy. Notice how different you feel when you're in a room filled with light, air, and empty space, where the temperature is just right and the furniture comfortable. You feel like taking a deep breath, sighing, maybe even kicking off your shoes and relaxing. That's the feel of good energy.

Within every environment the energy wavers. Opposite qualities compete for space, but too much or too little of anything causes an imbalance. Think of how life would be if it were always light or always dark. It's the balance that keeps life on an even keel. Many people suffer because their home or office is too hot or cold, is exposed to glaring sun or has too little light to read, is encased in air that's damp or stale. Equalizing or balancing opposite qualities is the simplest way to bring your space into harmony with nature. Just remember that too much of anything diminishes everything else.

In feng shui, we call the opposite forces yang/yin. Yang energy is light, high, bright, active, lively, forward, and positive. Large rooms with good light, an airy cross-draft, and oversize furniture; vegetable gardens ripe for the picking; lively football games on brisk fall days are all examples of good yang energy. On the other hand, a smoky, hot, noisy, crowded restaurant, or the incessant buzzing around an overturned hornets' nest, or subway and elevators packed with human sardines are examples of excessive yang energy.

Yin energy, the opposite of yang, is dark, low, subdued, inactive, calm, reflective, backward, and negative. Moonlight reflected in the calm surface of the lake, love songs sung by goddesses, monks chanting, supper by candlelight are all examples of good yin energy. Contrarily, excessive yin energy is expressed by dirty looks and snide remarks behind your back, the ominous drip of a leaking faucet, burned toast, broken lightbulbs in a beauty salon, a hole in the sidewalk that breaks your heel, warped floors, and bouquets of withering roses.

TOO MUCH YANG

Susan lived on the top floor of a beautiful steel-and-glass skyscraper in the heart of New York City. The Realtor had convinced her that living high off the ground would "give her a lift in life." So why was she so depressed?

A spectacular view can sometimes be a problem. When the view is 180 degrees or more, excessive yang *chi* inundates the space. Upon viewing the city below, Susan felt overwhelmed, bewildered, and confused about goals and relationships. The spectacular view offered more than she could handle.

High mountains and tall buildings are often harshly exposed to the elements. Strong winds assault the top, sweeping away money, love, or luck. If you live high off the ground, be sure there is a sufficient refuge from the elements by using screens, tall trees, awnings, and canopies to shelter and protect the space.

Living on the edge of the blue Pacific with a fabulous view of the crashing surf, John was fearful to the point of inertia. He trembled every time the waves crashed beneath the house, sure that at any moment he would be washed away with the tide.

Living too close to nature's untamed elements can produce excess *chi*. Wind, thunder, lightning, hail, snow, and rain blast the landscape like a fearful giant, engulfing the environment with energy. Without protection, you are at the mercy of those elements. The crashing surf of an ocean, a rushing river, and a booming waterfall can be particularly problematic. In such places, the atmosphere is charged with negative ions that disturb the electromagnetic field of the body. If you live in such a space, create barriers between you and nature by using wood or earthy materials such as ceramics, marbles, or stones. Glass and crystal tend to magnify the effects of water, but even transparent curtains over windows are helpful in toning things down.

If you live too close to a highway or heavily traveled street, a major shopping center, a police or fire station, a tourist attraction, a public building, or even an elementary school, you may experience excessive *chi* from crowds or cars. In the exterior, create a barricade with a fence, trees, shrubs, or plants between you and the source of the excess *chi*.

Inside a room or building, symptoms of excessive yang include an overflow of possessions, people, pets, furniture, equipment, or books. In the kitchen, excess yang takes the form of counters littered with bottles, jars, and dishes. In the living room it's end tables piled high with magazines and papers. Such a space is taking in more *chi* than it can expel.

To determine whether you have too much energy in your space, ask yourself the following questions: Is the space protected from the elements? (Uncontrolled exposure to the elements damages the good energy of any space.) Is the space too bright from neon lights or the burning sun? Is the atmosphere loud, pulsating, hot, or noisy? Are people packed in like sardines? Can you smell dogs, cats, birds, or other animals? Is the garden overgrown? If you answered yes to one or more of

The garden pictured above is dense and chaotic—too much yang. The garden shown below is more balanced because it uses empty space to display water bowls. The flowing water encourages the flow of the energy.

these questions, you might have excess yang *chi*. Here are a few simple things you can do to regain your balance and peace of mind.

- Close the drapes, turn off the lights, use spotlights to highlight special objects in darkened rooms; use muted lighting from invisible sources.
- Use subdued, quiet, cool, dark, secondary, subtle, or monochromatic colors, with static, still patterns.
- Cover, enclose, or contain areas or objects.
- Turn on the air conditioner; put a screen across the fireplace; blow out the candles; eat something cold, soft, and watery such as melon, grapes, or sherbet.
- Take a cold bath; collect water in bowls.
- Create stillness to cool off the *chi* with rock, sand, or moss gardens; dig in the dirt.
- Create silence, walk in your socks, keep your hands closed, turn off the TV and other appliances, hum or whisper.
- Favor short, fat, soft, limp, prone, crooked, irregular objects.
- Use absorbent, dull, wide-weave surfaces and fabrics.
- Add heavy, solid furniture and accessories.

- Use patterns that are horizontal to the flow of traffic.
- Remove clutter and make empty spaces where *chi* can flow. Ask visitors to leave, cover the birdcage, put out the cat.

TOO MUCH YIN

Arthur had been working at the same job for more than ten years with no hope of a promotion. He said he wasn't interested in "climbing the ladder to success." The boss said he lacked ambition. No wonder. He lived in a dark basement apartment with boxes stacked outside his doorway.

Remember old man Johnson's scary house? Blocked from the life-giving sun, it had too much yin energy. The space appeared gloomy, spooky, awful, and lonely. Too much yin energy is like death or dying.

Sam didn't have much heat in his house and always kept the drapes drawn, thinking it kept the place warmer. He loved to talk about get-rich-quick schemes and was "in the dark" as to why his plans never amounted to anything.

Excessive yin energy is cold and dark. Here you will find icy wind that freezes your fingers, clouds that cover the sun, barren gardens, sick and depressed people whose lives are absent, inactive, or in hibernation. Inside buildings and rooms, yin energy echoes through empty spaces and seeks moist hidden places away from the light. The environment is unappealing, even for sleep. Inside, yin accumulates in closets and storerooms, places with only one door and no windows. In these places *chi* can't exit or circulate freely so it becomes old and stale and cannot support life.

Arlene was a writer who had converted a large pantry into a home office. It didn't have a window, but she could close the door and escape from the demands of the kids. She had dreamed about this space for a long time, so why couldn't she spend even one hour there?

When there is excess yin, there is insufficient yang and no energy for life. Health, business, love, and every area of life are diminished. It is not a good idea to build or live where *chi* is weak or inaccessible. It is also difficult, expensive, and questionable to build in such places.

To determine whether your space has too much yin, ask yourself: Is the space so empty you can hear your voice echo or your heart beat? Is it cold or damp? Can you see mold spots, water stains, or rotten wood? Is the air stale and smelly because there is lack of ventilation? Is it dark and gloomy? If there is a window, is it so dirty that no light enters? Is the floor warped or damaged? Is your space lower than the street? Is it hidden or tucked away in a corner? If you answered yes to one or more of these questions, the space may be too yin. Here's what you can do right now to make things better.

- Open the curtains, let in the sun, or turn on some lights.
- Use primary, warm, hot, bold, bright, contrasting colors in dynamic, moving, open, vibrant patterns.
- Uncover, open, or dramatize areas or objects with bright or moving lights.

Workers sweeping a lonely, barren stadium (above) are in an excessively yin environment, with too much empty space and too much Earth and Metal. Shoppers in a busy marketplace (below) are experiencing an excessively yang environment, with not enough empty space, too much Fire and Wood.

- Turn up the heat, build a fire, light candles, use the stove.
- Take a hot shower; let the water run, splash, bubble, and spray.
- Eat something warm, such as soup, spicy chili, or red tomatoes.
- Make noise. Clap your hands, stamp your feet, turn on the radio, sing, shout, play the piano, pound on some drums.
- Add movement. Turn on electrical appliances, fan yourself with folded paper, hang wind chimes or pieces of fabric where they catch the air, let your hair blow in the wind.
- Use reflective surfaces and shiny, smooth fabrics that bounce the light.
- Use patterns that run the same way as the flow of traffic.
- Favor tall, thin, clear, light, firm, delicate, or irregular shapes such as erect, open-leg chairs and tables.
- Fill in the space with form. Invite friends over, uncover the bird, let in the cat, add plants or cut flowers.

NEGATIVE CHI (SHA)

Negative *chi* is called *sha*. *Sha* is naturally produced by geographical faults and fissures in the earth. During earthquakes, it rises to the surface, shaking and splitting the earth. Fault lines exist all around the globe. No place is immune to them, and living near known fault lines, whether in California, Missouri, or Japan, tends to engender corresponding patterns of human behavior. For example, angry retorts and tension-filled lives are common experiences to New Yorkers, who live near a major fault line. Southern Californians near the San Andreas fault line are subject to shaking standards; the rich and famous come and go as quickly as fast food gets cold. San Francisco, also located on the San Andreas fault, has a certain dynamic tension expressed first by the Forty-Niners who rushed to the gold-filled hills and currently by those who lead the pack in promoting gay rights. Japan, China, India, Pakistan, Mexico, Central America, and Australia all have fault lines. Thanks to the information explosion, we immediately know when disaster hits anywhere on the globe. Is it any wonder we are so tense? But it is not only through earthquakes that *sha* is produced.

Sha is the carrier of unfavorable currents adversely affecting each of us. *Sha* seeps, drips, and oozes through cracks, holes, and broken windows. It accumulates and stagnates in dead corners and sharp angles. It gains speed when it is forced into straight lines. It occurs in places dense with people, animals, or things—for example, barnyards, insect nests, rat holes, overcrowded elevators, trains, planes, and rooms. It is aggravated by bad smells, glaring lights, and irritating noises. It is the cold wind blowing in the dead of night and the aura surrounding dead or dying things. It can be seen, smelled, heard, felt, tasted, and sensed by the intuition. It is sharp, rotten, contaminated, polluted, toxic, vile, painful, and dangerous. No place is immune to *sha*. It is external or internal, apparent, hidden, or secret, and it affects physical, mental, spiritual, and social conditions.

SECRET ARROWS

Gerry complained to Dr. Morgan that she always felt worse after visiting his office, which was located at a T-intersection of two straight, busy roads. The view from the windows was of oncoming traffic and it was an unnerving sight. Imagine lying on the treatment table, in pain, and watching the cars headed directly toward you.

Good energy is always in motion, winding its way through space in a gentle curve. When it is forced into straight lines or sharp angles, instead of gently falling and rising like the tummy of a sleeping baby, *chi* compresses into a barb, like an arrow, as sharp as the tip of a knife or a cruel, cutting remark that wounds anything in its path.

Whether you live in the city or the country, there are many secret arrows around you. Most roads, driveways, pathways, walkways, and sidewalks form straight lines. In the city, buildings are crowded together with rooflines pointing at one another. The profusion of corners, walls, television antennae, billboards, tunnels, railroad tracks, crosses on churches, and other straight or angular features that can be seen from the windows of houses or offices are all capable of producing secret arrows that can attack the building. Telephone poles, traffic and advertising signs, and tall, straight trees make shadow arrows. Any straight lines leading toward a main entry encourage *sha* to be directed there. Straight lines that lead directly toward a main entry or that come almost to the entry and then turn to make a sharp right angle are especially dangerous, as they combine the effects of *sha* and secret arrows.

There are secret arrows inside as well. The corner of a wall or screen; sharp, angular counters; square or rectangular tables, chairs, and benches; and architectural features such as pillars, posts, and cornices can create arrows. Even items of decor, such as framed pictures, masks, trophies and awards, indoor plants, artificial flowers, cracked mirrors, or broken items can produce secret arrows. Make sure no straight lines, sharp angles, or points are directed toward you as you sit at your desk, eat your lunch, sleep, or even watch TV. If you feel tense at home or at work, look around to see if you can find the culprit arrow.

The boss was unreasonable, constantly criticizing hard-working Jane. Her desk was near a square column whose edges formed secret arrows aimed at her desk. When she received a coworker's postcard with a picture of the pope, she casually placed it against the in-out box on her desk, facing the square column. There he was, the white-robed pope with his arms outstretched, symbolically absorbing the secret arrows. The next day, Jane was ten minutes late coming back from lunch, and the boss didn't say a word.

There are several things you can do to protect yourself from an arrow. First, try to remove the object causing it. If this is not possible, cover the offending angle with a basket, a piece of fabric, whatever is available. When this is impractical, create a subtle and symbolic wall between you and the secret arrow. Use plants, objects, boxes, filing trays, pictures in small frames, or even a postcard to create some type of barrier, as Jane did. Another solution is to use a small mirror, reflective side toward the offending angle to send the arrow back to its source.

Madison had been trying unsuccessfully to sell a house. She blamed the recession. A big oak tree in the front yard, facing the front door, blocked the view of the entry from the street. She couldn't move the tree and didn't want to cut it down. What could she do? Placing a small reflective plate or mirror at eye level on a post or tree makes an imaginary hole in it, allowing the energy to penetrate. Madison did that, and within a week a neighbor asked if the house was for sale.

If an arrow comes from the shadow of a tall tree or pole, break up the straight shadow by placing round or fluffy objects in the shadow's path. When all else fails, consider positioning yourself out of the shadow's path.

BEAMS

The Smith family always argued, and Mrs. Smith had indigestion. The dining room table was under a large wooden ceiling beam. Beams act like horizontal arrows. Imagine how it would feel if a beam fell on you. Symbolically, it can do the same type of damage—splitting, cutting, crushing, and separating anything that is underneath it. A beam "split" the Smith family in two; Mrs. Smith, who sat directly under the beam, felt the pressure in her stomach. If you must sit or sleep under a beam, try to arrange the furniture so that it is parallel to the beam. Crystals, wind chimes, lights, or airy objects can be hung from the beam to symbolically disburse the strong energy. Tiny pieces of reflective tin or mirrors create symbolic holes in the beam, allowing the energy to pass through it and reducing the problematic effects.

Theresa, always the picture of good health, complained of feeling sick and tired. The billboard across the street from her house had recently changed its sign to read, ARE YOU SICK AND TIRED? MEMORIAL HOSPITAL IS WAITING FOR YOU. The messages on billboards and signs can also act as secret arrows, sabotaging even the most aware individual. Every time the sign changes, so does your life. If you live in the city, graffiti and gang markings must also be considered. You share the fate of the young people in your neighborhood, the mayor of your city, the governor of your state, and the leader of your country.

GETTING *CHI* TO FLOW

Chi can flow fast as a rabbit or slow as the turtle who won the race. It climbs up and down, spirals in and out, rises as smoke in a fire, clings like dust on a mirror, ascends to heaven, and sinks into hell. It disperses into the wind, pulses through electrical lines, trickles through walls, and oozes as sap from trees.

Good *chi* is always in motion, but it cannot exit the same way it enters. When it is unable to leave a space or its motion is stopped, *chi* quickly becomes stale and stagnated—sour *sha*. When there are obstacles in its path and its motion is inhibited, obstructed, blocked, or trapped, *chi* loses motion and buoyancy. It collects in pools, settles into corners, lurks behind doors, slithers under furniture, and sneaks into tiny, hidden spaces behind heavy appliances. It's *chi* that stretches a balloon and makes it full. The *chi* from a pin can also pop the balloon and leave you with a shred of colored rubber, the magic all gone.

Don't you hate to sit behind a post at a ball game or a concert? Do you like how you look in a warped, curved, or distorted mirror? Stepping on a crack in the sidewalk won't really break your mother's back, but these and other kinds of blocked, abnormal, or unbalanced perceptions can destabilize your nervous system and create all kinds of problems. Even when the distortion is not immediately visible, such as a broken shelf in the closet, the *chi* can be thrown off balance. All matter, whether it's blowing in the wind, just got off the bus, or was dragged in by the cat, alters the *chi* quickly and dramatically, changing its properties, characteristics, and intentions. Things that can impact or alter the *chi* include:

- Forms or shapes of all kinds
- Colors, patterns, and textures
- Images such as pictures, postcards, signs, symbols, and masks
- Amulets, icons, graphics, and statues
- Objects that catch the wind, such as flags, sails, wind chimes, mobiles, and running or active water
- Objects that block the wind, such as fences, posts, trees, bushes, buildings, mountains

- Sound, heat, electricity, natural and artificial light
- Reflections and shadows
- Smells: good, bad, familiar, offensive, engaging
- The weather: temperature, moisture, rain, snow, hail, dew, fog, frost

Every space, whether it is a home, an office, a loft in the sky, a carpenter's basement studio, a factory, theater, restaurant, gymnasium, nightclub, or zoo, has an energy and personality, just like you do. Those who occupy the space interact with its energy in the same way we interact with family, coworkers, or friends. But unlike most people, who change slowly over a period of time, healthy space changes quickly and continuously.

The energy of a space is different each day and each hour. Why? Because people, pets, and the elements leave their mark; the most diligent cat burglar will leave a clue, no matter how small or seemingly invisible. Even a space you are obsessed with keeping shipshape will change whether you want it to or not. We live in an ever-changing world. Get used to it. Monitor a space and make the necessary adjustments before you occupy it. Then don't make yourself crazy trying to keep things exactly the same. You may be resisting natural changes.

After you adjust the yin/yang to balance the *chi,* make sure the *chi* flows freely through the space, touching every room without obstruction before it exits through a door or window that is different from—and if possible far away from—the entrance.

To analyze the flow of *chi* and discover how it moves through the space, walk slowly from the driveway, walkway, or path to the front door. Is there enough space on the porch or landing to support your entire body as you open the door? Can you get the door open? Once the door is opened, walk into the entry space and take a look around. Then walk through the space, going into every room, upstairs and down, and finally out the exit. Two-story buildings should have a downstairs exit plus a window or door upstairs where the *chi* can get out. As you explore, look at your feet and let them determine your route. If you trace your path looking straight ahead at eye level, your body will automatically adjust to and move around obstructions, giving you a false indication of the flow. When you're looking at the ground and following your feet, they will automatically stop and will not be able to pass by the obstacles or blockages that the *chi* encounters as it moves through the space.

The *chi* will probably go along the traffic pattern you envision before starting your investigation, but you might be surprised. Often the way the furniture is arranged directs the *chi* into a closet, a wall, or a dead-end corner.

Carol lived in her parents' house in Honolulu. She wanted to move out, but for some reason never had enough money or energy to do so. Before entering her bedroom, the *chi* was stopped by a white, free-standing wall with a red/gold picture in the center, like a bull's-eye. As the *chi* moved down the hall toward her room, the wall stopped it before it could enter her space.

Inhibited, obstructed, or confused flow of *chi* is probably the number-one problem to solve with feng shui. Since we humans adapt quickly to any environment we're in and are trained to consider space inconsequential to well-being, we step over boxes, shove aside bags, leave clothes lying around, don't take out the trash, and excel at procrastination, promising we'll do it later.

Here are some common situations: Something inhibits, obstructs, or blocks the flow. The way things are placed confuses and disorients the *chi* or directs it to a place it doesn't want to go, like in a straight line or upside down, backward, or downward. Maybe the *chi* is directed right out the door, into a corner, or against a wall, where it may become stuck, frustrated, and uptight. Perhaps the flow of *chi* has holes in it from penetrations by the arrows of pointed-leaf plants or the corner of a table. It could have been cut to bits by a beam, slowed or made frenetic by the colors and patterns on the walls or the shapes of the furniture. Possibly the flow of *chi* is split in two by a half wall, a divided walkway, or a staircase. Any of these conditions can frustrate, anger, even enrage the *chi*, causing the occupants to feel the same way. Tension, poor health, and bad luck await those who occupy the space.

There are many ways the *chi* can be blocked, inhibited, or damaged. Just look around you. Now remove obstacles in the flow of *chi*. Cover, block, deflect, scatter, disperse, break up, or remove any secret arrows caused by interior or exterior features. Create a traffic pattern natural to the *chi*, one that rises, curves, and moves gently forward from north to south and east to west, from the entrance to the exit. Guide the *chi* to where you want it to go.

To Access Chi

When the *chi* is not accessible, for example, when it is deep in the ground, high in the sky, far away, confused, or unable to get to where we are, then we must invite it to come to our space and must welcome and encourage it to stay. Light attracts *chi* and can be used to direct *chi* around corners and toward other areas. *Chi* seeks living things and anything that might catch your eye, such as a plant or a colorful picture. *Chi* is attracted to reflections from mirrors, glass, or shiny objects that send the light rays to penetrate small, dark, angular, or "dead" areas where the *chi* often gets stuck. In a room where you sit with your back to the door, mirrors can give access to *chi* as well as provide visibility of the door and anyone entering the room. In areas where the ground is sunken, mirrors placed at the low point will raise the *chi*. Mirrors can also be used to raise ceilings and expand the apparent size of the room.

Call the Chi

Sometimes you'll have to call the *chi* with displays of bold colors or pleasant sounds that come from bells, chimes, flutes, or even electrical appliances. *Chi* responds to water in any form, bubbling or calm. Plants and flowers, pretty objects, and whatever attracts your attention is bound to attract the *chi*.

Direct the *Chi*

Consider how you give someone directions to find your space, mentioning things he or she will see as markers ("turn right at the street sign, go left at the red fence, cross over the bridge, go around the oak tree, look for the light, and I'll be waiting"). You have to do the same with the *chi*. A loud bell can announce the arrival of *chi* and give it a boost as it enters your space. A bright light in the entry says "*chi*, come here." Inside the house, a plant placed near the entrance to the living room instructs the *chi* to flow into the room. A fancy table lamp and a red pillow on the sofa instruct the *chi* to enter. A wind chime hung near the only window shows the *chi* where the exit is. Patterns on the floor, colors on the wall, and paintings all are creative devices that direct the *chi* where you want it to go.

Stimulate the *Chi*

Movement stimulates *chi*. Electrical tools and appliances, objects that turn or sway in the wind, running water, or anything that moves can be used to stimulate *chi*. Sometimes when the *chi* gets stuck, it gets very heavy and dense, sinks, and loses motion. Then it must be stimulated using something sharp, such as a pointed-leaf plant or a lamp on a thin, tall pole, to puncture the *chi*, making it lighter so it can flow again. You would not want to use this same antidote, punching holes in the *chi*, in an empty space. For example, the points of a sharp-leafed plant in the center of an empty room deflate and damage the *chi* before it can enrich the room or move on to another space. The points also act like secret arrows, attacking anyone seated in or walking through it.

Encourage the *Chi* to Stay

If you are attracted to a space and feel good while you occupy it, the *chi* will also feel welcome and want to stay. *Chi* likes plants, water, life, light, heat, color, reflection, movement, and curved spaces where it can circulate and escape when it wants to.

In conclusion, remember that the *chi* is the most important consideration in feng shui. Free-flowing *chi* is a river, stocked with the gifts of long life, prosperity, and health. Make sure there is enough *chi* and that it is flowing freely through space, bringing you every rich treasure you deserve.

Part 2

FENG SHUI AND
THE HOME

CHAPTER 3

The Feng Shui of

Regions, Cities, and

Neighborhoods

THE INFLUENCE OF PLACE

We are attracted to one place more than another place. There are many reasons for this but, basically, it is because the inner self, comprised of instincts and intuition, knows better than the outer, or conscious self, why we need certain experiences and why we live where we do. That inner knowing directs us to the place where we can best fulfill our destiny. Some people can live only in the mountains, surrounded by trees. Others languish without city lights. Sometimes it seems we have no choice and that circumstances force us to live in a particular place for a specific time and there's nothing we can do about it.

If you do have the luxury of choice, and you are considering where in the world or country or city or neighborhood you want to live, feng shui can help, because every location, no matter how large or small, has its own energy. If you can attune yourself to this energy and how it makes you feel, you'll know intuitively when you've found the right place to live.

To perceive how *chi* flows into, through, and out of a particular geographic area or neighborhood, look far and wide, above and beyond, within and without. Use all your senses to go beyond the obvious dimensions to the subtle realities, the shapes, patterns, smells, and sounds. Be like Master Po in the television series *Kung Fu,* who asks Kwai Chang Cane if he hears the grasshopper at his feet. Cane says, "How can you hear such a thing?" Master Po replies, "How can you not!" Listen for the grasshopper at your feet, the wind as it blows through the trees, birds singing and crickets chirping. Traffic noises, sirens, machines, and even dogs barking can be disturbing. Many beautiful neighborhoods are ruined by the sound of lawn mowers and leaf blowers. Grating, obnoxious sounds contribute to low-level anxiety and tension. Sniff the air: What do you smell? Lilacs, diesel fuel, or garbage? Pollution and other odors affect well-being, and you might not be happy living within nose range of a fish store or a garbage dump.

An ideal place fulfills the primary needs of the moment: shelter, protection, privacy, room for pets or significant others, comfort and easy access to and from the outside world. If the space satisfies the basic needs and also suits your lifestyle and temperament, it has good potential. A gardener is not happy in a skyscraper, a city person suffers when living in isolation. If you don't consider these basics when choosing a place to live, you are probably wasting your time, energy, and money, and will create unnecessary stress, which leads to problems. Interestingly, we are willing to sacrifice some basic requirements when we love the environment. The five elements describe the contrasting types of natural and human-made landscapes available. Some of these environments will attract you more than others. The trick is to find the one that inspires, comforts, and motivates you.

Wood Landscapes

Connecticut, northern California and its Redwoods, the Pacific Northwest, the jungles of Central America, and the Amazon are characterized by plants and trees of all kinds, and this makes them Wood landscapes. Abundant plant life, forests and jungles, column-shaped mountains, tall, narrow, rectangular buildings, or a profusion of telephone and telegraph poles define a Wood landscape. Parts of New York City are a Water environment because the city is on an island, but the city could also be classified as a Wood-type landscape because of its many tall and narrow buildings. This type of neighborhood is beneficial for those desiring a more creative, growth-oriented life and is suitable for businesses that nurture others, such as restaurants, advertising, and the healing arts. Basically, anytime you need a spurt of creative energy, put yourself in a Wood environment.

Fire Landscapes

Fire landscapes are distinguished by sharp angles, peaked mountains, pyramids, pointed roofs or steeples, or other sharply angled architectural detail. Houses situated at the base of the Alps and other sharply peaked mountain ranges enjoy the benefit of a Fire landscape, which is suitable for intellectual, academic, or spiritual pursuits. Sometimes meditation practices suggest looking into the flame of a burning candle. This is because Fire inspires the spirit. Anytime you need to be more thoughtful, put yourself in a Fire environment.

Earth Landscape

Driving through the panhandle of Texas or Oklahoma, the panorama is vast, the earth is flat, and the mountains are square or block shaped, typical of an Earth-type landscape. Plateaus formed by canyons, such as the Grand Canyon in Arizona, also characterize the Earth landscape, which may appear lifeless but often hides a wealth of treasure. Much oil has been found in these areas, and oil is a Metal-type substance found deep in the earth. Once it's tapped it provides material abundance for a gas-hungry world. The Earth element is particularly suited for those looking for an enduring, stable environment.

Metal Landscape

Landscapes that feature gently rounded hilltops, such as the rolling hills in Tuscany, Italy, or Rolling Hills Estates in California, identify a Metal landscape, as do metal arches from bridges or freeway supports. Metal environments are suitable for those interested or involved in the material world of finance or government and civic issues. This type of environment is very good for focused or highly detailed work. Just being in a Metal environment can make you feel more efficient, sharp as a tack! Because Metal aids in the process of letting go, anytime you feel the need to release the past, put yourself in a Metal environment.

Water Landscape

Ocean, lake, river, and canal, as well as all beach, river, and lake communities, are considered Water environments. Sites or cities on islands, such as New York, Hong Kong, Victoria Island, Honolulu, Sydney, and Melbourne, in addition to all other Water-type landscapes, are particularly suited for communication and the transmission of ideas—for example, literature, the arts, music, media, advertising, and publishing. Businesses involved in seagoing affairs obviously are well suited to a Water environment. Anytime you want to feel more social, relaxed, or at peace with the world, put yourself in a Water environment. If you sit by a river watching the waters pass by, all the answers to complex questions can be answered.

DOMINANT FEATURES

In addition to being aware of the five elements—Wood, Fire, Earth, Metal, and Water—when choosing your ideal place to live, you should be aware of the dominant human-made and geographical features, because they have a very definite influence on the flow of *chi* into, through, and out of an area or city. In the next few pages we'll look at how such things as mountains, rivers, skyscrapers, and streets can influence feng shui.

Mountains, Skyscrapers, and Dragons

Mountains and water serve a crucial purpose in feng shui. They are interdependent, creating perfect vehicles to pump beneficial *chi* through the earth's veins. Earth needs water to nourish crops in the same way you need water to sustain your life. Earth needs hills to avoid floods, and you need hills for protection from the wind and as a barrier against those who might invade. Before the discovery of the telescope, mountains were used as fixed points against which to watch the movement of the sun, moon, and stars. Mountains symbolized the stairway between heaven and earth, the path traveled by the gods who lived in the mountains and by the spirits of the dead, who also traveled this transition road.

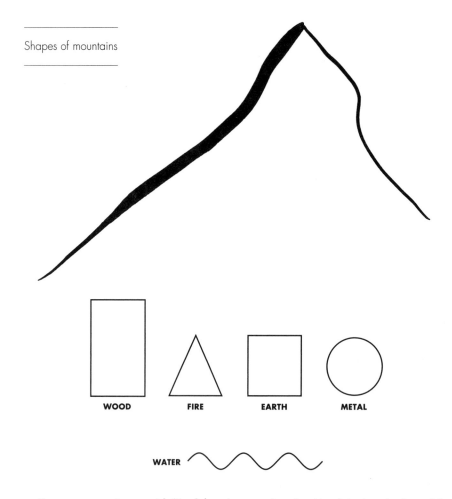

WOOD   FIRE   EARTH   METAL

WATER

Every mountain was idolized by the people who lived in its shadow: Mount Olympus, rising 9,000 feet above the Aegean Sea, was home to Greek gods and goddesses; Mount Fuji, to the Japanese, was a goddess much celebrated in art and song; Mount Sinai was revered as the place where Yahweh handed down to Moses the tablets of the Ten Commandments.

Mountains also take their meaning from one of the five elemental shapes. For example, a tall, narrow mountain, a Wood-element shape, brings much growth and nourishment to the surrounding communities. Living near a pointed mountain, which is a Fire-element shape, supports high-quality thinking because Fire also is associated with intelligence. The peaks of the Bürgenstock, Glärnisch, Tödi, and many other pointed mountains in the Alps can be seen from the entry of the World Congress Hall next to Lake Luzern, Switzerland. The Congress Hall is the site for many highly intellectual affairs. Gently rounded mountains mimic the Metal-element shape, which is associated with money. Communities living in the shadow of a round mountain are often wealthy. Plateaus and flat-topped mountains are symbolic of the Earth element, enduring, like the pueblos of the American

Indians in the United States Southwest, while a Water-shaped (irregular) mountain promises much social activity for the communities living in its shadow. Regardless of its shape, a mountain influences those who see it. Mount Rainier, one of the highest mountains in North America, casts its magic on the people of Seattle who "stay high" through the beauty of nature, spiritual pursuits, and music. In Los Angeles, the Sierras are hundreds of miles to the northeast and, notwithstanding earthquakes, riots, and fires, Los Angelenos enjoy the security of living within visual distance of an extensive mountain range that protects the fertile California valley from the harsh Nevada desert.

It is preferable to live in the shelter of a mountain, with your back protected from the cold north winds. Living in the shelter of a high building, however, may not make you feel protected. As a matter of fact, you might feel the building was overwhelming and oppressive. Living at the apex of a mountain or too high up in a building is also dangerous because of the strong winds that bombard the top of mountains or skyscrapers. Living in a basement apartment or on the bottom floor of a tall building is like living at the base of a mountain; the occupant tends to take on the problems of the upper floors. (Of course, if you are in the healing or helping professions, this may be just what you need and may suit you just fine.) The feeling of security and coziness in a basement apartment could become oppressive to some. Also, because you usually have to go upstairs to exit your house, you may feel it is a struggle to "rise in life" and may somehow regard yourself as less than successful.

Living in the shadow of a mountain or a skyscraper might make an individual feel "in awe" of life, or insignificant and inadequate compared to the size of the neighboring massive feature. Do what you can to exaggerate your entryway, and make your space important. You could place a mirror, reflective side up, on the top of the roof to reflect the larger structure back to itself. A bowl of water can be used as a reflecting pool to serve the same purpose.

Dragons figure prominently in Chinese legend and are the most frequently used symbol for mountains, particularly in the School of Forms, the oldest known type of feng shui. Different parts of the mountain mass embody different aspects of a dragon; a line of ridges leading to the summit are the vertebrae, ridges running to either side are the arms and legs; mountain streams and underground springs become the veins and arteries, exhaling "dragon breath" and pumping *chi* to the surface from deep within the earth. The highest elevation in the east is considered to be the Dragon, and the Tiger will be in the west; they are always together and cannot exist independently.

The ideal site or building is embraced by the dragon and the tiger and does not disturb them in any way. Basically this means that buildings are best located in a valley with mountains on either side. Progress and urban development have blasted tunnels through mountains, sliced off their tops, and generally rearranged their shapes to make way for roads and progress. This means that many mountains have been disturbed, which is the equivalent of cutting into the veins of the dragon or slicing off a tiger's tail. It is likely that the builders and occupants of these properties will experience bad luck. When you see the tops of mountains cut off and roads running through tunnels, you know the landscape has been altered and that you will have to work doubly hard to create a natural environment in your own space.

Remember that every place is good for something. It is your awareness of the benefits and problems that will enhance your ability to create a harmonious environment.

Rivers and Waterways

Water is life. And all people, from desert nomads to city slickers, need it to live. The banks of great rivers—the Tigris/Euphrates, the Nile, the Huang, the Amazon, the mighty Mississippi—all have mothered great civilizations. In the absence of nearby rivers, streams, lakes, oceans, natural wells or oases nourished the community. Wells provided water for the people and were also considered to be sacred sites, the source of spiritual nourishment, where oracles could be interpreted from the netherworld.

Think of what the Seine does for Paris, the Thames for London, the Charles for Boston. Rivers are the lifeblood of the earth. Like the fate of mountains, however, the natural courses of many rivers have been rearranged for the convenience of city planners or for the benefit of food crops. Los Angeles, for example, once had a river, which is now just a trickle down the middle of a concrete bed. Florida's Everglades, once a thriving watery ecosystem, is now endangered because so much of its water is being diverted for crops and to supply water to the burgeoning Miami metropolis.

In feng shui, water is synonymous with money, and good, clean water equals good money or the ability to attract money and resources. All environments containing water are superior to those without water. The most beneficial sites are those with a view of water, which is why beachfront property throughout the world, from Malibu to Malibar, is expensive and desirable. In most cities the financial district is located near the water. Even the inland financial district in Los Angeles is located on Spring Street. Natural features such as lakes, ponds, rivers, streams, waterfalls, and oceans are beneficial. Artificial waterways such as canals, sluices, conduits, reservoirs, and dams can be sources of good or bad influence. Aquariums, bowls of water, fountains, and birdbaths can be added to improve the quality of any environment.

Water can also be a destructive force. Tidal waves, hurricanes, floods, or tsunamis can destroy entire communities, erode foundations, and sweep the earth into the great sea. Water running too fast or straight creates what the Chinese call "killing *chi*," which can destroy property and lives. When water is too still it becomes stagnant and contaminated, and then problems occur.

The desert had never been considered a particularly favorable place, but with the addition of water, life can flourish. Las Vegas, Palm Springs, Santa Fe, even

The Ritz-Carlton in Marina del Rey, California, does good business, in part because of the bubbling water fountain outside the front entry.

Death Valley have become tourist attractions because of the addition of water. Like a smooth-flowing river, water flowing freely brings with it all the riches of the earth.

A young man from San Francisco complained of a lack of sex drive. The plants around his bed were sick and dying and he had allowed dried leaves and old water to accumulate on the supporting dishes. He cleaned up the dead leaves and replaced the sick plants, and his love life improved tremendously. The presence of stagnant water, whether it's in the river nearby or in the dish of your favorite houseplant, can cause all kinds of problems. Cover or hide sewers and cesspools with rocks or plants. Keep rain gutters clean. Clear away all stale water.

Even today, the Chinese go to great trouble to have a view of the water. The Regent Hotel in Hong Kong was not doing well. Its location blocked the view of the harbor from the nine dragons, represented by the peaks of the surrounding hillside. On the advice of a feng shui master, glass windows were installed in the lobby, thereby allowing the "dragons" access to their favorite bathing place.

You don't need to live on Lake Shore Drive to bring water into your life. If there is no water nearby, a pond, waterfall, fountain, birdbath, swimming pool, spa, or even a bowl of clean water can add water to any environment. The pollution of the oceans and bays, the realignment of rivers, the destruction of the rain forests all contribute to the negative energy of both planet earth and humankind. The addition of good, clean water to any environment, even if it is only a picture of water, improves the feng shui considerably.

Streets and Avenues

When there are no mountains, monuments, large buildings, rivers, or natural waterways, the main thoroughfare becomes the prime conduit of *chi*. Gently curving roads are best, and the ideal road has various elevations such as gentle mounds, valleys, and rolling hills. A variety of dimensions creates a lively and active landscape, while a one-dimensional landscape is boring and depressing.

The Imperial City, built during the Ming dynasty and rebuilt in the Qing dynasty, is a perfect example of the principles of feng shui and can be used as a model of perfection. Built on symmetrical lines to imitate the form of a human body, the palace enjoyed a north-south orientation with the main gate facing south. A southern orientation blessed the city with golden sunlight throughout the day, while a hill was erected to block the cold winds blowing in from Mongolia to the north. Even now, the tradition carries forward, and in Beijing, many houses do not have windows or other openings on the north. The gate of the Forbidden City at the center of the Imperial City was placed in front of the Golden Water Stream. Water flowing by the entrance symbolized wealth and, enclosed by a moat, the city was surrounded by wealth-giving water. The main buildings were placed in the position of the main organs of the body, with the emperor residing in the heart. The entire palace complex was decorated in auspicious colors and motifs.

Just as the subjects of the Chinese emperor were influenced by the feng shui of the Imperial City, so are we influenced by the feng shui of the city in which we live. Whether the influence is good or bad, everyone in the city is touched. Visitors to that city may also be affected to some degree. People throng to New Orleans for Mardi Gras; Las Vegas attracts gamblers; and most people go to the theater when in London.

The shape of a place can determine its fate. For example, Sicily, once the home of kings, is shaped like a ball in position to be kicked by the toe of boot-shaped Italy's mainland. You can kick a ball so many times before it deflates. Once the crossroads of the Mediterranean Sea, Sicily has been in economic decline for centuries. That's an obvious example. Others may be a bit more subtle.

Consider the town of Cuzco, Peru. Cuzco, once the center of the Inca empire and thought to be the center of the world, is now a small town serving as the drop-off point for travelers venturing up the steep mountain slopes of Machu Picchu, sacred site of the Incas. Cuzco was laid out to form the shape of a puma, with the fortress of Sacsahuamán as its head and the buildings and streets in the city below as the body, legs, and tail. Much of the city was destroyed during the Spanish conquest and subsequent uprisings, but enough Inca stonework remains to give you a sense of what Cuzco was like.

The destiny of the people follows the fate of the city. All along Highway 49 in California, the remnants of towns that flourished during the gold rush days are now shells of their former substance. Once the gold was gone, the town slid into decline. At one time, New Orleans enjoyed a stellar reputation, first as a busy seaport, then for its world-famous French Quarter. Already situated below sea level, New Orleans sinks a little more every year. And every year the political, social, and economic situation of the city also sinks a little more. Crime, pollution, and graft speed the decline. The continued pollution of the Mississippi River as it empties into the Gulf of Mexico in New Orleans ensures that the overburdened harbor will also have to process the problems of the Midwest, accumulated by the river as it flows southward.

A successful city includes all five elements—Water, Fire, Earth, Wood, and Metal. New York is a good example of a city that takes advantage of all five elements. First, it is a Water environment because it is surrounded by water. The skyscrapers, whose primary building materials are Metal and glass, add a tall, rectangular Wood shape. Central Park, located near the center of Manhattan island and in the area of prime *chi,* pumps life-giving energy through the arteries and veins of the city. Its streets, which are made of concrete, add the Earth element. Because New York City is located on waters so close to the ocean, resources could easily flow out to sea, but the resources of the city are held in check by the Statue of Liberty in New York Harbor. Lady Liberty, a gift from France, holds on high a beacon of light, welcoming immigrants and foreign imports with the warmth of the Fire element.

ASSESSING THE FENG SHUI OF A NEIGHBORHOOD

Once you have considered the major geographical features of a particular region or city, the next step is to choose a suitable neighborhood.

One of the first steps is to investigate who the neighbors are or will be. Landmarks, amusement parks, public beaches, famous people, or scandalous events attract tourists and activity. Living near factories, transit stations, police and fire departments, or other nonresidential types of noisy environments could be a deterrent to good feng shui. Even living near a gymnasium, which might at first be appealing if you are an athlete, exposes you to extra cars and people in the neighborhood. Choosing space near a garbage dump, high-power utility pole, nuclear power plant, or other source of contamination is asking for trouble.

Some places have an excess of one element, which makes them extreme and unlivable without moderation: additions of water and wood. An excess of Fire characterizes Death Valley, California, which has seen the demise of many a traveler. Antelope Valley, situated northeast of Los Angeles County, is brutalized by the Fire element (hot, dry winds that blow in from the Mojave Desert) but is a fine place to grow cactus and other desert plants.

PLACES THAT REQUIRE SPECIAL CONSIDERATION

In ancient times, feng shui automatically considered some locations as unfavorable, such as swamps and graveyards. In the following pages, we'll examine some of these environments in closer detail. If you live in a traditionally unfavorable place, don't panic. Your attitude about the place can have more effect on you than the place itself.

Graveyards

It is not preferable to live near a graveyard, cemetery, or mortuary because the energy around these places is sad, regardless of how beautifully landscaped they are. Many people do live in such areas and do just fine. London is virtually built on a graveyard.

A young woman got married in a chapel commonly used for marriages as well as funerals at Forest Lawn Cemetery, which is like a theme park for the dead. Her husband died eighteen months later at age thirty-three of a heart attack. Probably it's not good luck to get married at a graveyard or hang out around dead people. See the film *Poltergeist* for Hollywood's version of graveyard feng shui.

Hospitals

If you don't work in a hospital or are not in a healing profession, you might not be too happy living so close to a hospital that you can see the entry or ambulance entrance. You may be subtly influenced by the coming and going of sick people or you might be disturbed by the ambulance sirens. Hospitals are places of death, but they are also sites where miracles of healing occur. Just remember that you could be influenced by what goes on there; use your own judgment.

Churches

Living near a church is another situation that could be a curse or a blessing. Churches conduct funerals and would therefore expose you to sadness and death. Many churches have crosses that can become potential secret arrows of negative *chi*. Also, a cross is a constant reminder of suffering and sin. On the other hand, churches are places of hope, where faith is renewed or restored and where marriages and baptisms, which are joyful ceremonies, take place. An awareness of the influences and a proper attitude can do much to overturn the negative influences.

Deserted House

Living next to a deserted house has several problems. If the house has been deserted for a long time, the yard is bound to be overgrown and unkempt, and the house will be an eyesore. Every time you look at it, you will be reminded of ruin and decay. If it is deserted but not abandoned, the yard might become the resting home for old, rusted cars and washing machines. A house like this gives off a smell of failure. Many times deserted homes become hangouts for homeless people or teenage gangs, so you will not only have to look at an unsightly view, but you also might be in danger of vagrants or other disreputable characters who may build fires to stay warm in these old houses. The house could catch fire, which could spread to your house.

Mouth of a Bay

A bay holds in water, close to the shore. As a result, a house at the mouth of a bay enjoys and can hold on to the wealth produced by the nearness of water. Think of Genoa, Italy. For centuries it has enjoyed prosperity because it is situated at the mouth of a bay, making it an ideal, well-protected, safe harbor embraced by the Apennines behind it. Not only Christopher Columbus, but also many other prosperous merchants set sail from Genoa's lush, verdant shores. Palatial homes, some more than six hundred years old, are still occupied by the city's most successful merchants, who exemplify the benefits that can come from living at the mouth of a bay.

Peninsula

At the point of a peninsula, water rushes by on both sides and joins the ocean or lake. As the water flows past the point, money and luck run out. Add water close to entry to compensate.

Where Water Is Stagnant or Dirty

When water gets caught in fallen trees at the sides of rivers, in swamps, or murky tidepools, it ceases to flow and can become stagnant. Stagnant water is great for snakes and mosquito larvae, but it does not nurture human life. When you live near standing water, there is a possibility that energy in your life has ceased to flow. There may be blockages, which can lead to contaminated affairs and health. If you've ever experienced a bout of constipation, you understand this concept. If there is stagnant water near the property, try to provide a barrier between you and the bad water, using plants, fences, or statuary. If the stagnant water is on the prop-

A house situated at the mouth of a bay is likely to hold and retain wealth for its occupants.

A house situated at the point of a peninsula cannot hold the wealth offered by the water.

erty, plant lotus flowers or other water plants in it. Such plants love the mud and will thrive, providing you with a colorful garden of water flowers. If the stagnant water is from rain gutters, clean out the gutters.

Water Flows by Too Quickly

If water flows by too quickly it cannot nurture the living things it passes. Rushing rivers do not nourish their shores. Money and resources go with them. Use large stones, statues, plants, or rock fences with lights on the posts to create a barrier between you and the rushing water. Mirrors placed close to the structure will call the water and encourage its energy to linger by your property.

Water Too Close

With water too close to the property, there may be danger of flooding or swamping. Water flowing past the side of a building does not enhance its feng shui. Water that passes by the front door is more auspicious but should be gentle and slow-moving. Think of a moat surrounding a castle, protecting the wealth of those living within.

Water Too Far Away

If the water is too far away but you can still see it, use mirrors to bring its reflection inside the building. When water is not visible, add either still or active water to the space, get a wave machine or an aquarium, or use images of water in pictures or photographs as part of the decor. Hang crystals in the windows to magnify the negative ions released by the distant water. Use glass objects such as bowls or plates to decorate your home.

Pond in West

If there are ponds or pools on the property, make note of their location. A pond located on the west side of the property is not as fortunate as one located in any other direction because the West symbolizes endings and can swallow the good fortune promised by the water. Use a mirrored garden ball (popular in Victorian times) or any reflective surface in the east to reflect and "move" the western-placed pond to the more favorable side. If the water in the West pond is still, cover the surface with water plants so it looks more like a garden than a pond.

On a Canal

A business executive lives on a canal in Naples, California. The water rises or falls depending on the tides and the moods of the local government officials. Her fortune goes up and down with the water in the canal. When it's not moving, no opportunities come to her. When it is flowing, opportunities abound. Life that rises and falls with the tides is not as stable or pleasant as life next to a deep, calm, and clear lake or a gently flowing river. Still, it is beneficial. Just adjust your expectations and energy to the tides and don't lose faith. Every tide that goes out eventually comes in.

Unless the water in these canals becomes stagnant or overflows, this house will reap benefits from having a flow of water past its front door.

Near an Arroyo

Arroyos create cracks and fissures in the surface of the earth, and these can become secret arrows. Because water is associated with life, a view of a dried-up arroyo can coincide with infertility in the body and the mind. The American Southwest is full of arroyos, but many people manage to live there and still have happy, artistically creative, and successful lives, especially when the structure is in harmony with the environment. Low, flat structures built of earth materials, stone, and adobe plus the addition of active and still water enhance and enliven a dry environment. Indoor desk fountains, even a bowl of water, or a clear glass of water, can serve as a fountain. Wind chimes or light, airy things that flutter in the wind stimulate the *chi*. A birdhouse encourages living things to come to the property, and this, in turn, brings life and energy into the environment.

Gullies

Sha chi is found in natural gullies or dried-up river beds that form straight lines. Here there is danger during times of extreme rainfall because such formations tend to fill and overflow, flooding the surrounding areas. Create a barrier through the use of landscaping or fencing that blocks any arrows created by straight lines in the ground and spares your property from flooding.

Swamps

Living near a swamp has a few problems, including muggy weather, alligators, giant mosquitoes, weak soil, and quicksand. Sound awful? Not to those who live in New Orleans; Key West, Florida; or the Amazon Basin in Brazil. Abundant life thrives in the fertile, fecund, rich, steamy, sexy swamp.

Where the Ground Is Sandy and Wet

It is best to avoid areas where the ground is sandy and wet because it is difficult to lay a strong foundation, usually essential to the building. However, in certain environments such avoidance is not possible. In the Amazon Basin of Brazil the preferred construction style is on stilts, which can accommodate a river that rises as much as twenty-three feet during the rainy season. Structures built on logs that float and rise with the river are also suitable there. Houses built in the sandy soil near an ocean or lake often have relatively small foundations, and the second stories are supported by steel beams balanced on poles. (This is similar to a stilt foundation; it just doesn't look that way.) If these are the conditions where you live, match the building to the soil and you'll be in tune with nature and have a good space.

On Land That Has Been Burned

Nothing grows on burned ground, and the soil is easily washed away. Land that has been burned should be left untouched for seven years. However, if you have to rebuild on burnt ground, remove at least three feet of topsoil from the entire lot and replace it with fresh soil before any construction begins.

On Hard Rocky Soil

In the West, we are so willful that we insist on building on hard rocky soil even though it is difficult, expensive, and often requires the use of dynamite to blast into a mountain. This activity disturbs the natural force of the mythical dragons that reside there. If you live in such a place, in some small way honor the mountain that has been damaged and cover the wounds with vines and plants.

Where Ground Is Sunken

It is considered unfavorable to live where the surrounding ground is high and the actual site is sunken, because of danger from flooding or being engulfed by fire. However, many successful spiritual retreats are built on this type of property because it offers solitude and withdrawal from the world at large.

In Malibu, California, there is a successful mini-mall near the Malibu Creek, which empties into the Pacific Ocean. The mall is built on sunken ground, and when the creek floods, so does the mall. When the creek dries up in the summer, mosquitoes irritate the customers. It's not good feng shui to live on sunken ground, but it is done all the time. Businesses last about two years at the Malibu mini-mall and then move to higher ground. Consider the kind of water that is near the site. If it is dirty or polluted or stagnant, so might be your business interests.

Mountains

A mountain in front of a building might block energy from entering. If the mountain is in the back, it protects the structure from the elements—wind, rain, and snow. If the mountain is too close to the back of the structure, however, there is danger from mudslides, avalanches, and fires.

When there are no mountains, the largest constructed mass, building, or monument is interpreted as if it were a mountain. An odd-shaped mountain can bring misfortune. A Chinese-born friend blamed her harelip on her ancestors. She said their graves faced a cleft in a hill and, because of this, each generation gave birth to one child with a harelip.

In the Shadow of a Mountain or Large Building Next to a Mountain

Living near a mountain is generally favorable but is dependent on the placement of the structure relative to the mountain. Some people may feel protected and safe living very close to a mountain or large building; others might feel overwhelmed. Living near a mountain gives us the opportunity to use the mountain as a model to emulate the great and have compassion for the small. Whatever feeling a mountain inspires in you, remember that we all have our own destiny, and that what is suitable for others may not be the best for you.

Living in a small structure overshadowed by a bigger one is like living too close to a mountain. You can symbolically "raise its roof" by placing a mirror, reflective side up, on the top of the roof to reflect the larger structure back to itself. A bowl of water placed on the roof or in the garden can be used as a reflecting pool to serve the same purpose.

Closed in by Mountain or Building

Many structures are built too close to a hillside or mountain and, unless they are actually built into the hillside, with the entry in a different place, are not considered favorable because the entry gets no light from the sun and, basically, the

The house in the center is overshadowed by larger houses on both sides and by a huge tree that blocks the light. Notice how small and dark the house seems. A solution is to remove the tree and/or place reflective material on the roof to bounce the energy from the bigger houses away from the smaller house.

energy is blocked. There also is danger during rain because of mudslides. An entry canopy or covering trellis can help focus the *chi*. Lights will do what the sun cannot, and water will circulate the *chi* by the entry. It is very important to keep this area free of debris, garbage, boxes, etc. Living very close to a larger building gives you a brick wall for a view. Keep the window covered with drapery or screens. If there is natural light, use tall bushy vines or long hanging plants in front of the window to disguise it. If possible, build a window box outside and grow tall plants, herbs, and tomatoes in it.

Squeezed Between Two Larger Buildings

If your house is squeezed between two larger buildings, try to incorporate some element of design, color, or texture of the larger structures into your overall design scheme to make your building look as much like the adjoining ones as possible. For example, if the adjoining structures are painted gray, paint your house gray; if they have cypress trees, plant cypress trees on your lot.

Under a Cliff

Living under a cliff could feel very protected or oppressive, depending on your point of view. Just make sure the roof and supporting beams are strong and made of metal or concrete rather than wood. Use electric lights to replace unavailable

This house seems to have been built without consideration of the mountain or the laws of gravity. It is not a place for the timid or faint of heart.

sunlight and make sure you don't develop a hunched-over stance from thinking the weight of the world is hanging over you.

On the Edge of a Cliff

Living on the edge of a cliff is just right for an adventurous type, nerve-racking to the more timid. Make sure your protecting fences are strong, check for erosion daily, and contemplate why you choose the edge of a cliff for your space.

Next to Elevator, Staircase, Exit, Bus Stop, Subway, Train Station, School, Fire or Police Station

If you live next to a frequently used exit, you may often see people leaving the building. This may make you feel like you always have to go somewhere, and it may be hard to settle down and stay home for very long. A client had trouble keeping household help. The maid's room was very close to the exit. Maids came and went until the client moved the maid's room farther from the exit. Now she can't get the maid to take a day off!

If your apartment is next to an elevator, there is bound to be a lot of traffic coming and going, which may have the same effect as living next to an exit. Also, people waiting for the elevator and the mechanical effects themselves may disturb your peace and quiet. Of course, an apartment placed near an exit or elevator is good for a quick getaway, which can sometimes be an advantage. Occupants of an apartment next to or across from an incinerator or close to the trash and to fire may see some plans or dreams go up in smoke.

A client in a retirement village in Laguna Hills, California, lives in a condominium in the front of a single-story building and next to a stairwell that goes to underground parking. She is in her eighties, has a busy social calendar, does volunteer work, has been awarded many honors for her involvement with the community, and is in fairly good health. There is an adjoining unit in back of her, out of the line of *chi* from the entry next to the stairwell. Everyone who moves into that unit withdraws and then dies because any energy coming from the street goes into the front units or down the stairs. The back unit is quieter and so seemingly more desirable, but it does not receive life-giving *chi*.

Next to Reflective Glass

Living next to a building clad in reflective glass is like living next to a giant mirror. There may be too much light/heat *chi* because sunlight plus mirrors equals glare, which then bounces off other buildings, creating hazards for passersby as well as occupants in nearby buildings. Inside, if there is a panoramic view, the occupant may feel overwhelmed by all there is to see. If the view is blocked by a neighboring building, the view becomes a kind of blank wall, which is not inspiring. People who live in mirrored or glass houses are also in danger from flying objects coming in through the windows. To ensure privacy, window coverings must be used. Glass, as a primary construction material, is not a good insulator. In winter, the heat cannot be retained. In summer, the air conditioning is lost. Just remember: Every place is good for something. Your awareness of the benefits and the problems can enhance your ability to create a harmonious environment. For example, glass walls can act as giant windows, through which we can happily watch the clouds go by.

Placement on a Mountain

Frank Lloyd Wright liked to build structures on mountains, but he never choose the top as the site, saying he didn't like to put a building, like a hat, on the top of a mountain. He preferred a placement about 20 percent down from the top, which he called "an eyebrow on the mountain."

If you live in a multiunit building, it is like living on a mountain. Your placement within the building and your relationship to the units above, below, to each side, and across from you also affect the feng shui of your unit.

Top of Mountain/Top of Building

The benefit of living at the top of a mountain or building is the million-dollar view. The high life, however, is somewhat dangerous, because winds that barrage the tops of structures can be overwhelmingly strong. Put barriers between you and the prevailing winds or you'll be blown off the mountain.

CHAPTER 4

The Feng Shui of a
Home's Exterior

W hether you are looking for a new home or just want to make the best of where you are, feng shui can help you find or create a home that is in harmony with the environment, and one in which the flow of *chi* is abundant and healthy.

APPROACHING YOUR HOME: THE IMPORTANCE OF YOUR STREET'S NAME, DIRECTION, AND CONDITION

What's in a Name?

The name of the street is important because it sets the tonal vibration for the house. Every time you say or write your address, you set this vibration in motion. A very successful woman lives on Royal Oak Drive. She is affectionately called "Czarina" by those who know and love her. A young boy used to go to school on Hayter Street. It was a running joke that when asked about school, he'd say, "I hayter." He eventually had to leave the school in the middle of the semester because the school went bankrupt and was evicted from the site. A writer lived on Neptune Street, a gently curving street along the ocean that unfortunately ended in a dead end. Many women who lived on the street were alcoholic widows. The writer wasn't a widower when he moved to Neptune Street, but while he was living there, his beloved pet was run over by a car, giving him "widower's status." Still, his experience there was not all bad because it coincided with a tremendously creative time for his work and he wrote a wonderful musical there.

Know Where You're Coming From

The direction from which you approach a house can influence how you feel on a day-to-day basis. This is because different directions tend to produce different feelings. When going east, the energy tends to be enthusiastic, bright, and eager, because the east is where the sun rises. If you approach your home from the east, home is a place of high activity and energy, a very busy place. When you approach your home from the west, the direction of the setting sun, home is a place of entertainment, retirement, and rest, or maybe children, because the west is associated with the "children of the sun." Approaching home from the west makes your home a very relaxing place. If you approach your home from the north, business, money, career, and status preoccupy your thinking. You may spend a lot of time "keeping up with the Joneses" or being the Jones family that sets the standards for others. If you approach your home from the north, you might find yourself feeling efficient, organized, and successful—all attributes of the north. If you approach your home from the south, you'll have a more philosophical and easygoing point of view and not be so hard driven at business. Let's review the directions:

> **EAST:** *Lively, dynamic, ambitious energy*
> **WEST:** *Retirement, rest, children, and family*
> **NORTH:** *Efficiency and business orientation*
> **SOUTH:** *Relaxed and philosophical*

What if you don't like the direction from which you approach your home or business or bank or supermarket? Simple! Before you get to where you are going, go around the block, and make your final approach from the desired direction. This may sound kind of crazy and like a waste of time but it's fun to experiment. Keep a compass in your car and make note of what direction you're going, how you feel, and what happens when you get there. Keep a diary of this and soon you will discover what directions are best for you.

The Final Approach Street

As you approach a property, analyze the flow of *chi* by considering the condition and configuration of the streets, driveways, and walkways that lead to it. The way the final approach street is maintained as well as its configuration affects those who live and travel upon it. A broad, tree-lined, gently curving avenue in good repair surely leads to a successful home. Whenever possible, travel along curved, well-maintained streets to approach the site.

Streets in need of repair, or that are narrow, steep, crooked, winding, blocked, dirty, messy, broken, barren, smelly, congested, poorly lit, not clearly marked, or that have too many cars and people can cause problems. Living, driving, or walking along streets that end in T-junctions, culs-de-sac, or dead ends can drain us of hope and energy; we seem unable to follow through on anything. Living at the tip of a peninsula, crossroad, or Y-split, or living near railroad tracks, bridges, tunnels, or overpasses can give rise to tension, anxiety, and stress. The noise and vibrations created by these high-traffic situations can make you feel constantly on edge.

When poorly configured or damaged streets inhibit or prevent *chi* from entering the buildings, you will have to use your talents as a host or hostess to invite, direct, and welcome the *chi* to your space, encouraging it to stay indefinitely by creating curves and imitating nature whenever you can.

PROBLEM STREETS

Street Too Narrow

Driving or walking along congested or narrow streets suggests a pathway to narrow lives with limited potential or resources. If this is the type of road to your home or office and there is no other road to take, you need to develop an attitude that interprets "narrow" as "focus" rather than complain about something you can do nothing about. If you live in an apartment building where the corridors (your "approach street") are narrow, use mirrors, light colors, and good lighting to widen the hallway. Always remove debris or other objects that have accumulated in the hallway.

A Flat, Featureless Street

A flat, featureless road produces a feeling of desolation and death. Traveling to work on such a road might leave you feeling uninspired; going home on such a road could be a depressing prospect. As you travel along such a road, don't focus on the details but rather look as far as you can see, beyond the road, traffic, and buildings. Look to the sky or the open space and think about the big picture. Then make sure that the landscaping and exterior features of your house offer you a welcome sight.

Street in Disrepair

A broken street (or shabby carpeting or flooring in an apartment building) means broken promises and broken lives. Unfortunately, these conditions are the government's or management's problem. All we can do is watch our step, try not to drive into potholes, and petition for repairs. We can make sure our own path or driveway is in good shape and watch where we're going.

Road with Sharp Turns and Twists

A road with sharp turns may lead to reversals and fast changes in a topsy-turvy life. A twisting, winding road can portend a complicated life, filled with changes and surprises. In an apartment building, a hallway that leads to many corridors may confuse the *chi* and, in turn, confuse the occupants. If you must drive or live with sharp turns and twists, develop flexibility and the ability to adapt instantly. Don't fall prey to crooked thinking with hidden agendas. Be honest, think straight, and keep your goals always in sight.

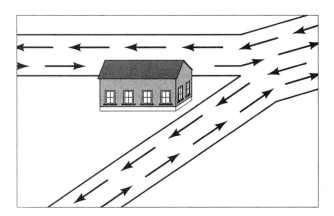

A house located in a fork in the road receives energy from all four directions and is in the flow of *chi*.

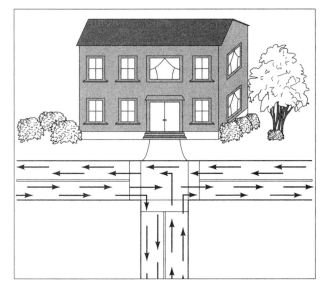

At the base of a T-intersection, the flow of energy can become so complex and congested that none reaches your door.

Split or Fork in the Road

If your home is located near a split or fork in the road, it can benefit from the energy that flows along both streets. There can be internal conflicts, however, if one family member wants to go one way and another doesn't agree. If there is a split or fork in the entry path, there may be arguments among the people who inhabit the house. Try to connect the fork with a hyphen by painting red marks between the split. You can use red stones, tile, paint, chalk, or even nail polish to indicate the connecting marks. The size of the marks is not important.

Streets with T-Intersections

When your home is located at a cross in the road, or at a place where the road forms a T-shape, the energy becomes extremely congested and confused. Cars from three or four directions all converge at the intersection. If you live close to the T-junction, you may experience problems in making decisions, your life may always seem to be at the crossroads, and your movement may seem constantly blocked by others who want the same things you do. Develop patience. Let others go first. Have confidence that your destiny and personality will take you where you need to go.

When you live at the crossroads or near a T-intersection, you need to call and direct the *chi*. Make sure your entry is well lighted. Put down a half-circle door-mat in front of the door. Paint your door a different color from the window trim. Place circular pots of plants on either side of the entry.

Street Too Straight

Straight roads are especially treacherous because their shape imitates that of an arrow being shot from a bow. The arrow points directly to anything located at the end of its path. Energy naturally flows in a gentle curve. When it is forced into straight lines it tends to pick up speed. Think of a shooting bullet.

If your house is at the end of straight road, erect a barrier in the form of trees or a fence between the house and the street, or install a bubbling fountain in front of the entrance. The bubbling water can act as a filter—a kind of "speed bump"—for the energy coming toward the house. Or hang a mirror near the entry, reflective side facing the street, to draw the energy from the straight line away from the entry door. Do not put a mirror directly *on* the entry door or inside the entry facing out, because this prevents good *chi* from coming into the house.

In apartment buildings, the entry to the apartment is commonly off a long, straight, and narrow corridor. Apartments at the end, facing the corridor, are subject to the energy traveling swiftly toward them. Hanging a picture on the inside of the entry door will protect the interior from the vibrations of the hall. A client living in New York City hung pictures of guard dogs on the inside of her door and she says she always feels safe.

Culs-de-Sac and Dead-End Streets

Living in a cul-de-sac may pose a problem because the energy from the street tends to accumulate in the center house. This could make the house the focus of the neighborhood, a place where friends gather for barbecues and good times. Or the house could accumulate all the problems of the neighbors and be the focus of negative energy. For this reason, it is best to live in one of the side houses and not at the end of the cul-de-sac.

Living on a dead-end street is very safe, especially for small children who like to play in the street. The energy that comes down the street, however, is stopped by the dead-end so it is easy for houses located here to accumulate all kinds of stuff, just as if all the energy from the street stopped at your house and wouldn't leave. Excess *chi* can create an unmanageable life with so many responsibilities or commitments that there is no time for self-development. Also, because a dead end stops energy, projects, careers, and relationships stop short in their tracks. Life may

A house built at the end of a road with no outlet must contend with all the built-up *chi* from the street.

STREET ENDS no outlet

appear to be a dead-end. Also, living on a dead-end street offers only one way in or out, dangerous in a fire or flood.

If you live at the end of a dead-end street or in the center house of a cul-de-sac, just be aware of the problems that can occur when energy is stopped. If you place still water in the form of a pond or birdbath in the front opposite the street, this encourages the energy to fill the pool and nurture the house. Running, active water, whether from a waterfall or water fountain, will ensure that the energy is recirculated, creating a healthier environment. Place a flag, windmill, wind chime, or other object that twirls in the wind in the backyard to circulate the energy and ensure that it doesn't become stagnant.

House Located Between Streets or Corridors

A house located between two roads may have trouble containing resources, which could go out as fast as they come in. Also, maintaining security in such a place could be difficult, exposing the occupants to burglaries or other intrusions. Try to separate your property from the streets with trees and landscaping or fences that are the maximum height allowed in your neighborhood. Have only one opening through these barriers and keep the actual entry to the structure as far away from the streets as possible. If there are other entrances and exits, keep them locked or designate them as large windows.

House Located at the Corner

Energy comes from both sides, and an entry slanted to take in both sides has the benefit of attracting greater amounts of *chi*. Think of successful hotels whose entries span an entire corner. Corner houses, corner apartments, and corner offices

This grocery store has been successful for more than 25 years. It has an angled entry, which benefits from *chi* coming from both streets and from straight ahead. The mailbox (Metal) provides a nice focus that attracts money for the store.

Here a dramatic driveway leads to a fountain but not to the entry, which is to the side and out of the picture. Life-giving *chi* goes to the fountain, stops at the fence, and bounces back to the driveway without ever reaching the entry.

are valued for their ability to attract good resources. A very successful mechanic's shop is situated to take advantage of energy that comes down the main street and into his shop. He is known as "the Prince of Mechanics," maybe because his shop acts like a funnel for positive *chi*. Cars come in and go out, leaving large amounts of dollars behind.

THE DRIVEWAY AND PATH TO MAIN DOOR

The driveway and path to the entrance are the main conduits of *chi* into the house. In ancient times, the king's path was preceded by young girls who threw flowers in the walkway. Today the wedding aisle is covered with rose petals to ensure a sweet and fragrant entrance for the bride. The red carpet is still laid down for Very

Important People. Flowers in the path and red carpets protect the walker from the grime and dirt of ordinary life and transmit the idea that those who walk upon it are special. Buildings become more impressive when designed with a walkway and entrance that are impressive and grand. Think of Vatican City in Rome with its many columns and decorations. There is no one more important to the Roman Catholic world than the pope, and the pathway to his house certainly proclaims it.

While it may not be covered in rose petals or red carpets, a well-tended, clean, and neat path is preferable to a dirty, weed-infested one. Remember that *chi,* life energy, flows in a curve. A curved walkway becoming wider as it approaches the front door makes way for sufficient *chi* to enter. If a narrow path or driveway joins abruptly to a wide front landing, the proportions and flow are off. Like a small hose filling up a big pool, not enough *chi* can get to the front door.

The driveway, like the path to the front door, directs the *chi* from the street to the house. When it is smooth, life also tends to move along smoothly. When it is level, there is a good chance those who live there avoid the extremes of life and are well balanced, living a calm and steadily progressive life. A level walkway is similar to a first-floor apartment. Even though occupants of the first floor tend to be burdened with the problems and cares of the upper floors, because the walkway to the apartment is level with the street (usually), these occupants tend to have steady, even progress through the years. Living in such a space, you can easily develop a well-balanced, level point of view.

Elevated Entry

A house whose entry is elevated above street level is considered to be yang—and receives an automatic "boost" that can help you rise to success and prominence. When you leave the house, you travel downhill, making your exit an easy one, which can lead to an easy kind of life. The difficulty here is that life may take a "downslide," and all your efforts may go downhill, with fortune turning into decline. Energy may have trouble getting to the house, while resources, luck, and health may flow away from the house, down the hill. To counter this negative flow, plant bushes or place flowerpots on both sides of the path near the street, or install lights low to the ground near the side of the house nearest the street. Another solution is to install brick posts on either side of the entryway or driveway, at the base of the slope. This can inhibit the downhill slide so that more energy stays with the house.

Living in an apartment at the top of the stairs is similar to living in a house at the top of an uphill path. You might develop a "king" complex and begin to develop a conceited or arrogant point of view toward the people living below you. If this is your problem, contemplate the oneness of all living creatures and count your blessings. Living in such a space might have the opposite effect, causing anxiety and pressure. Ambition and self-esteem may be low, making you feel isolated and alone—as if climbing the stairs is all that can be accomplished. If you live in such an apartment, make sure the light above the entry is bright and keep it on even during the day. If you can paint the door, use light colors. A warm, inviting doormat also encourages the *chi* to enter this type of apartment.

Entry Below Street Level

If the driveway or walkway is sloped, it might be difficult to maintain equilibrium; life may seem to go up and down with some crisis always occurring. A house situated lower than street level is considered to be yin—and can make the occupants more receptive, creative, compassionate, and empathetic. When you leave the house, however, you travel uphill, which may make you feel that life is an uphill struggle or overwhelming challenge. Also, when the entry is lower than the level of the street, you might be inclined to "sink your fortune" into unsuccessful endeavors or be tempted by unethical activities. Something about your life may be hidden, or need to be hidden, because houses lower than street level are often protected by shade trees offering protection from the light and the business of everyday activities. These places are excellent for rest and recuperation, for deep inner psychological or spiritual work. Esalen Institute in Big Sur, California, is built on sunken ground with the main entry far below the street. It has been a successful metaphysical, psychological, and spiritual center for many years. If your entrance is lower than the street level, install a light on a tall pole behind the house, pointed up toward the roof, to bring up the energy. Another solution is to hang wind chimes from the eaves to call the *chi* upward.

Those who live in houses built on sloping ground may have problems holding on to resources, because *chi* and money run out. If your house is on sloping ground, make sure that the platform or foundation upon which it rests is level. Living at the bottom of a hill is like living in a basement apartment. The problems of the neighbors living farther up the hill run down to those living below. Living at the bottom can be oppressive, giving the feeling that the world is caving in. Occupants in such a place might find themselves at the "bottom of the barrel," always struggling to rise in life.

Living in a basement apartment is similar to living in a house whose front door is below street level. Here you may feel oppressed and burdened, but, at the same time, there is warmth and total security in these cozy places. Basements can be rather dark, so artificial lighting is important. A couple lived in a basement apartment in Chelsea, England. There were only two windows in the front, which looked out at people's feet as they walked by. The woman was very creative and worked in the healing arts. She managed to grow beautiful plants in her little space with the help of artificial lighting. She lived in the same place for more than thirty years and was quite happy and successful.

Basically, every place is good for something. Just be aware that your placement can have a great effect on your well-being. If you live on the edge of a cliff, turn those "edgy" feelings into something more positive by admiring the view, working in your garden, or cleaning your house. If you live next to a freeway, pretend the roar of cars is the roar of the ocean. Embrace your space, wherever it is. Feng shui can make good space sensational and bad space healthful. A lot depends on your awareness.

Paths and Driveways

The best type of path or driveway is the same width throughout, then widens as it gets to the landing. Energy travels in a curve, making curved and circular driveways particularly favorable and beautiful. If the driveway is angled and formed by two straight lines, it becomes a secret arrow and may encourage negative *chi* to approach the house. Also, an angled path or driveway makes it difficult to see oncoming traffic. If it is possible, place round objects over or near the corners of the angles, turning a straight line into a curve, or install a mirror to see what you cannot.

Steps leading to the entry should be gradual and wide. Steps that are steep, narrow, or broken foretell disaster within. A man lived at the top of such a stairway and had experienced ill health for some time, which caused him to stay home a lot. He spent some money and time fixing the stairs, and his health improved considerably. If the stairs leading to your house or apartment are not in good repair, do what you can to fix them. Install banisters or handrails for safety, and paint the stairs white or a light color. In interior stairwells, use mirrors or other reflective objects on the staircase walls to give the illusion of width, and make sure the space is well lit by installing lights at both the top and bottom.

If there are stairs opposite the entry, there is a chance that resources as well as luck could roll downstairs. Place a basket at the base of the stairs to "catch" the flow.

THE SIGNIFICANCE OF YOUR HOME'S ADDRESS

The address of the building as well as the address of your particular unit in a multi-unit building are as significant as the name of the street. In feng shui, numbers mean more than their use in adding, subtracting, and multiplying. They are symbols that have esoteric meaning. Systems and techniques for interpreting numbers are varied and numerous, but because feng shui's origins are Chinese, it seems logical to use Chinese numerology to assess the meaning of a particular address.

Chinese numerology is based on homophonic principles. Many Chinese words, when spoken, sound alike. If a number sounds like something good, it is considered to be a good number. If it sounds like something bad, it is considered to be a bad number.

In Chinese numerology, numbers can be either yin or yang. Yin numbers are even, and yang numbers are odd. Yang numbers are considered more fortunate than yin numbers. Zero represents nothing, perfection, completion, and harmony. A favorable address combines yin and yang, as in 183 or 2176. Addresses that contain all yin or all yang numbers, like 44 or 113, seem to coincide with lifestyles that are heavily weighted toward one function: all work and no play; all play and

ONE: *In Chinese, the word for "one" sounds like the word for "honor." One is considered to be a lucky number. It represents the Water element and the north direction.*

TWO: *Sounds similar to the word for "sure." Two stands for "doubling up" (as in "double your happiness") and for symmetry, and is considered a good number. It corresponds with Fire and south.*

THREE: *In Cantonese, the word for "three" sounds like the word for "growth" or "alive" and is considered to be lucky. It represents Wood and east. The Chinese regard a three-sided house as unlucky because a three-sided object is unstable. Three fish are considered lucky or to represent abundant growth.*

FOUR: *Sounds like the word for "death" and is considered very unlucky unless it is combined with a favorable number, e.g., 45. Four represents the west direction and the Metal element.*

FIVE: *In Cantonese sounds like "nothing" but is a popular number because of the five-element classification. It represents the central position and signifies balance. When combined with two, four, six, or eight, it becomes extremely auspicious because each pair of numbers is balanced.*

SIX: *Sounds similar to the word for "wealth," making it an extremely popular number. Also sounds like the word for "deer," which makes the deer an auspicious symbol. Represents the element Water and the north direction.*

SEVEN: *Sounds like the Cantonese word for "sure" and is considered to be a very fortunate or lucky number. Represents Fire and south.*

EIGHT: *Sounds like the word for "multiply" and represents good luck. It is considered to be a "fertile number." If you desire many sons, live in a house with eight in the address. Represents the Wood element and the east direction.*

NINE:: *Is considered one of the luckiest numbers because it sounds like the word for "longevity" and "long life." Represents the Metal element and the west direction.*

TEN: *Last on the decimal scale, it implies completeness. It is not, however, particularly auspicious, because it is a yin number. It is not associated with any element or direction.*

ONE HUNDRED: *Sounds like the words for "very much" and "forever." It is a very auspicious number and represents longevity. Associated with heaven as a direction and the Metal element.*

TEN THOUSAND: *Represents plenitude. The emperor in China was addressed as "wan sui" (ten thousand years old) to signify his long reign. It is associated with Earth and the direction center, because this was the emperor's realm.*

no work; tribal style with lots of ex-wives and children; living alone; and so on. A mixed address, because it contains yin and yang, offers a better chance for a balanced life while living there.

The meaning of certain number combinations is based on the similarity between the sounds of the numbers and other words.

1 + 2: very easy in Cantonese, a popular number

1 + 2 + 8: easy to succeed

1 + 4: sure to die (avoid it unless a third number can be added)

1 + 4 + 8: sure to prosper to the end

2 + 3: double the growth

2 + 4: easy to die or easy to the end

2 + 6: double wealth or double your money

3 + 6: abundant wealth or abundant gold

3 + 1: plentiful honor

4 + 8: succeed to the end

5 + 4: do not die

5 + 6: nothing but wealth

6 + 1: wealth with honor

6 + 8: wealth multiplies

7 + 5: sure to get nothing

7 + 3: sure growth, have more sons

8 + 100: multiply forever

9 + 100: long life

100 + 3: forever wealthy

In summary, remember that Chinese numerology is based on the way the number sounds when pronounced and its similarity to other words having the same sound. For further information, consult Evelyn Lip's *Chinese Numbers* (Union City, California: Heian International, 1992), from which this material was adapted.

THE HISTORY OF THE PROPERTY

Money does not determine good feng shui. Still, it is very easy to understand why the rich get richer and the poor get poorer. The rich can build beautiful homes with gracious entries, with pools and fountains, and surrounded by nature—all of which enhance the *chi*. These properties feel rich, and the lives of the occupants show it.

Upon approaching your home, office, or any other structure, feel its "presence." Does it impress you with its grandeur or send shivers up your spine? Does it remind you of Grandma's house or the Bates Motel? The site should feel protected, with sufficient distance between the house and the street to afford the occupants privacy and some space from the outside world.

Every property has a history, and the history stays with the space long after the occupants have gone. Ask when the original house was built, because this will give you some idea of the condition of the house and the attitude of those who built it. Were any additions constructed and, if so, when and how much of the house was remodeled? If the roof was removed and replaced or if the roofline was changed by additions, the house changed also. For example, if the house was built in 1929, a year that coincided with the downfall of the Stock Market, the original owner might have experienced something similar. If it was remodeled in 1980 at the beginning of the real-estate boom, the house may have valuable additions. If more than half of the house was rebuilt, or if the roof was totally taken off and replaced, treat the house as if it were new. That means that the fortune that occurred in 1929 has been revamped for 1980 standards. Who lived there before? Were they successful, or did they fail? It is a popular trend to buy foreclosure property because it is offered at an extremely low price. If you are considering purchasing one of these properties, think twice. The reason the bank foreclosed was because the previous occupants could not afford the payments. Do you want the memory of failed lives lingering in the house?

Be sure to ask questions about the fate of the previous occupant. If you are buying something at a reduced price, it's usually because no one wants it at the regular price because there is something wrong with it, or the owner can't afford it himself, which means the property is not particularly lucky. If the previous owner died of a brain tumor, got a divorce, or filed for bankruptcy, think twice about moving into the same space. Remember, the karma of the previous occupant lingers.

Ask questions about the neighbors and about their pets. Nothing ruins the peace and quiet of the evening like a barking dog or party music blaring through the night. Offensive neighbors and dogs can be deflected by hanging a mirror with the reflective side facing the intrusion. Plants, shrubs, trees, and fences can also provide effective barriers. Common sense, however, must prevail. If you buy a house near a nuclear power plant, you're asking for trouble. But people adapt to whatever is around. Students keep registering at Cal State Dominguez Hills, California, even though the smell of sulphur is everywhere. People living near JFK Airport have learned to stop talking when the jets take off, just as actors in San Diego outdoor theaters have learned to stop performing during takeoffs and landings from nearby Lindberg Field.

We adjust, but should we? Is it really necessary to live next to the fire or police station, with bells ringing and engines roaring constantly? It is better to find a property with good feng shui than try to correct what is wrong with a bad one. Further, if you live in a building that has the owner's name plastered across the top, like Trump Tower, the fate of the owner of the building will rub off on you, for good or bad.

Sometimes, however, negative energy can be healed. One woman's backyard swimming pool was the scene of a tragic drowning. Every time she looked at the pool she was reminded of the incident. Finally, since she loved the house, she filled in the swimming pool and covered it with grass. This created a lovely garden and she stayed in the house. Not to be ghoulish, but death is a natural occurrence, and not every house is cursed because someone died in it. Death doesn't necessarily make for bad feng shui. A television producer purchased the house of a film star who had lived in the house for twenty-four years, dying in the arms of her long-time lover. The house is charming and romantic, and everyone who has lived in it since her death has prospered.

I'm getting a little ahead of myself here, because a house's *interior* feng shui is the topic of a future chapter, but you should know that the old vibrations from any space can and must be cleansed before you take possession of the space. This means that when you move into a new space (new for you), whether it is a home or a hotel room, an office or a desk in a typing pool, you need to cleanse it. If your household relationships break up and you are staying in the same place, treat the space as if it were new and follow the same procedure as if you were moving into a new space. This can help you to get on with your life. The following procedure is simple to do and you will notice an immediate affect on your emotions and fortunes.

1. *Clean everything.* Look in all closets and drawers; check outside rain gutters, drains, and other places where water or dirt can accumulate. If you can, purchase a new bed and new bed linens. If you can't or don't want to do this, make sure the linen you put on the bed is absolutely clean. Pillows, too.

2. *Wash the insides of all the door and window frames.* Wash especially those around the entrance and exit, with strong soapy water, or use citrus water made from a mixture of the rinds of five pieces of citrus fruit (lemon, orange, tangerine, grapefruit, lime) in one gallon of water.

3. *Make sure everything works.* Turn on all appliances, heaters, coolers, etc., to make sure they work. Don't leave them on. Check them and turn them off. If they don't work, throw them out or get them fixed as soon as you can.

4. *Use good-quality incense or sticks of sage, cedar, or sweetgrass to smoke your new house.* Walk the perimeter of the property with your smoke stick burning. Then go through the front door and walk through the space, clockwise, smoking all the corners in every room. Be sure to include the attic and basement. While you are smoking the house, say, "This is my space. All spirits, living or dead, follow the smoke and leave this space."

   An empty fireplace looks like a big black hole. It sucks *chi* into the chimney and out of the house and allows negative *chi* to enter the room through an open draft. Check the condition of the fireplace. If it works, start a large or small fire and burn cedar needles or sage. The smoke will carry all chimney spirits away and cleanse the fireplace. If the fireplace is fake, if it is inoperable, or if it is summer and you don't want to build a fire, you can use a small ceramic dish with sand and burn some incense. If you feel uncomfortable doing this, put a plant (real or artificial) in front of the opening, or cover the opening with a picture (sometimes you can balance a picture on the hearth and lean it, to cover the opening).

5. *Run the water.* One at a time, turn on all the taps in the house and flush all the toilets. While you are doing this, say, "I am washing away the presence of anyone or anything in this space."

6. *Choose an auspicious moment to take possession of the space.* Consult your local astrologer, feng shui consultant, or the Chinese or Western almanac for an auspicious date. If you have a lunar calendar and know how to read it, try to find a time between the new and first quarter moon phases. These occur the two weeks preceding the full moon, which is visible from anyplace on earth.

7. *Announce your presence and take possession of the space.* In a loud voice, announce that you are the new occupant. "I am (say your name out loud) and I am taking possession of this space. Everyone else, human or spirit, GET OUT. Let this place support and encourage a healthy happy life with good to all concerned." If you have your own words or prayers you prefer, say them now.

THE IMPORTANCE OF PROPORTION AND POSITION

The ideal building is situated in the center of a square or rectangular lot, facing south to a water view and protected from the northern winds at the back by mountains. Buildings located to take advantage of this configuration are regarded as prime real estate. A house situated to view a beautiful scene or other enviromental feature can benefit from "borrowing" the landscape. Streams or natural water courses integrated into the space promise success, abundance, and life-giving vitality. Green areas provide "lungs" within the space, particularly important in densely populated areas. There should be open and semi-open landscaped courtyards so there is a contrast of yin and yang, or a balance between the open and built-up areas. Amenities such as porches and covered walkways give easy and safe circulation of *chi.*

A building with a southern exposure is always preferable to one with any other exposure. The south side of the lot receives the light of the sun throughout the year, and this can bring much positive energy to the occupant, particularly if the lot is kept empty except for landscaping or ponds. For greatest harmony, flowing streams and low hills in the east symbolize wealth. In the south, ponds and lakes ensure health and wealth. In the west, low hills and roads offer protection from the glaring light of a setting sun. The east, west, and north sides of the lot can be enclosed in order to accumulate *chi* for the property.

Looking toward the entry of the building from outside, the right side of the building is considered to be more powerful than the left. It is best for a home to be arranged so that the most important rooms in the house are on the right and the landscaping or parking is to the left. Look for buildings that include curves or other interesting features and avoid buildings with many sharp angles.

It is important to consider the relationship of your home or building to other buildings around it. Is it larger or smaller than its neighbors? If it is larger, it demands more attention than other buildings. If it is smaller, it might be overshadowed. Neither condition is balanced.

A HARMONIOUS ENVIRONMENT IMITATES NATURE

Mother Nature, when creating a harmonious environment, includes all the five elements—Earth, Wind, Fire, Water, and Metal—so you should look for these in the exterior of house and in the surrounding property. One of the elements will usually dominate the others, and this is as it should be, but all the elements should work together to create a pleasing and proportionate balance. Improper proportions make odd, ugly, unbalanced creations.

For a home's exterior, balance is established when the lot, the shape of the building, and the size of the entry are proportionally correct. The size of the building compared to the size of the lot determines the balance of yin-yang. When the structure is built to the limits of the property line, it's too big (yang) for the lot; there is no empty (yin) space. Large houses with tiny windows are out of balance, as are tiny houses with giant-size doors or outdoor furniture and accessories that are too big or dense or otherwise out of proportion.

When elements are combined unnaturally, the result is an odd, crazy, mixed-up, chaotic space. When the elements are combined in proper proportion, nature is imitated and harmony achieved. Too much of one element and not enough of another produces an unsupportive environment. When the proportions are correct, balance and beauty are achieved.

Symmetrical balance appears serene, static, and eternal. In facial structure, this results in a classic beauty. Symmetrical balance is obvious in the tombs and chambers of the ancient Egyptians and in the temples of the ancient Greeks, who established harmony through what they called the "golden mean," setting architectural standards for centuries to come. Symmetry is dynamic in the works of Renaissance artists, such as Michelangelo; the ancient Chinese, who built all of their cities and towns according to geomantic principles; and architects throughout the world who strive to achieve beauty that will last forever.

Symmetry is achieved when both sides of a line are mirror images of each other. In architecture, symmetry is easy to achieve by using identical features spaced equally from each other: windows on both sides of the door; pillars to hold up the porch; posts next to the staircase, identical rosebushes bordering the front walk.

Asymmetrical balance is more organic. It appears to be animated and changing, mimicking nature through the inclusion of contrasting elements and features, variety of size, mass, density, shape, height, texture, color, light or dark patterns, combined in unequal proportions with spacing that seeks to imitate a triangular shape. It achieves balance through dynamic tension. An example of asymmetrical

Two examples of asymmetrical balance. The design of the house above works beautifully. Notice that all five element shapes (Wood, Fire, Earth, Water, Metal) have been included to create a pleasing and interesting structure. The design of the house below does not work. Only four of the five element shapes are included (no Fire), and the right side is much heavier than the left. The garage door takes up almost half the front of the house. (What's more important here—people or cars?) Locating the palm tree directly opposite the front door blocks *chi* from entering the house and creates a shadow arrow.

balance can be seen in arrangements based on the principles of ikebana, the Japanese art of flower arrangement. A tall, narrow stalk of grass, placed in the center of a shallow bowl, along with a dense, medium-size rock and a small but bold blossom synthesizes three diverse features and achieves balance through dynamic tension.

Asymmetrical balance is much more difficult to achieve than symmetrical balance because it requires imagination and forethought. When attempted without a plan, it can look chaotic, confused, and tasteless. Rock, sand, and water gardens are examples of asymmetrical balance in landscaping; in architecture, look for anything designed by Frank Gehry, including his new American Center in Paris.

This house is not in harmony with its environment and would be more suitable as a commercial building in a commercial area.

This hotel of floating logs on the Amazon River includes all five elements and is in harmony with its environment.

A building with good feng shui is located and built to harmonize with surrounding buildings, including any outstanding natural feature, blending streams, large trees, or boulders into the overall plan rather than removing them. Some homes allow trees to grow through them, while other places incorporate rocks, streams, and pools of water into the house and garden, adjusting to nature rather than imposing personal preference on the landscape.

It is best if the essential form of the structure is suitable to the environment. When it's not, it looks out of place. In the jungles of Mexico the palm frond roof structure is the prevailing style because it provides shelter from the brilliant southern sun and protection from the rain. Walled on three sides, it is easily heated when needed yet is open enough to be cooled by the breeze. In the jungle it is ideal, but imagine how ridiculous it would be in a northern or suburban climate! Conversely, a brick house perfect for the snowbelt is inappropriate in the jungle.

In nature, unity is achieved through inclusion of a wide variety of life forms, shapes, sizes, textures, colors, functions, and philosophies. This is natural. Monochromatic landscapes, neighborhoods, houses, and rooms are not balanced. The only time you see homogeneity in landscaping is in agriculture where hundreds of acres are planted with the same crop. The land in these areas is quickly depleted, and supplements must constantly be added to keep the land fertile. When an environment is homogenous, it has usually been made so for the sake of expediency and cost-effectiveness. For example, in the army everything is olive drab.

Land developers find it economical to build hundreds of houses with the same design and construction materials, a plan that is taken to extreme in suburban housing tracts where everything has the same form and function. Suburbs fail to re-create nature because homogeneity is favored over diversity. The vibrant atmosphere of a city is missing in the suburbs because functions are not allowed to mix. Nature creates unity through diversity, and we should try to do the same in our environment.

UNIFYING ARCHITECTURAL OR CONSTRUCTION FEATURES

A city imitates the diversity of nature by allowing mixed usage of buildings for living, working, shopping, and playing within walking distance of one another. Each building is unique, but unity is achieved through similarity of various exterior or public features. Understandably, form does better when it follows function. A building should look like what it is. A factory should not appear to be a temple. A garden shed should not appear to be a teahouse. A home should not look like a bank.

Not discounting the uniqueness of some buildings, it is preferable for a building to be in harmony with the surrounding natural and artificial elements. A building that is somewhat ordinary and similar to others in the same area is automatically more successful than one that makes an individual statement.

Similar architectural or construction features help structures with diverse sizes, shapes, identities, and purposes blend with the surrounding buildings. If one building is made of bricks and horizontal lines, those built after it and next to it should imitate the design and use brick trim and horizontal lines. Rows of buildings with completely unrelated heights, shapes, forms, sizes, colors, textures, and landscaping are not as favorable.

Imagine a block with one red house and the rest brown. The red house would look out of place and not in harmony with the neighborhood. A house in which every window and door is painted a different color looks like a cartoon; this is also unfavorable. Window frames and doors along the same wall should be the same size and color. The only exception is the front door, which should be painted a dif-

This house uses similar images and shapes throughout (railings, windows, roofline) to create a balanced and attractive structure. The tree, unfortunately, blocks the energy.

This house looks unbalanced because it employs too many types of window, door, and fencing treatments. But at least the tree doesn't block the entry.

ferent color from the window and roof trim. Painting the main entry a different color emphasizes the door and makes it a kind of target so the good *chi* can easily find the entry.

WALLS AND ENCLOSURES

Walls should be built at an appropriate height to the structure and without any openings, except for the entry and exit gates. A wall enclosing an open courtyard in the central space is a good feature. A wall that surrounds the entire building with only a narrow space between the wall and the building is not considered good. High walls with many openings are bad. A single-story building can have a wall that is six to ten feet high. A ten-story building could have a wall as high as twelve feet. A building more than ten stories has to use landscaping to provide imaginary walls.

If you are building a house, finish the building first, then build the wall. Remember, too, that the gate must be in proportion to the scale of the building.

The wall or fence around your home marks your territory. It should be in proportion to the house, neither too big nor too small. It's your protection from the outer world; keep it well tended.

THE LOT'S CONTOUR AND LANDSCAPE

When one side of a lot is lower than the other, it is easy to be caught off balance; one activity of the life pattern is exaggerated while the others are diminished. Occupants in such places may have strong family bonds (if the west part of the lot is elevated), but may have financial difficulties (if the east part of the lot is sunken).

To fix such a problem, place mirrors, reflective side up, along the sunken side. Or use lights along the sunken side.

Live plants are one of the best antidotes available to heal bad space. Trees, shrubs, and flowers are all good and can add much to enliven an area. Too many plants, however, can block the sun, encroach on the passageways, or crowd the environment, and it is best to remove them if this is the case. Providing privacy and protection, trees and plantings can greatly enhance any environment, but plants should protect, not overwhelm. Fast-growing trees should be avoided because they seem to coincide with fast-growing problems, like an escalating telephone bill or diseases out of control. A property overgrown with too many bushes and trees might create a feeling of claustrophobia for the occupants. An overshaded landscape is too yin, too passive, and the occupants might not feel ambitious or have enough energy to deal with life's challenges. They might also be living in the dark and not even realize it.

When a property is overgrown with trees and plants, the life-giving light of the sun is blocked and the occupants suffer in various ways. Living in a dark home for a long period of time is extremely unhealthful. The addition of plants, flowers, trees—anything growing or natural—can do much to improve the environment, as long as they don't block sun or crowd space.

THE FOUNDATION

The house rests upon its foundation. Without a good, solid foundation the house is unstable, and the basis of your life could also be unstable or weak. Plans, goals, and life may not seem grounded in reality. A house is like a tree. A tree is only as sturdy as the soil in which it grows. When it is planted in gravel or sand, the sapling is easily uprooted. When the foundation of the house is unstable or weak, the occupants are easily uprooted. When the soil under the foundation is too dense, occupants tend to be stuck in one spot, unable to make changes. If its roots are in granite, a tree is impossible to dislodge. Good solid soil allows the tree to grow straight and tall, just as a strong foundation gives us strength and stamina in life.

The foundation must be on level ground. If it is not, place lights on tall poles or at the corners of the low end to bring the foundation up, or use ground lights with the light directed up. Weak foundations can mean the occupants have no support in life. When the foundation is crumbling or has been eroded by termites, the house and the occupants are in serious trouble.

THE ROOF

Each building has a unique roofline, and the roofline and construction material of the roof can affect the destiny of the house. The first consideration must be the condition of the roof. A leaking roof means water is falling on your head. Symbolically or not, this is not a favorable sign. Fix the leaks as soon as possible. If they can't be fixed, place plants under the leaks so the dripping water will water the plants. If you can't do that, place buckets under the drips. When the bucket is full, use the water for something useful, like watering your lawn.

A roof supported by upward eaves is considered to be lucky, because the eaves are believed to catch evil spirits before they can enter the house. If the eaves point down, hang wind chimes to "bring them up," or focus lights up to the roofline.

Different-shaped roofs bring different energy. In feng shui, we can determine the element of the house based on the shape of the roofline, and then compare it to the element of the neighborhood. If the house and neighborhood are in harmony, the chances for success improve. If the element of the house is not in harmony with the neighborhood, then there might be problems, which can usually be fixed by the addition of another element near the entry, but don't worry about this now. (See page 111 for more information on the roof). Just remember that there are five basic roof shapes, one for each element, as follows:

Wood/rectangular roof (tall, narrow building)
Fire/pointed roof
Metal/round roof
Water/irregular roof
Earth/flat roof

Secret Arrows

Check to make sure there are no secret arrows of negative energy directed toward the front door. Also look through the windows of the house to inspect for these subtle intrusions—imaginary straight lines caused by the shadow of a tall tree or pole or the angles formed by the corners of roofs, buildings, or walls, television antennae, or other angular features. Since *chi* travels in a curve, when it is forced into a straight line it takes on the power of a shooting bullet or a flying arrow. In feng shui, we must be sure to protect the house from any flying arrows coming its way.

The home of a schoolteacher had been burglarized the previous night. Since she had lived in the same place for more than twelve years with no apparent problems, I asked if anything had changed in the neighborhood. She paused for a moment to look out of her living room window only to discover that a tree had fallen over in

A secret shadow arrow attacks the sidewalk entrance to this home.

a recent storm. The broken part of the tree was pointing directly at the door that had been burglarized. She spent all day getting rid of the tree and the remaining stump. She said chopping all the wood worked out a lot of her frustration at being victimized. Since then, she's had no more problems.

A seminar leader waited patiently for students to show up at an afternoon workshop that was being held in a student's home. Unfortunately, there was a tree directly in front of the entrance. No one came to the workshop. If the front door opens onto a tree, energy is inhibited from coming in and going out. If it is possible to remove the tree, do so. If not, place a small mirror, facing the house, in the middle of the tree, post, or pole, to act as an symbolic "hole." When the secret arrow is from a neighboring roof, wall, or building, use mirrors hanging from the interior window with the reflective side facing the offending arrow. Don't place a mirror on the interior wall directly opposite the entrance because this may deflect the good energy coming into the house. If there are plants or trees nearby, hang mirrors in the tree so that their reflective sides face the intrusion.

If there are too many secret arrows directed toward the entrance, and there is no possibility of deflecting them with mirrors, pottery, or drapery, you might want to consider using a different entrance for your main entry.

EXTERIOR MAINTENANCE

Like the shell of a crab, a house's exterior protects the soft interior. If the shell is damaged, the interior is injured. If the shell is shabby, the fortune is bleak. Note the general condition of the exterior of the structure. Its color, texture, and constitution will tell the story. The exterior maintenance pronounces the well-being of the structure. If the paint is peeling and the rain gutters are blocked, if there are broken windows, missing roof tiles, downed fences, torn screens, then you can anticipate problems for the building and subsequently for the occupant. Check for any blockages, plugged rain gutters or drains, cracks in the walls or foundation, and general appearance as you approach the site. Broken equipment, weeds, and dog droppings stink of failure. Tulips along the path, clean, neat walkways, and freshly painted exteriors smell of success.

Just as your clothes, coloring, and overall appearance hint of your own inner health, so does the exterior of a building indicate whether the space and its inhabitants are in good health, vibrant, and successful. Keep the exterior in good condition. The life of your house as well as your potential for success may depend on it.

CHAPTER 5

The Feng Shui of a

Home's Interior

W hether you live in a mansion, small apartment, loft, trailer, or boat, you instinctively know that there's no place like home. Modest or grand, our homes provide respite from the external world. They are our safe space where we can do whatever we want.

A house shows off who and what you think you are and reflects not only the outer circumstances of your life but also the inner workings of your mind. A house is like a living entity, a body with its own metabolism. Just like you, without proper nourishment it will die. If the house is healthy, you will also enjoy good health. If the house is sick or weak, you could be experiencing less than the best of health and strength.

THE MAIN ENTRANCE

The main entry door sets the tone of the building. It offers protection from the outer environment and serves as a threshold to the inner world. When you close your front door, no one else exists and you are in your own private world. If the main entry is too close to the street, you may not feel safe and you may be disturbed by the noise of the street. A fence, bushes, trees, or even a screen door or screened windows can do much to provide separation from the street, but they should not inhibit the flow of *chi* by blocking the entry. Look for secret arrows from straight lines or angles in roads driveways, rooflines, walls, fences, signs, shadows, or any straight features that aim toward the entrance. If there *are* arrows, block or deflect them.

One of the first considerations for the entry is its relationship to the exit or back

The main entrance is the most important aspect of a home. Lower right: Where is the entry? If you can't find it, neither will the *chi*. Upper right: A nice solution to a problem entry. The straight path is softened by the palm fronds and glass gate. Below: Curved steps and plantings make this corner entry feel inviting.

door. If you can see the back door from the front door, the energy runs right through the house and out the exit without nourishing the house. Your goal is to encourage sufficient *chi* to enter the house and move in a gentle curve through the house to the back exit. Use statuary, plants, furniture, lights, paintings, rugs, or other objects to create a curved path between the front and back doors. Another solution is to hang wind chimes, crystals, lights, fabric hangings, or plants from the ceiling, along the line between the front and back doors. If the back door is solid, you can hang a mirror on it to bounce the *chi* back into the room. If the back door is made of glass, use a curtain to keep it covered and stop the *chi* from exiting as quickly as it otherwise might.

The ideal entry is well lighted and protected from the elements. An exposed entry offers no security from the external world. Rain pouring over the front door may make your life a study in crisis management. Such an entry is not welcoming to you or your guests. A canopy or other feature protects the entry from the weather, while a bright light on the exterior, near the entry, makes your home appear warm and inviting. If your entry is dark, keep a light on even during the day.

Entrances should open inward to allow the *chi* to enter; fire doors must open out to let the *chi* out. If the building is in a closed space—a theater or a club, for

The walkway is too narrow for the width of the doors. The doors open out instead of in, which discourages the *chi* from entering. There is no landing to define the entry or to support *chi* or people as they knock on the door. The two sets of doors so close together can confuse the *chi* and cause it to lose its primary focus.

example—then the entrance doors definitely must open outward. The ideal entry has a door or doors that open into the house. When the opening is wide enough to allow sufficient *chi* to enter, there is a good chance the house will be healthy, promising the occupants the same vitality. Bigger is not necessarily better, however. It's more important for the entryway to be in proportion to the size of the house. Big doors should open into big spaces. An entry door that opens onto the broadest part of the room allows the widest view of the interior and gives a feeling of space and openness.

Once the *chi* enters, it should flow gently through the space without interference from walls, pillars, or other obstacles. A wall directly in front of the entrance will stop the *chi* once it comes through the door. If on entering the home you are confronted by an empty wall, you may feel that the future is blank. Hang a pretty picture on that wall, particularly one with a distant vista, and suddenly the entry welcomes you with beauty and long-range vision. Just don't hang a mirror directly opposite the entry, because this will bounce the *chi* back into the street every time you open the door. If you are confused when entering and don't know which way to go, neither will the *chi,* and you will have to direct, guide, call, and encourage it to flow from the entry toward another area or room. If you can easily see where to go from the entry, the *chi* will also know where to go.

After the *chi* enters it must be able to exit or exhale from a different door, ideally from the west and back of the house. It can also exit through a side door, and, if there is no other door, *chi* can exit through a window. Windows represent the "eyes" of the house, expelling used *chi.* When *chi* cannot exit, as in rooms with no windows and only one door, it becomes stagnant and stale. These rooms are best used for storage. If you must live or work in such a space, hang a picture of a door or window, or use a mirror in a window frame on the west wall to give the *chi* a symbolic exit. In cartoons, when a character wants to get out of the room, an exit is drawn on a wall. Presto! A door or window has been created. In feng shui, symbolism works as well as the real thing. The further addition of plants and bubbling water can create an inviting and healthful atmosphere, even in an enclosed space.

Sometimes it seems convenient to store furniture or other objects behind doors, but this blocks the flow of *chi* coming into the room. A writer who worked in her bedroom had placed a file cabinet behind the entry door, and this kept the door from opening fully. She had also placed her business telephone on the file cabinet. As she was moving the file cabinet from behind the door, the phone rang with the offer of a new job. An artist complained of lack of opportunities and poor health. She had placed a heavy wooden table in such a way that it blocked the front door from opening fully. She said it would be impossible to move the table because it had been her grandmother's and that area was the only place it would fit. The table had to stay. She wasn't ready for change, and that's okay. Change happens only in its own time. If you don't want to change, maybe you're not ready.

To invite opportunity, remove blockages from doorways and remove stored items from behind doors. If the door can't open fully, you are not getting the full benefit of potential *chi,* and the stuff that is behind the door may somehow be the obstacle to your success.

Consider the way you open the door. The doorknobs, locks, and other hardware should work properly and not stick or rattle. An advertising executive had been unemployed for more than six months. The doorknob of her front door had been pulled off, leaving just the lock on a metal plate. It had been that way for quite a while because she didn't have the money to get it fixed. Her mother bought her a new doorknob for her birthday, and the day after it was installed she was called to two different job interviews.

If you have trouble entering your house because the doorknob wobbles, the energy may also find it difficult to enter. Successful front entry doors have well-tended, working hardware that doesn't squeak or wobble. If the paint is peeling, the screen door is rusted or broken, and the doorknob wobbles, you may feel that your home is not your castle but something much less. To invite opportunity, make sure all the hardware on the door is clean, rust-free, and in good working condition.

The entry is the most important part of your house and speaks of the health and safety of those within. Dramatize the entry in whatever way you can. If it shouts of success, so will you. If it mumbles, stutters, and spits, you will, too. Give the entry the importance it deserves. A good entry usually coincides with a healthy interior.

Entries to Multiunit Structures

To enter a multiunit structure such as an apartment or office building, you have to find an entrance to the building. If the building is placed in such a way that the parking is too distant, or the entry confused, you may never accomplish what you set out to do there. A college student stopped going to UCLA because she could never find a parking place. Some buildings have underground parking. In that case, the elevators or escalators should be prominently placed and visible so that the path to the entrance is clear.

As you enter a building, pay particular attention to the lobby. Its condition and "feel" give you (and visitors) a first impression of the life within. The lobby has a presence that is determined by its color, smell, temperature, and lighting, and by the location of the furniture. A spacious, well-lit, well-appointed lobby is the sign of a successful building—and successful tenants. A shabby, dark, and musty lobby gives a depressed attitude to anyone entering and is reminiscent of shady business. Remember, the most important openings of a building are the gate, the main door, and the back door. Make sure the front door of the office/shop does not align directly with the back door. If it does, *chi* will come in one way and go out the exit without nurturing the space.

In a multiunit building, the main entry to the building, the lobby, and the staircases or elevators affect the feng shui of all the units. Your unit may have wonderful feng shui, but if there are problems with the entry of the building, you will also be affected.

NONTRADITIONAL ENTRIES

Houses are customarily built to be entered through the front door, but every structure is unique. In many locations, the car is king and must have its own house— the garage. If the commonly used entry is through the garage and the garage is congested with boxes, trash, and papers, there might be obstacles in the path of life. Also, when you store articles that should be sold, given away, or thrown out, it is difficult for transformations or changes to occur. It may be impossible to finish projects or complete tasks. Subconsciously, you are holding on to the experiences associated with the objects. If you are holding on to unused or unnecessary items, nothing new can come into your life. Can you catch a ball with your hands closed? Besides, the garage holds all the vibrations picked up by the car as it traveled along the roads. Think of what your car tires have passed over. Every person, in every car, leaves his or her mark on the road. Who wants all that to come into the house?

When the interior of the house looks like a picture from *House Beautiful* and the garage is reminiscent of the Addams Family, something is out of balance. Someone is putting on a good show, but the inner workings are contaminated. It's like a couple who appear to have a perfect marriage, but behind closed doors, all hell breaks loose. This same idea applies to the closets in the house. The expression "skeletons in the closet" is more than superstition. Remember, everything you save has an energy. When entering your home, if the first thing you see is garbage, bills from creditors, or pictures of ex-lovers, home may be less happy than it could be. On the other hand, if the garage is so immaculate that you could eat off the floor, it might be an indication of a preoccupation with cleanliness, which can lead to an unbalanced and fearful attitude about life. A little bit of dust is natural and doesn't hurt anything.

Many of us enter our homes through the garage and still lead successful and well-balanced lives. Just make sure the garage is clean and well organized and that the door leading into the house opens as wide as possible. Be sure not to store unused objects behind this door and, if it's possible and convenient, hang the door to open out, into the garage. If the door opens into the house, place a light above or to the side of the door on the garage side, or hang a wind chime inside the front door high enough so that it doesn't interfere with the movement of the door.

The back, side, or secondary entries into a home are usually reserved for service people. If you always enter your home through a secondary entry, you might never feel as if you were master of the house or lord/lady of the castle. Entering through the rear, traditionally reserved for servants or deliveries, may make you feel subordinate in life. If only visitors use the front entry and then only when their feet are clean, ask yourself if you're living your life for yourself or for your visitors. Remember: A problematic entry affects the occupants, while visitors are hardly influenced.

If it is impossible or inconvenient to use the front door, designate whatever door you use as the front door. Make sure it is free of obstacles and kept clean. Put your address close to the door you designate as your front door. It is amazing how many people fail to put their house number near the entry. If your house is not marked, how will anyone ever find you?

A social worker complained that no one ever came to see her. She lived on a river, and her official front door faced the river while the back door faced the street. Of course she always used the back door to enter her home and the official front door was never used except on the weekends when she was enjoying her garden by the river. When she designated the back door as her official front door, her social life perked up considerably. She moved the numbers of the house to this back entry, making them visible from the street. She further emphasized the special quality of the back entry by painting the door a different color from the window trim on the house, placing flowering plants in pots on either side of the door, increasing the wattage of the outside light, and clearing the path. Since it was only a back door, she had allowed trash and other unused objects to collect by it. After she made these changes, she got involved in local politics and became quite popular and well-known.

The entry is the most important part of the house because it is the main conduit of energy into the house. Its condition, shape, and design can affect how you feel about where you live. If it is large enough to allow sufficient *chi* to enter, you automatically have a better chance at life. Act like a VIP. Enter through the front door, even if it's only once a week, so that you can see what your visitors see.

A tree blocks the entry, and a latticework overhang creates an unwelcoming shadow.

Above left: The builder wanted to spare the tree but should have placed the entry door farther to the side. Above right: The offending phone pole is by the street and obviously can't be moved. Plantings or a fence would shield the entry from secret arrows.

HOW TO REMEDY PROBLEM ENTRIES
Tree in Front of Entry

If the front door opens onto a tree, energy is inhibited from coming in and going out. If possible, move the tree or pole. Disguise the tree or pole by using tall round-leaf plants in front of it to block and soften the obstructing straightness, or use low round-leafed plants at the base of the pole or tree. Make a round or curved planter in front of the pole or tree, or use round patterns in pavement design. Another antidote is to hang a mirror, reflective side out, at eye level, facing the door on the outside center of the pole or tree. You can use a wad of tinfoil as a substitute mirror.

A writer had been trying unsuccessfully to sell a house for six months. A large tree was directly in front of the doorway. She absolutely did not want to remove this grand hundred-year-old oak. She made an imaginary hole in the center of the tree trunk by placing a small, shiny object—a wad of tinfoil—in the crook of the tree. As she was positioning the foil, she said, "Tree, this is the door for *chi* to come in and go out." This was enough to allow the *chi* to flow to the house. Within a week, a neighbor called saying he had been dreaming about buying the house. If the entry receives the secret arrow from a tree, cut down the tree or make an imaginary hole in it with a mirror or other shiny object.

This entry has problems. The overhead latticework casts oppressive secret shadow arrows across the entrance. The plants in Earth pots are too small for the size of the entry. Vines growing over and through the latticework would break up the arrows and soften the entry.

Make sure you don't cross yourself out of the picture. The jail-like trim on the garage and the dark front entry make this house seem uninviting.

This entry has many built-in problems, but they've been nicely solved: The half-circle in the barred gate softens its lines and encourages *chi* to flow through; the angled stairs create a curve in an otherwise straight pathway.

This dark entry faces a wall, and the tall windows to the left of the door compete with the door for attention. To help *chi* find the door, it should be painted a bright color appropriate for the direction in which it faces.

Secret Arrows Aim Toward Entry

Check to make sure there are no secret arrows (negative energy) directed toward the front door from any exterior source. Look through the front and side windows of the house to inspect for these subtle intrusions. *Chi* forced into a straight line takes on the power of a shooting bullet or a flying arrow. When the secret arrow comes from a neighboring roof, wall, or building, hang mirrors from the interior window with the reflective side facing the offending arrow. Don't place a mirror on the interior wall directly opposite the entrance because it can reflect the good energy back out the door. If there are bushes or trees nearby, hang a mirror or mirrors in them, with the reflective sides facing the intrusion.

Shadow Arrows Aim Toward Entry

The shadows from trees, poles, telephone lines, rooflines, buildings, walls, or other angular features cause offending arrows. To remedy this, you can place a terra-cotta planter in the shape of a chicken and filled with red flowers between the offending item and the door. The chicken and the color red represent the element Fire, which can reduce the effects of the tall or rectangular objects, which belong to the Wood element. Secret arrows can also be deflected by using curved, circular, arched, semi-circular, or round shapes and patterns in all elements of your landscape: the shape of the paving stones, leaves, and ceramics; the patterns in textiles, fences, and flowerbeds. The addition of small round tables or narrow straight tables, decorated with round bowls or vases, can also counter secret arrows and bad shadows.

Ugly View When Entering or Leaving the Building

When an unpleasant sight across from the entry greets you on exiting your home, create an open-space wall, like a trellis, in front of the entry to block the view. This wall should be as far away from the entry as possible. Grow vines on this trellis, but don't let all the holes get filled up. A trellis arch will frame the view, and if you grow flowering vines on such an arch, your attention will be drawn to the flowers and not the view.

If the entrance faces a wall or an undesirable feature such as a column staircase, bathroom, or exit, mirrors can draw the energy into the space and away from the entrance. If you can easily enter a house or other building, so can the *chi*.

Doors That Don't Match

In places with extreme weather, two doors are common. Usually there is an outer door to face the elements, and another door leading inside the house. In this case, both inner and outer doors should open in the same direction. A porch between the inner and outer doors should be big enough to allow the outer door to open inward into it. Both doors should be hung on the same side; if the outer door is hinged on the right, the inner door should also be hinged on the right. Whenever there are two doors in close proximity, leading from one area into another, both doors should either line up *exactly* or they should be distinctly different and placed in such a way that it is obvious they are not meant to be aligned. Doors in close proximity that are not exactly alike or that are not distinct from each other make the space look crazy and distorted, which causes the occupant to feel uncomfortable without knowing why. If they are almost alike, but a few inches off perfect alignment, you can use a tall mirror or a column of mirror tiles to create the illusion of a wider door or opening alongside the appropriate door.

The gate at the bottom of this entry staircase helps to keep the *chi* from rolling back to the street. The railing at the top, however, casts secret shadow arrows across the entry and could be remedied by a planting in a round pot.

Where is the main door? If it is upstairs, a wind chime hung at the top of the stairs and small lights placed along and up the stairway will help guide the *chi*.

Entry Located Near T-Junction

If a T-junction is present at the entry, choose another entry or keep the entry door covered, use a circular design on a picture hung on the door facing the T-junction, or hang wind chimes in the doorway, high enough so that they do not to interfere with the flow of traffic but so that they will move with the breeze. Any of these antidotes can disperse the overly strong energy of a T-junction.

Entry Elevated Above Street

A house whose entry is higher than the street is considered to be yang: strong, vital, and active. Living above the street is like living at the top of a hill. A house elevated above street level receives an automatic boost that can help its occupants rise to success and prominence. The problem is that the occupant may develop a conceited, arrogant, or superior point of view. Living high up, you may feel on top of the world. But it is also possible for fortune to run down and out, and you may find it difficult to hold on to what you've earned. Living at the top of the hill also exposes the space to strong winds, leaving you in a defenseless position.

Entry Lower than Street

A yin house is one whose entry is lower than the street. Occupants may feel that all the problems of their neighborhood and of the world reside on their doorstep. Also, secret arrows formed by the surrounding rooflines, poles, trees, and other objects may be directed to the house, making the occupants feel as if they were always under attack. Living below the street is similar to living in a basement apartment. The occupant is burdened with the problems of others (living on top of him or her), which may contaminate the vital energy of the house. Fortune, honor, and prestige may be just out of reach, making it difficult to climb the ladder of success. If you live in such a place, make sure there is plenty of light—real or artificial—near the entry and in the interior. I know a gardener who lives in a basement apartment and grows beautiful fruits and vegetables by artificial light. Her basement apartment is lively, inviting, and warm.

If your entrance is lower than the street level, install a light on a tall pole behind the house and point the light up toward the roof to bring the energy up. Another solution is to hang wind chimes from the eaves to call the *chi* upward.

Entry off Straight Corridor

When the entry is off a straight corridor, as is common in most apartment complexes, the *chi* has a tendency to speed down the corridor without stopping at the entry to the apartment. Think of a rushing river, swallowing towns in its course. If you live in such an apartment and it is possible to do so, place a light outside your apartment, use an attractive, semicircular doormat outside the door, and make sure the apartment number is prominently displayed. If the numbers are metal, keep them clean and shiny. These simple additions can encourage the *chi* to stop by your entry door.

Too Many Entrances or Exits

Some places are not successful because they have too many entrances and exits— too many people coming and going but no one stopping. Too many entrances and exits make security difficult. Designate one door and one exit as the primary entrance and exit. Keep the other exterior doors closed, locked, and covered with posters or pictures. When there are too many interior doors, there is too much activity. Be sure to keep all closet and cupboard doors closed, and if you can keep some of the extra interior doors closed, do so.

Entry Opening onto Space with Many Doors

Entries open onto a narrow corridor with many doors leading to various rooms that tend to confuse the energy coming into the house because it doesn't know which way to go. The home of a widow who was having trouble getting on with her life had glass double entry doors opening into a wide entry, facing larger quadruple glass doors that opened into a patio. The *chi* came in the front and went right out to the patio without having a chance to nourish the interior rooms. Inside the house, the woman hung mirrors on both sides of the entry doors, which made them appear to be equal in size to the patio doors. She then covered the patio doors with sheer fabric, which let in the light but added a sense of steadiness to the doors. This reduced the amount of *chi* that escaped to the patio. She placed a lamp inside the living room close to the door, to direct the *chi* once it entered the house. After making these simple changes she felt confident enough to join a community group and finally felt she could get on with her life. You can encourage the *chi* to enter the other rooms by placing lights, bright colors, or plants at their entrances.

Entry Is Too Near Bathroom

Entries and bathrooms don't mix. A local Chinese restaurant had so much trouble enticing customers that they finally gave up and served lunch buffet style on the sidewalk in front of the restaurant. What was wrong? The main entrance was directly opposite the ladies' bathroom. Upon entering the restaurant, the first thing you saw was the toilet. Not good. Bathrooms should not be placed in the center of the room or where they are clearly visible to customers. If they are, use mirrors on the opposing walls to draw the offending room to a different area.

Entry Too Small

When the entry is too small, not enough *chi* can enter the space. This is like a person with asthma who can't take in enough air. The space begins to choke and cough, and it will eventually expire from lack of *chi*. The occupants will manifest this by never getting what they need or want and always having to reduce expenses, limit activities, and otherwise suffer deprivation. To make a small entry appear larger, reduce the size of furniture and plants that flank it. Use mirrors, light colors, and other tricks to create the illusion of larger space.

Entry Too Large

If the entry is too large for the size of the house, too much energy enters and the house cannot accommodate the excess. Like a person gaining weight, the house will begin to accumulate furniture, books, and unnecessary objects as the occupants become increasingly burdened and overwhelmed by the challenges of life. A very small house had tall, wide, double-glass French doors as entry doors. The doors were much too big for the house. The interior was crowded with furniture, boxes, papers, very large plants, and assorted exercise equipment. There was too much *chi* in the house. The family who lived in the house was overcommitted with community affairs and children's appointments. The wife was on the verge of a nervous breakdown. Covering part of the doors with drapes to make them appear smaller or placing statuary or special rocks by the entry door, either inside or out, can inhibit excess *chi*. When the entry doors were covered with drapery, life became more manageable. The kids stopped some of their lessons and the wife started saying no to activities that didn't interest her.

Shabby Entrance

Nothing is less inviting than a shabby entrance. If the door is in need of paint, choose a color that harmonizes with the direction it faces. Paint it a different color from the rest of the house or the trim, making it more important than all the other exterior details of the house. This gives you a very noticeable or bull's-eye-type entry, a sure sign of success. For example, if the door faces east, paint it green, black, or red; south-facing doors should be green, red or yellow/earthy tones; west-facing doors are ideally yellow, white, gray, or blue/black; north-facing doors are gray, blue/black, or green.

The first thing you see upon entering the house determines your overall attitude about the space, and this in turn influences your family and other relationships. The most important room should be in the center of the house, some distance from the entry and protected by walls, drapes, differences in wall and floor coverings, or other methods of providing privacy from the front door and street. If the first thing you see when you enter your home is the laundry room, clothes may be your life. A seamstress in Chicago is happy and successful. She enters her home through the laundry area and the first thing she sees are baskets of fabric. However, if your primary focus in life is not laundry, entering through this room may encourage you to become obsessed with cleanliness, picking out the spots and stains of life and missing the big picture.

If the bathroom is the first room you see, life may focus on changes and transformations. Health problems may cause you to spend a lot of time in the bathroom, or vanity may keep you primping at the mirror. If this is the case in your home, keep that bathroom door closed all the time and, if you can, hang a pretty picture on it.

If the first thing you see upon entering your home is your office, you may become a workaholic or suffer from guilt because you are not working all the time. Spend a little "social time" at your desk entertaining your friends so that it can become more homelike. Also make sure to keep your desk neat all the time, especially if it's the first thing you see when you enter your home.

If the first thing you see upon entering your home is your bed, expect to spend a great deal of time there. If all you do there is watch TV and eat, the energy enters the house and lays down, which may cause you to spend time in bed because you are sick, tired, or lazy. Do something to disguise your bed so that it looks more like a couch. Rearrange the pillows so that they appear to be throw pillows on a couch, and cover the bed with a fabric instead of a bedspread.

Remember that the first thing you see as you enter affects how you feel about your home. Fill the entry of your home with plants, flowers, good books, pretty pictures, or lovely objects of art. Move bills, dirty laundry, the cat's litter box, and anything else not conducive to a happy, loving vibration.

ROOM PLACEMENT

The center of the house is usually where a concentration of good *chi* is accessible and should contain the most important room in the house. In ancient times, the kitchen was placed in the center of the house. Today the activity of the house is usually centered around the television, so whichever room contains the TV is usually the most important room in the house.

If your bedroom or kitchen is in the center of the house, your life may become focused on those areas. If the bathroom or laundry room is located in the center, money and resources may go down the sewer lines. To counteract this possibility, use mirrors on all the walls inside that bathroom. Or draw the offending room to another part of the house by hanging a mirror so that it faces the outer wall of the offending room and reflects the wall toward another part of the house.

Homes are happiest when each room or area has its own defined purpose and energy. When functions are inappropriately mixed, for example when faxes and file cabinets are kept near the bed, when meals are eaten in front of the TV, or when clothes are stored in the bathroom, the *chi* becomes confused and flows erratically. Even if you live in a one-room apartment, separate the functions of your life as much as possible. Designate space for sleeping, cooking, bathing, working, and playing. You will find that your mind becomes much calmer and more organized.

SHAPE OF THE ROOM

Rooms whose walls are not at right angles or that are L-shaped are troublesome because it is difficult to arrange regular-shaped furniture and because parts of the room are dangling or missing from the *ba gua,* indicating a missing or dangling area of life (see the Appendix, pages 173–179). To bring missing areas back into the room, place a mirror on the wall or walls that, if removed or pushed back, would create a square or rectangular space.

An L-shaped room can be made into two rooms by using screens, plants, or other dividers. Odd-shaped rooms can be made into regular shapes by arranging furniture and floor coverings to create squares, rounds, or rectangles. Straight, boxy pieces of furniture can be placed against the offending angle to create the appearance of a square. When the room is odd-shaped, square, straight furniture and accessories look better when they are free-standing with empty space around them. Odd, angular, curved, or irregular pieces can be placed in the odd corners or angles.

THE BEDROOM

You spend more than one-third of your life in the bedroom, which makes it the most important room in the house. It should be a place where Morpheus, god of dreams and sleep, would feel welcome. The importance of sleep is underestimated. It is not only sleep that we require. Dream time or REM sleep is what keeps us healthy. Dream images and symbols tell us things hidden in the light of our waking moments. Is your bedroom conducive to rest and relaxation, or is it just a place to continue your work while you eat your dinner in the semiprone position? Let's consider some of the details of the bedroom, such as its placement within the house, the color of the walls, the height of the ceiling, and the type and color of floor covering. Look at the placement and direction of the bed plus the material used in its construction. Take a hard look at the condition of your mattress, and get a new one if necessary (twelve years is considered the normal lifespan for a mattress). Assess the color and fabric and condition of your linens and replace those, too, if they are worn or a disharmonious color. Notice other furniture in the room, the mirrors, the closets, the inner doors and windows, the temperature and ventilation, the lighting, and the electrical connections. Replace or repair anything that is cracked or chipped or not working as it should. Keep everything dust free. The covering on the floor can affect your mood. Again, this is a matter of personal taste and what you can afford. Whether it is covered in oak, tile, or the latest in carpets, keep it clean. Dust and dirt settle into the carpet. Molds accumulate in the foam padding under the carpet. Both can cause allergies and other breathing problems.

Colors can greatly affect your mood in the bedroom and can influence the activities that take place there. White is good because of the variety of colors that can be added. Plus, it's easy to see when it's dirty. However, there are millions of colors and textures of wall coverings that can engage your senses. Basically, the decor should be conducive to rest and relaxation. Glaring colors and bright, bold patterns and textures stimulate the *chi*, which is why the walls of whorehouses in times past were covered in red velvet with lots of gilt-edged frames, furniture, and mirrors. Unless you desire that effect to improve your sex life, the *chi* in the bedroom should be subdued, quiet, and gentle.

Placement of the Bedroom
The placement of the bedroom within the house determines the status of its occupant. The placement can also determine whether the *chi* in the room is restful or active. The master bedroom should be as far as possible from the entry and from the main street. If the bedroom is too close to either, the occupant will lead a less peaceful life. If you sleep in such a room, arrange the furniture and plants so that they are between the bed and the wall next to the main street.

A young woman asked me to look at her bedroom for clues as to why her relationships were constantly failing and "going down the toilet." We discovered that the head of her bed was against the same wall as the toilet in the adjoining bathroom. She was able to move her bed away from the common bathroom wall. This apparently solved her problem, because she married soon after moving the bed. If you can't move the bed, place a mirror in the bathroom on the wall opposite the toilet to "move it to the other part of the room." Or place a mirror on the wall opposite the bed to symbolically move the bed to the opposite side of the room.

In a home with more than three bedrooms, the bedroom next to the kitchen is traditionally reserved for servants. If the master or mistress of the house sleeps in such a room, he or she may feel less than equal to other family members. This attitude might then affect self-esteem or ambition. Also, this room is not particularly favorable because of the constant presence of cooking smells and the proximity to Fire sources. Keep one of the doors closed and, if there are no doors, arrange a partition for privacy.

In some modern buildings, the bedrooms are built directly over the garage, which is like sleeping on the top floor of a warehouse. All kinds of vibrations from the street ooze up through the ceiling, and when vibes are not oozing up, there is a big, empty, hollow space below the room. If the bedroom is above the garage you may feel that "home" is temporary and not feel like unpacking your boxes. Even if you live in the room for ten years, you will still feel as if it is only temporary. It's hard to build a foundation in life with an empty room below you. In this type of room, a special carpet on the floor can really improve the energy, acting like a filter for the vibrations below.

A man asked how he could prevent his mother-in-law from staying as long as she usually did when she came to visit. While she was there, she stayed in the upstairs bedroom, next to the master suite. The house also had a large, lovely servant's room next to the kitchen and across from the back door and that was not being used. The next time the mother-in-law came to visit, the man put her bags in the downstairs maid's room. She stayed only one night.

In lofts and studio apartments, there is usually only one room, which serves all functions. Sometimes the bed is a Murphy bed. It comes down at night and, during the day, returns to its niche in the wall. It doesn't really matter how big a room you sleep in. It could look like a deluxe suite at the Ritz or it could be a single bed in a humble apartment. No matter what its size, the sleeping area should have its own space, defined by different colors, textures, or lighting around, above, or beneath it.

Many people crowd their bedrooms with office equipment, or they may even work on or from the bed. The telephone is close to the head of the bed in case an important call comes in the middle of the night, and there may be file cabinets, typewriters, computers, fax machines, exercise bikes, gym equipment, ironing boards, and other items that really don't belong in the bedroom. Some of us, however, do not have separate space for all the functions of our life and we must make do with what we have. If this is the case, arrange your bedroom so there is space for work and separately defined space for sleep. Try to remove all nonbed objects before you go to sleep.

Make sure there is some visual identity and separation between where you sleep and everything else in the room. You can do this by using free-standing walls, partitions, and screens; plants; carpets; drapery; a bright bedspread; or decorative pillows. In the movie *It Happened One Night,* Clark Gable hung a sheet to provide Claudette Colbert with privacy when they had to sleep in the same room. If the space is really cramped, you could hang mosquito netting over the bed to give your sleeping space an exotic and natural look. It is important to your rest and dreaming that your bed is private and separate from the rest of your life. Do what you can to achieve this effect. Be creative.

The Bed

"Who's been sleeping on my bed?" said the three bears to Goldilocks. Beds are very personal, intimate, and private. While visitors are welcome in the living room, they are seldom invited into the bedroom. Only lovers and family are allowed, and sometimes close friends. The kind of bed you sleep on can affect your life. Maybe you sleep on the iron bed you had when you were a child and you're having a lot of trouble growing up. Maybe you sleep on a big, ornate bed with four posters and run your life like a dictator. Beds see you when you are most vulnerable—when you are weak, tired, or sick. Beds are the recipients of your good and bad dreams, your stomach flu, your headache, your aching bones. Just like other furniture, they carry memories of the past.

An old Chinese adage says "the shape of the bed shapes the marriage." A client called crying. Before her marriage, she and her fiancé had a great sex life. Now that they were married and living in his old home, they were fighting and having no sex. I asked about the bed and was told it was a wonderful antique bed that the ex-wife had died on. No wonder the marriage was falling apart. A new relationship requires a new bed or at least new linens. When you change your life or end a relationship, begin anew by rearranging the furniture in your bedroom. Nothing maintains an attachment more than continuing to look at the same things. If a relationship breaks up, move your furniture. When you start something new, be sure you're looking at a different, new view.

Remember the story of the princess and the pea? The princess was so delicate that even when she lay atop one hundred mattresses, she felt the pea underneath. Believe it or not, you are as sensitive as that princess. Even though many chiropractors recommend it, a mattress placed directly on the floor creates back problems. It is best if the bed is elevated, but no more than three feet off the ground. If possible, the bed should be on castors so it can be easily moved. Don't store stuff under the bed unless you want to dream of what you've stored. The exception is blankets and extra linens. One Chinese superstition holds that before a baby is born, its spirit hovers around the mother and clings to the dust near the bed. If you're pregnant, you are advised not to dust under the bed until after the baby is born.

The element of the bed can influence you. A bed with a wooden frame is a Wood bed—nurturing, creative, and good for procreation. The element Fire rules animal products such as cotton and silk, so a Fire bed is basically a cotton futon on the floor. This type of bed is good for meditating or thinking. If you sleep on such a bed you might spend a great deal of time in contemplation or mental activities. An Earth bed is one with a concrete, stone, marble, or tile base. You can feel particularly safe and stable on this type of bed. A Metal bed is one with a metal, brass, or iron frame. Sleeping on a Metal bed is good for a diplomat, one who can be charming and conciliatory while still being firm in morals and ethics. A bed ruled by Water is, of course, a water bed. Sleeping on a Water bed will increase your ability to attract friends, and you may find your social calendar booked. Adding the following colors will add the element to the bed regardless of its material: green, Wood; yellow, Earth; red, Fire; white or gray, Metal; black or dark blue, Water.

Place the bed with the head in the north and feet in the south because this follows the natural flow of energy.

An architect placed his bed at an awkward angle in the room, in an inconvenient and unattractive spot, because he had read somewhere that it was best to put the bed in the north. The awkward angle was the only way he could place the bed in the north. This doesn't make sense. Never place the bed at an awkward angle to accommodate the direction. Place the bed so that you have a maximum view of the entry. This usually puts the bed in the corner farthest from the door, or catercorner to the door.

Some people prosper when they sleep with their head in the west. Others feel out-of-sorts, like they're riding backward in a car. The west is counter to the natural movement of Earth and is the position of the setting sun, the end of the day, and, thus, symbolically, the end of life. An actress placed her bed so she could watch the sunset. The sun went down and so did her marriage. (Of course, there were other problems, too.) If you sleep alone (and enjoy your solitude) you may find a west-facing bed relaxing and joyful. Many do.

The bed should not be placed directly opposite the door or so that your feet point toward the door. This position has a tendency to drain energy, so you may feel just as tired when you wake up as when you went to bed. This is the way a dead body is stored at the morgue. If the bed is positioned lengthwise across the back of the room, the placement is similar to how a casket is placed at a funeral.

Place the bed against a solid wall. After moving into a new house, a client placed her bed against a fake wall that separated the sleeping area from the bathroom. Shortly thereafter, her long-time partner quit after embezzling the company bank account. Friends turn false and support seems to disappear when the bed is placed against a glass or fake wall. If the bed is too close to window, there might be drafts or external influences that affect the sleeper.

Even if you are not a sleepwalker, sometimes you have to get up in the middle of the night. Because of this, avoid clutter or heavy furniture next to the bed. You might trip over it when you are not quite awake. Clutter also acts as an impediment to subtle energy forces and may cause many problems. Some bedrooms are filled with bookcases, televisions, computers, and all kinds of furniture. As a result, the individual is restless, has difficulty making decisions, cannot start anything new, and may suffer from chronic illness. Many people sleep with their telephone next to their head, or with their bed next to an electrical outlet, and then wonder why their sleep is disturbed. One particular tragedy occurred during California's January 1993 earthquake when a sleeping man was buried alive under tons of his stuff!

A widower complained of a lousy love life. His room was decorated like a child's room with toy airplanes and cars. When he replaced the toys with erotic pictures and black satin sheets, he stopped complaining. It is amazing how many adults save childhood toys. A divorced woman asked how she could improve her sex life. A large, stuffed bear sat on a chair between the entry and the bed, welcoming her into the room. She said the bear's name was Bob, after her dead husband, and that she talked to it every night. She realized that keeping a toy bear was not conducive to romance, so she moved the toy into the kitchen near the honey jar. Childish toys, pictures, and furniture keep you in a childlike state. This is not a sensual state but one of innocence. If you want an adult love life, get the stuffed animals and children's toys out of the bedroom. Similarly, if you are married, consider that nothing ruins the mood more than children interrupting. If their toys are around, you are reminded of them and can't really relax. That goes for trying to make love next to a basket of dirty laundry or the vacuum. How can you relax when you are reminded of all the work to do?

To activate your sex life, make sure your bedroom conveys a sense of privacy with low lighting. Stay out of drafts, use lively, colored sheets, light some red candles, place flowers in the room. A very sexy opera singer always sleeps on black satin sheets. He also has a white grand piano in his living room, and his love life is fertile and satisfying.

Rules for Placement of the Bed

- A new relationship, new job, or new life deserves a new bed, or at least new and differently colored bed linens. Move the bed so that you have a new view. You can't move ahead when your view remains unchanged.
- Avoid clutter, as well as heavy or inappropriate furniture in the bedroom.
- Protect yourself from wind, drafts, or exterior influences that might awaken you during the night.
- Create a cushion of *chi* for the bed by elevating it above floor at least five inches but not more than three feet. Let *chi* circulate above and below on three sides. Place the bed on castors for easy movement. Don't use the empty space under the bed as a storage unit. If you're pregnant, don't dust under the bed until after the baby is born.
- Use low-wattage lightbulbs in fixtures that are close to your head.
- A bedroom or bed close to the house's main entry promotes a busy, active life filled with turmoil. The master bedroom should be as far as possible from the road and main entry. If it is close to either, hang a mirror in such a way that it draws the energy from the street or entry and reflects it toward another area. (For example, if the bedroom is immediately to the right of the entry, place a mirror to the left of the entry so that the entering *chi* will go to the left rather than to the bedroom on the right.
- Place the bed against a solid wall, not against a window or a glass wall, half-wall, or false wall.
- Place the bed in the corner farthest from the entry, with the greatest view of the entire room, preferably on a north/south or east/west axis.
- Don't place the bed directly opposite the door or a window. If this is unavoidable, create a barrier between you and the door or window by using low furniture or tall plants. Cover or close the window or door at night.

- Don't place the bed so that your feet are pointing toward the door.
- Don't place the headboard of the bed against a wall backed by a toilet or sink. If this is unavoidable, place a mirror above or opposite the toilet or sink in the bathroom and opposite to the common wall in the bedroom.
- Avoid placing the bed under a beam. If this is unavoidable, place the bed parallel to the beam, not across it.
- Don't place the mirror so that the first thing you see in the morning is yourself.
- Don't place a hand mirror on the dresser opposite the bed.
- Don't place the dressing table opposite the door because this can lead to a bad temper and emotional problems.
- If the mattress is against an electric plug that is not being used, cover the plug with a childproof guard.
- To bring more love, compassion, and understanding to your relationships, hang a round mirror in the bedroom.
- To bring a partner, make sure the bed can be accessed from two sides.
- To bring more life and vitality into the bedroom, use three plants (or five): one close to the interior entry, another near the bed, the third near the exit door or window, making a curved path for the *chi*. Add fresh flowers whenever you can. Don't put too many plants in the bedroom, though, because they will suck up the available *chi,* leaving none for you, which defeats their purpose.

Sleep and the bedroom are crucial to your well-being. If you are in a relationship or want to attract one, the bedroom is the place on which to focus. When the bedroom is romantically designed, cupid shoots his gentle arrow. The more comfortable you are there, the better you'll sleep. The better you sleep, the more your life will be like a beautiful dream.

THE KITCHEN

A Chinese proverb advises: "If you have two coins, buy a bread with one and a flower with another. One will give you life and the other a reason for living." Food, like air and water, is *chi* that we take into our bodies. Without it we starve and die. Many social customs, behavioral traits, addictions, and problems surround eating and food because eating is the common denominator that links all people. We must eat to live, which makes the kitchen, after the entry, the most important room in the house. Some people spend their lives in the kitchen, and some never enter. If you never go into your kitchen, then where you eat takes the place of the kitchen. Is it the dining room, the bedroom, or the corner restaurant? The place in which you prepare and eat food becomes symbolic of the internal fires that keep the spirit going.

Many childhood memories start with the smell of freshly baked bread or the delicious aroma of hot chocolate. Cooking and the kitchen have always represented warmth, comfort, and the security of home and family. They can also be used as a metaphor for spiritual cultivation. "Burning" or "cooking" symbolizes the process of internal examination via external experience. Cooking teaches us the benefit of allowing ourselves to mature, mellow, and ripen, and it shows us the benefit in serving others. Cooking transforms hard and raw materials into soft and delicious morsels that are nourishing to both body and soul. Cooking helps us to understand our duties and responsibilities to ourselves and others. In light of this philosophy, it is easy to see why the Chinese attach such great importance to the kitchen and compare a great leader to a great cook. The kitchen is the channel through which we take in the *chi* that creates a healthy body and a happy mind. We have to eat to live, which makes the kitchen one of the most important rooms in the house. Basically, kitchens are as individual as people. Any style is acceptable as long as all the plumbing and equipment work.

In ancient times, the kitchen was the center of the home, which is a good place for it, even today. But regardless of where it is placed, it is the condition of the kitchen itself that is important. If it is well lit, spacious, and airy, we feel happy. If the kitchen is dark, dirty, or cramped, we don't feel like being there. If the kitchen is too narrow, paint it a light color, increase the wattage in the lights, and/or hang mirrors to help create the appearance of a larger space. When you stand at the sink or stove, you should be able to see the entry and anyone coming into the kitchen. If you can't see the entry to the kitchen from the working stations, hang a shiny pot, silver tray, or mirror to reflect the activities of the entrance.

If the kitchen is visible from the entry, you may spend all your time eating or worrying about food. Try to create some kind of screen that separates it, or use objects and light to draw attention to another part of the house. A kitchen facing the living room sometimes causes the occupant to suffer ill health and family members to argue. It is easy to create an unobtrusive partition using wind chimes, plants, or other items placed between the two rooms. If the kitchen faces a bathroom, especially if you can see the toilet, keep the door to the bathroom closed and hang a pretty picture on the outside of the bathroom door.

A kitchen placed in the south is not considered favorable because Fire rules the south and the food may tend to burn. You can use glass bowls and plates to add more water to a south kitchen. The north/Water is not favorable either because the pipes may leak or the domineering Water will somehow put out the Fire, which means problems with the ovens, cooking, and burners. Add Fire accessories (red, knives, animal objects). A kitchen in the west is preferred because Metal/west does not incite Fire or consume Water. Unless you're building your own home, this is not always easy to achieve because we are at the mercy of the city's utility connections. If the kitchen is not in the west part of the house, the *chi* can exit the kitchen through a window or door that faces west. When there are no west-facing exits, a mirror placed on a west wall helps direct the *chi* to the west.

Within the Kitchen

The kitchen has a different quality from the rest of the house, and the nature of the equipment in the kitchen sets it apart from the other rooms in the house. Even though there are Fire and Water elements in other areas (heating units and bathrooms), nowhere are they more prominent than in the kitchen. The element Fire is represented by the burners on the cooktop and inside the oven, whether the Fire is created by solid fuel or electricity. Water, mortal enemy of Fire, lurks close by in the sink, refrigerator, or freezer. Water combines with Fire in water heaters, dishwashers, washing machines, and other machines. This could be a disaster, but the other elements are also represented and act as mediators to the Fire/Water problem. Metal is a common element in the kitchen because of the pots and pans, as is Earth, represented by ceramic or porcelain tiles for counters and floors. Wood is also represented by the food that is cooked there, thus re-creating a microcosm of nature in the kitchen. Fire and Water are combative, and thus should be separated with Wood, Metal, or Earth counters, cupboards, or partitions. (Note: Formica is a kind of plastic that can be molded and that has similar properties to Water, so it is considered a Metal material.)

The most beneficial placement of the stove is in the east or the south because these directions are associated with Wood and Fire, thus cooking. The sink, dishwasher, refrigerator, and freezer seem to function most efficiently when they are located in the western part of the kitchen, which is associated with Metal, the primary construction material of these appliances. Use colors from the elements on or near the appliance to bring the direction to it. For example, a red spoon holder placed on or near the stove brings Fire (south) to the stove.

A grandmother was constantly burning the cookies she loved to bake for her grandchildren. Even though she kept her eye on the time and temperature, the oven couldn't maintain a constant temperature. The oven was next to the refrigerator. When she had a carpenter build a Wood partition between the refrigerator and the stove, the oven problems stopped and her cookies no longer burned.

A woman who lived in a trailer also had the stove next to the refrigerator and couldn't keep the pilot light of the stove lit. She had changed jobs several times in one year and was having trouble maintaining her focus. She didn't have the space to create a partition between the appliances, and all she could do was wedge a tiny wooden match between the refrigerator and the stove. This was quite effective. The stove stayed lit and she stayed at her job.

Remember that in feng shui, cooking is synonymous with money. Just think, every time you cook something, you may be bringing in extra cash. Some miscellaneous tips: Keep your ovens and burners clean in order to increase your cash flow. Place a mirror or other reflective surface such as a silver tray or shiny griddle behind the burners to double their number. Even Metal cooking spoons can be used to reflect the burners. Double the burners, double the money. Make sure all the appliances, including clocks and timers, work. If they don't, discard them or have them fixed. Keep the refrigerator clean and free from any items that have turned into "science projects." A bowl of baking soda absorbs any food smells. Make sure there are no drips or leaks, because this causes resources to "drip" away. Keep the trash well contained and remove it often. Don't let garbage pile up, or all kinds of "psychic" garbage will accumulate.

The kitchen is where *chi* is channeled into the body. Keep this channel clean, clear, and in good working condition and you'll find yourself "cooking on high." *Bon appetit!*

Rules for the Kitchen

- If the cook cannot see the entry to the kitchen, place mirrors so that he or she *can* see the entry while cooking.
- Keep the stove clean and the burners uncovered.
- Hang mirrors, shiny pots, or reflective surfaces behind burners to double their number and double your cash flow.
- Create a separation between the sink (Water) and stove (Fire) with Wood.
- If the kitchen faces the living room or bathroom, keep the doors to those rooms closed or use screens or plants to separate them.

DINING ROOM OR EATING AREA

The dining room is an important room in the house, but only if you use it. Many houses have formal dining rooms that are used only once or twice a year on holidays, and the rest of the time the room is used for other household activities. In some houses, it serves as the office space, the place to pay the bills. If your dining room is used frequently, a round or oval table is best with four, six, or eight chairs. If there is only one chair at the table, don't expect company. Who would come when there's no place to sit?

Chi should not be allowed to stagnate in the dining room or the atmosphere will become stuffy. It is preferred that there be at least two ways for the *chi* to enter and exit, but they should not be opposite each other because the room will look like a hallway or corridor. It's better if the two doors are in the same wall or in adjacent walls. This goes for the windows in the dining room, too.

A round or oval table tends to be more harmonious than a square one, which divides the diners into opposition. Place the table in the center of the room so that there is a maximum amount of space around the chairs. Avoid placing the table under a beam, but if you have to, position the table parallel to the beam. Place as many chairs as you need around the table, but realize that if you need only one for yourself, and use only one, no one will ever join you for dinner. Three is the minimum number of chairs that should be placed around a dining table. If you live alone, change places every night so that all the chairs are used periodically.

TV OR GAME ROOM

The west and north quadrants of the house are both good locations for a television or special viewing room. Just don't sit facing the TV with your back to the door. A favorable location for a game room is south, where the sun is likely to cast its good fortune on winners. A client complained that her father had lost the family fortune gambling. Could I do anything? Upon entering their house, my eyes were immediately drawn to a gaming room to the right. The gaming room also held the back door for the house. The game room served multiple functions in the home—a sewing and crafts room, a party room, an office for the father, and a storage place for bicycles, skates, toys, and other outside play and garden equipment. These items blocked the pathway to the back door and I noticed that the back door was blocked on the outside with overgrown bushes and trees. I suggested she move the father's office to a different part of the house, organize and divide the room to create space for all the other functions, unlock the exits, and screen the entire room from visibility from the entrance. Another solution is to use colors, shapes, and materials from west/Metal and north/Water to symbolically add these directions to the room.

LIVING ROOM

Sometimes the living room is used only by guests, in which case, unless you have a lot of guests, you are wasting your space. Many houses have perfectly wonderful rooms that go unused, while the occupants cram their lives into small, inappropriate spaces. If this is your situation, ask yourself if you are living your life for your guests or for yourself.

BATHROOM

Did you ever notice that when life goes through changes, usually there is a problem with an appliance, a car, or the bathroom? The bathroom is an important room in the house because it is where transformations take place. The purpose of a bathroom is to cleanse the body externally and internally, and the *chi* in the bathroom should be encouraged to flow through quickly without settling down or being allowed to get stale. According to Chinese tradition, the more simple the bathroom, the easier it is for the *chi* to get in and out. Elaborate, ornate rooms tend to hold the *chi,* which is not a good idea because transformations should take place as quickly and easily as possible. It *is* a good idea, however, to have a window in the bathroom for ventilation, even though extractor fans can keep the air fresh. If you don't have a window in the bathroom, is it because you are living so high off the ground that an open window is not possible? Or is it because the bathroom is in the center of the house? Since the center of the house usually holds the *chi* of the entire building, a bathroom in the center means all the *chi* may be going down the toilet. If this is the case, use a mirror to draw the image of the bathroom to another part of the space. Or place mirrors on all four of the bathroom walls to cancel out the position entirely.

The home of a drive-by shooting victim was in terrible shape. The kitchen trash was overflowing, the garbage disposal was broken, and all the toilets were plugged, emitting bad smells throughout the house. The family was having trouble making sense of this senseless event. The toilets told part of the story. The bathroom, to be blunt, is where the shit goes, literally as well as metaphorically, so when a bathroom is not in good working order, there may be blockages, health problems, and difficulty making major changes. The main water lines and drainage system usually dictate that the bathrooms and kitchen be placed near each other. If you can see into the bathroom from the kitchen or from the bed in the bedroom, always keep the bathroom door closed.

A once-successful actor came upon hard times. His money was running out and he hadn't had a job in some time. When asked if there were any leaking or dripping faucets in the house, he said, "No, but my water bill was over $400 this month." A plumber discovered a massive underground leak where a pipe had broken. As soon as the leak was repaired, the actor was offered a new television series.

Many bathrooms are not current. Medicine cabinets and drawers overflow with old prescriptions, cosmetics, and magazines. Separate first-aid supplies into a special box, then go through your bathroom and discard anything that hasn't been used in six months. Be sure to discard old medicine. Who wants to be reminded of a winter cold in summer?

STUDY, OFFICE, OR LIBRARY

If you are lucky enough to have an office in your home, refer to Chapter 7, "The Feng Shui of the Workplace." If you don't have extra space in your home for an office, designate an area where you can keep important papers and bills, and set a specific time to take care of household accounts. This will help create the discipline required for paperwork. Just don't put the unpaid bills where you see them as soon as you enter the house. Imagine how discouraged you will feel if, upon entering a room, the first thing you see is a mountain of debt. To support your efforts, sit at a desk or table that is spacious, allowing room for the expansion of your ideas.

Read the section on The Desk (pages 159–166) for specific information regarding the desk. The rest of the office furniture should be placed so you can see the entire room, especially the entry, from your work station. If this is impossible, place mirrors in such a way that you can see the activities of the entrance and most of the room. Don't sit with your back to the door. If you do, place a reflective object where it will allow you to see the entry. If you have to sit facing a wall, put something on it—a picture, calendar, or mirror. If your "office" is too close to a window, you'll spend more time daydreaming than working. To help master New Year's resolutions, hang a brass wind chime above your desk.

ROOF, ATTIC, CEILING

The roof, the attic, and the ceiling all provide you with shelter from the elements. When the roof leaks, external influences seep into your life, causing you problems.

A political consultant lived in Connecticut in a house whose roof was caving in from the abundant winter snowfall. Inside, the house was packed to the ceiling with boxes of old papers, magazines, and the belongings from generations of the same family who had lived there. She was involved in so many different businesses and activities that she was feeling overwhelmed. A little at a time, she started getting rid of some of the stuff that wasn't needed or used. As she cleared away the excess in the interior, the snow on the roof began to melt. Soon her roof was clear and dry. Her mental clarity improved tremendously. She was able to create new goals and set about improving her life.

The shape and material used for the roof can affect the destiny of the house. Compare the element of the house (determined by the shape of the roofline) to the element of the neighborhood. If the house and neighborhood are in harmony, the chances for success improve. If the element of the house is not in harmony with the neighborhood, then there might be problems, which can usually be fixed by the addition or subtraction of another element near the entry. Roofs come in five types that are defined by the construction material used for the roof and the shape. On a tall building, a slightly rounded roof or a green roof or one made from wood is considered a Wood roof. Severely pointed or red roofs are Fire; flat or yellow/brown roofs on square boxes are Earth; round, domed, curved, or white, silver, or gray roofs are Metal; a black roof or one in the shape of a wave, or that includes various shapes, is a Water roof.

Keep the attic clean and organized unless you want to have "bats in your belfry." Try not to store too much stuff up there. If the baby carriage is still in the attic and your children are now adults, you're holding them and yourself back. Think about it. What do you really want to have hanging over your head? Don't you want free space so ideas can expand?

Ceilings provide a covering, and their height affects the quality of the space. The ceiling's height should be in proportion to the room. A high ceiling can make a room feel either lofty or drafty. A small room with a high ceiling is top-heavy. Use fabric hangings, false ceilings, chandeliers, and a dark color on the ceiling to "lower the ceiling." You can direct the eye down by using low furniture or by adding floor details such as stenciling or parquet or patterned rugs. A low ceiling can make a room feel either cozy or cramped. A large room with a low ceiling is bottom-heavy. Paint the ceiling white or another light color and use lights from the floor, pointed up to illuminate the ceiling. Recessed lighting is unobtrusive. A low ceiling in a confined space debilitates the *chi,* making inhabitants depressed and prone to headaches. If this is the case, paint the ceiling a light color and install mirrors on the walls to expand the space.

A low ceiling can be used to create an intimate, cozy, and private room. Here lighting is extremely important and should be used to create mood as well as be useful. Use vertical lines, high-back chairs, straight draperies, and dramatic, eye-catching objects at eye level. Use light colors on the ceiling. In corners, use tall, skinny, narrow objects and pointed-leaf plants.

Slanted ceilings are unlucky and may shelter slanted activities. You can cover a slanted ceiling with fabric, something like the inside of a tent. It's very attractive and hides problems. An uneven ceiling tends to produce uneven feelings, mood swings, contact with unreliable people, even an irregular cash flow and uneven opportunities. An uneven ceiling in a place with more than one person could cause feelings of inequality. If this is the case in your space, paint the ceiling black to disguise the irregularities (black is also a money-inducing color), or install a false ceiling to cover the problem.

THE BASEMENT

The basement can be compared to the subconscious—the place where we hold onto things below the surface. The basement is where things fester, get moldy or dusty, and go stale. Keep the basement fairly well organized and as clean as possible without becoming obsessive. Make sure there is good lighting and some type of ventilation.

THE FLOOR

An even, well-kept floor symbolizes a solid foundation in life. With a floor that's slanted, the occupants may have a warped point of view. If the floor is warped near the bathroom, there may be problems in making transformations, letting go of the past, or forgiving self and others. Near or in the kitchen, there may be warped ideas about eating, food, or nutrition. A damaged bedroom floor may cause sexual problems or problems sleeping. The best solution is to get the floor fixed. If you can't, use a rug to cover the warped part as a temporary solution. But remember, it's like using cloves to deaden a toothache instead of visiting the dentist.

The type of floor you customarily walk on can affect you more than you realize. If it is uneven, you are liable to trip. An old office I inhabited for many years had a rocky floor (it had been an outdoor area previously). Until I understood feng shui (and changed the flooring), my life was rocky.

If the floor is shabby, you are reminded of past failures. If it is clean enough to eat from and you don't have crawling children, you're spending too much time looking down and are preoccupied with details that detract from seeing the big picture. The covering on the floor can affect your mood, and this is usually a matter of personal taste and budget. Whether it is covered with wood, tile, or carpet, keep it clean and clear of clutter.

Some corridors move *chi* too quickly. A rug holds the *chi* down, creating a more positive environment. Rugs hold vibrations, however, and can't be kept as clean as a bare floor. This is just something to think about. Of course, the color, pattern, and texture of the rug affect you. If the carpet is thick and soft, you have somewhat of a cushion in life. If the floor is hard, you may do everything the hard way. If the floor is dirty, the quality of your thinking may also be dirty, confused, or not clear.

Doors offer one of the richest symbols available in the house in determining personal relationships and possible opportunities in the world. To open a door is to have the wisdom or knowledge required to pass over the threshold. Not to be able to open a door leaves you out in the cold, in more ways than one. When you have the key, the world is yours. What goes on behind closed doors? A closed door is a separation between what is known and unknown. If a door is opened, opportunities abound. A door provides the transition between the inside and outside, the public and personal. A door provides protection from invasion and offers privacy.

The size of the doors should be in proportion to the room. Big rooms require big doors. Small rooms require small doors. An oversize door accentuates the importance of the room. The house of a Hollywood producer appeared to be quite important. All the doors, interior and exterior, were oversize, extending from floor to ceiling. Some of the doors opened into shallow closets. Some opened into very small rooms. The producer had purchased the house at a bank foreclosure sale. The previous occupants had put on a good show and appeared to be quite successful, but in reality they were bankrupt. The producer complained that the house cost so much to maintain that he couldn't keep up with his payments. He also couldn't fulfill promises he had made to his studio. He spent most of his time in the den, the only room in the house that had an appropriate-size door, and the rest of the house was virtually unused.

The main entry door should open into the house or office, allowing the *chi* plenty of space to enter. The exit doors can open out. If the room has a closed function, like a theater or a storage area, then the door should open out to let the energy out. If your doors open the wrong way, you can have them rehung.

If there are double doors, make sure both doors open the same way. Sliding doors allow only half the available energy to enter, but this is usually sufficient because half of a sliding door is about the size of a full single door. To double the amount of energy coming in, hang a wind chime on the open side of the door. This effectively doubles the *chi,* making up for the other closed side.

Make sure all doors open smoothly and are hung evenly. If a door is hung crooked, the result might be a crooked life. Drafts cause chills, and *chi* oozes through the cracks. If the doors are not straight, have them fixed, remove them, or cover them with drapery. If you can't afford to buy drapes, blinds, or curtains, do what you can to disguise a crooked or ill-hung door. Doors should be hung in the center of the wall or to either side, with the hinge closest to an adjoining wall. Doors opposite each other should be the same size and hung in the same way.

More Doors than Windows

If you have more doors than windows—a situation that can cause adult occupants to be too serious, conservative, or afraid—keep the unused or unnecessary doors locked. Add pictures of windows, emphasize the windows you do have by painting the window frames or by using decorative drapery. You can also place mirrors to reflect the window and hang wind chimes from the windows to emphasize them.

Door Too Big

If the entry door is too big for the structure, make it smaller by covering the sides with vines growing on a trellis, or large plants in pots on both sides. Make sure the door opens onto the widest part of the room. If it doesn't, use mirrors to the side of the entry in the interior to draw the *chi* away from the door. You can also cover the sides of the door with drapery on the inside and use plants on both sides.

A real estate agent purchased a beautiful Spanish-style house with thirty-foot ceilings on the lower floor and doors that were totally out of proportion to the average human being. There was a false quality about the house. The oversize doors opened into very small rooms and shallow closets. The last three occupants of the house had failed at business, gone bankrupt, and had to sell the house because they couldn't afford to live there. How could anyone ever live up to such a grand expectation?

Door Too Small

Do what you can in the way of optical illusion to increase the size. Paint the door and entry a light color. Make sure there is a bright entry light both on the interior and exterior and that the entry area is somewhat defined by floor covering, wall covering, or furniture and plant arrangement. Use mirrors around the door to make it look bigger.

Too Many Doors

When there are too many doors used for entrances, exits, room separators, and closets, the *chi* becomes confused and doesn't know where it is supposed to go. The result is confusion in the occupants' life pattern or style. There will be many people coming and going, many secrets to be held and kept, anxiety about things beyond ones control.

Three Doors in a Row

Three doors in a row create fast-moving *chi*. If, for example, the entry door, the door from the entry to the living room, and the door from the living room to the dining room are all in a straight line, the *chi* flows swiftly through the house. To slow this energy, hang crystals or colored cloth from the ceilings in the path of the three doors. Carpet runners on the floor are also useful in holding down *chi* that is running too fast.

Door at the End of a Corridor

A door at the end of a corridor is not favorable because it becomes the recipient of swift-moving *chi* from the hall. Use carpet on the floor to slow the *chi*. Hang a mirror or a pretty picture, preferably one with a vista, on the door. Unused or "dead" doors symbolize "dead" areas of life and inhibit the flow of *chi*. This sometimes results in arguments and tension among family members. If doors aren't being used, seal them and hang pictures on them. A mirror hung on a "dead" door cures the situation, making the door invisible.

Doors That Bang into Each Other

If doors are placed so that they bang into each other, paint a small red dot on the center of each door so that they can "see" each other. An artist who was involved in multiple lawsuits lived in a glass house in Colorado. The glass entry door opened in, and faced a glass patio door that also opened in but led to an unused concrete-enclosed space. A third glass door opening into the house from the garage created a very confused entry because the three doors banged into one another. He painted a red dot in the middle of the door to act as an "eye" for the main door. He rehung the door to the garage so that it opened out into the garage instead of into the entry. Because the patio was unused, he then locked the patio door and placed floor-to-ceiling bookcases in front of it. Finally the entry was more manageable and he was more in control of his life. His legal problems also took a turn for the better.

Alignment Between Front and Back Doors

If you can see the back door from the front door, the energy will run right through the house and out the exit without nourishing the house. Your goal is to encourage sufficient *chi* to enter the house and move in a gentle curve through the house to the back exit. Use statuary or furniture to create a curved path between the front and back door. Another solution is to hang wind chimes, lights, fabric hangings, or plants from the ceiling along the line between the front and back doors. You can use almost anything you have around that can be easily hung from the ceiling without its brushing your head as you walk from the front to the back. If the back door is solid, you can hang a mirror on it to bounce the *chi* back into the room. If the back door is made of glass, cover it with a curtain to stop the *chi* from exiting too quickly.

In any room, when the entry and exit are in line with each other or when you can see one door when standing at the other, the energy enters and moves quickly though the room. It is hard to concentrate, focus, or plan the future in this type of situation, and occupants may suffer a decline in fortune and health. If this is the case, place heavy furniture, screens, or statuary to the side of the path between the doors. Or cover one door with a curtain or screen. This will help to slow the enegy.

Glass Door for Exit

When there is a glass door for an exit it is difficult to distinguish whether it is a window or a door, and the occupant may vacillate between being flaky and being responsible. It is better to have a solid rather than a glass door as the primary exit. If yours is made of glass, keep it covered with a full or partial curtain or shade, or hang plants and objects in front of it but not so the door is obstructed.

Doorknobs

If you have trouble entering your house because the doorknob wobbles, the energy may also find it difficult to enter. To invite opportunity, make sure all the hardware on the door is clean, rust-free, and in good working condition.

WINDOWS

Windows are the eyes of the house. They expel used *chi,* take in the view from the exterior world, and watch the activities of the inner world. When they are clear and clean, our vision is likewise. When they are dirty or dust-streaked, our thinking can be muddy, our view of the world unpleasant. Broken windows toll the death knell for a house and mark the beginning of the end. *Chi* oozes in and leaks out of the cracks, coinciding with resources disappearing and vitality weakening. Vision is distorted, activities are contaminated, and relationships break. Windows should be in good repair and kept clean. There's nothing like a dirty window to give a negative outlook on life. Everything is so much brighter when the windows are clean.

When you look out of your windows, what do you see? Often, we see only what we want to see. We have selective sight and overlook details while we focus on what is outstanding or distant. Look out of the window and try to see what the window sees. Check for secret arrows aimed toward the house from antennae, poles, trees, or the corners of roofs, walls, and buildings. If a window looks out on a beautiful view, maximize it by using mirrors to draw the exterior view into the interior. Cover windows that receive secret arrows or that face ugly views such as alleys, garbage cans, or blank walls. If the window is in line with an approaching street, keep the window covered or use landscaping as a barrier. There is something very unnerving about looking out the window and seeing cars coming directly at you. Cover windows with a light material that lets in the light but blocks out the view. If you don't have access to curtains, fabric, or anything suitable, regular typing paper works very well as a window covering.

If your office has only one entrance with no windows or exits, hang pictures of pretty scenery with sweeping vistas to give you the feeling that you are looking outside. You can also use a mirror fashioned like a window—or any mirror, for that matter—to enliven a closed-in space. Fans and other electrical appliances can also activate and move energy around when there are no windows or exit doors. The addition of plants and water—real, artificial, or symbolic—does much to activate any space.

Regard the windows of the house as your extended eyes. Do they need glasses? Do you? If the windows are dirty, cracked, or broken, if the window frames are warped, if you can't get a window opened or closed, take care of the problem. If you ever need the answer to a complex problem, wash your windows. This can actually clarify your mind.

Windows should be protected from extreme heat or cold and placed so they capture *chi* and encourage the flow of air. Natural light should enhance space and color and not be a source of glare. The width and height of the windows should be planned to take advantage of any natural light.

Avoid having windows at opposite ends of room, because this encourages the energy to run through. A simple solution is to keep one of the windows covered. Don't place your bed too close to the window or you'll be exposed to drafts in the night. Don't place your desk too close to a window or you'll spend all your work time daydreaming. A broken window is a warning that the house is about to go into decline. Get it fixed immediately

Sliding Windows

Sliding windows give false impressions. Keep one half covered. Hang a wind chime at the open end to call the *chi* to the open side. This symbolically doubles the size of the open part.

More Windows than Doors

Too many windows in a room can overpower the room with too much *chi* or create a feeling of tremendous space in a room, depending on what the windows look onto and what size the room is. Unlike a room with no windows, however, it is much easier to fix this problem because all you have to do is use some type of window covering.

Sun Glaring Through the Window

Sometimes windows intensify sunlight, creating a devastating glare. Remember the Boy Scout trick of starting a fire with a magnifying glass and sunlight? Glaring light, strong enough to start fires, fades the carpets and drapes and virtually "kills" plants or anything else living in its path. An actress had placed her bed so she could lie on it and watch the sunset. The woman's marriage, like the setting sun she watched nightly, declined into darkness and ended in divorce. Of course, there must have been other problems. To fix this problem, keep the window covered during the glare time or hang a crystal in it to break the light into a colored spectrum.

No Windows in the Room

Some apartments and offices are closed boxes with only one entrance and no windows. These are deadly places where *chi* enters but does not circulate or exit, so the use of lighting and ventilation are extremely important. Fans, air conditioners and heaters, pink lights and diversified light sources (ceiling, desk, table lights), pictures of windows, mirrors in curved frames or window frames, pictures of landscape or waves or movement or flight can do much to enliven a room with no windows. The addition of plants and aquariums, or desk fountains, is also helpful.

Too Much Window, Too Much of a View

Often, in expensive properties and in many skyscrapers, there are large picture windows or entire walls made from glass, giving the occupant a spectacular view.

Sometimes this causes too much *chi* to enter through the windows. A person living in such a place might feel overwhelmed by life, or not quite competent or equal to what is seen. Janis Joplin said it was "the kind of crazy you get from too much choice," and that is what happens. Too much to see, too many choices to make, too many comparisons, criticisms, or judgments can cause confusion and anxiety. If you feel there is excess *chi,* it can overwhelm the interior. To provide a barrier without blocking the *chi,* use plants, statuary, or furniture between you and the view. Transparent or translucent drapery, paper screens, or other light covering let in the light while providing a thin filmy barrier between you and the excessive *chi.*

STAIRS

Stairs are the conduit of *chi* from the lower to the upper floors. In ancient times, people regarded mountains as stairways to heaven. Modern stairways seldom go to heaven, but the symbolism remains. Stairs should be wide enough and light enough to be safe and easy to traverse.

The pathway from the main entrance to the elevator or stairs is the main conduit of *chi* to the upper floors. Consider the flow of *chi.* If this pathway is blocked, nothing goes upstairs. If it is sufficient and flows smoothly, whatever transpires on the upper floors (sleep, dreams, sex, home office) has a better chance for success.

A poet lived in a house with a dark, unused staircase leading directly up from the front door. The upstairs was considered to be a separate unit and used another entrance. The stairs hovered over the rather small living room like an ominous ghost. When she lightened the stairwell by placing lights to shine toward the ceiling of the stairs and used the risers to hold trailing vines, the poet felt more comfortable. Further, she placed a lovely picture of nature and mountains on the wall at the landing, visible from the entry. These simple changes had the effect of creating a wall of light, supporting the growth of the plants and creating a nice atmosphere for the living room. Dead space became usable space. This coincided with the publication of her first book of poetry. The activities of the occupants increased: Life, love, and money were activated by enlivening the staircase. If a room receives negativity from a staircase, deflect its straightness by using baskets, plants, or pots to create a rounded visual effect.

Stairs That Are Broken or Too Steep

Steps leading to the entry should be gradual and wide. Steep, narrow, or broken stairs leading to the entry foretell disaster within. A man lived at the top of such a stairway and had experienced ill health that caused him to stay home quite a lot. He spent some money and time fixing the stairs, and this improved his health considerably. If the stairs leading to your house or apartment are not in good repair, do what you can to fix them. Install banisters or handrails for safety and paint the stairs white or a light color. In interior stairwells, use mirrors or other reflective objects on the staircase walls to give the illusion of width, and make sure the space is well lit by installing lights at both the top and bottom.

Stairs That Are Dark and Narrow

If the staircase is dark and narrow, make sure there is sufficient light. Mirrors on the walls can enlarge the space. Use light carpet with a round or curved pattern. On the walls use horizontal lines to direct the *chi*.

Stairs with Space Between Risers ("Floating" Stairs)

Stairs with nothing but space between the risers are not efficient channels for the *chi*. Install plants beneath the stairs to help accumulate *chi*. Keep a light on at the top of the stairs to call the *chi* upstairs. Don't let stuff accumulate under the stairs.

Spiral Stairs

Spiral stairs are not particularly favorable because they are dangerous and hard to climb. If you have a spiral staircase, wrap something green around the banister and place lights on the ceiling to illuminate the spiral at the top and bottom of the stairs.

Double Stairways

Grand, elegant homes often have a double staircase, sometimes called splayed duck stairs because they resemble a duck's feet. This type of stairway doubles the energy going up and down but may also "split" it, causing family members to use separate stairs or take separate paths in life, as when the father is a doctor and the son a rock singer. To correct this, position a round table and/or a round planter of tall, round-leafed plants or large round objects between the two sets of stairs.

Staircase Empties out the Door

When a staircase ends at the front door, resources and health may roll down the stairs and out the door. Putting a basket at the end of the stairs will catch the *chi,* ensuring that good energy is not lost. Placing a light at the top of the stairs encourages the *chi* to go up the stairs.

   If the stairs split and lead to a basement, make sure there is a light at the bottom of the stairs as well as at the top. Put a basket at the bottom of the basement stairs as well as a basket by the entry.

COLUMNS

Columns, both square and round, add a classic touch to any room but can block the *chi* and make it difficult to arrange furniture. Preferably, the columns are in the corners of the room. When they are placed in the middle of a room, they interfere with the smooth flow of *chi* and are considered unlucky. A round column is preferable to a square one, and both types can be modified by arranging vines to grow around them. Follow the architect's proverbial wisdom: When you make a design error, grow ivy to hide the flaws of the house. If you can't place vines around it, hang a mirror, reflective side out, at your eye level on the column, or tie a red ribbon around the column. An astrologer who works at home uses two telephone poles to hold up the second floor of her house. Unfortunately, the poles are almost directly opposite the front entry. Her business was virtually nonexistent until she tied a large red piece of cloth on one and hung a Greek eye on the other to symbolize an eye for the pole. These antidotes seemed to work; her business improved steadily.

BEAMS

Exposed beams are quite popular but, like angles, blank walls, straight lines, and long corridors, they create negative *chi (sha)*. Beams are considered bad because they act like a hatchet, ax, or sword, cutting into whatever is under them. If a beam fell on you, it could cut you in two parts. In feng shui, the area under the beam is cut into two parts. If the dining table is placed under an open beam, diners might suffer indigestion. Under a beam, there would be a tendency for the family to fight and argue (which also causes indigestion). A beam over a bed causes pressure to the part of the body directly under the beam.

If you live with beams, place the furniture in the same direction as the beam, not perpendicular to it. Imagine what would happen to the furniture if the beam fell on it. Would it cut what was under it in two? If you can, install false ceilings to cover beams. If this is not possible, arrange your furniture to avoid or take advantage of the beam. For example, use it to divide the functions of a room. If you can't move your furniture from under the beam, hang a crystal, mobile, wind chime, piece of fabric, or anything beautiful from the beam. If you cannot do these things, place a small mirror on the surface of the furniture (desk or table) to reflect the beam back to itself. Even a pen on a shiny flat pen holder works as a mirror. Light the beam, lighten the load.

ANGLES AND SLANTED CORNERS

Angles squeeze *chi* into a pointed shape or catch it, creating a "dead" corner. Place furniture in such a way as to make an angle into a square, or use screens and plants to hide the angle. Slants seem to coincide with a slanted point of view. It is easy to cover a slanted corner with cloth, curtains, tassels, anything to straighten it out. Dead corners also catch *chi*. After almost a year of debate, an astronomer finally put a mirror in a dead corner in her living room. She was astounded at how quickly the energy began to move. Her business didn't exactly improve, but the quality of her life did. For the first time in a long time, she was able to take some time off, relax, and enjoy herself. Hanging mirrors on one or both sides of the dead corner activate and stimulate the corner. Hanging crystals in that corner, or placing plants, especially growing vines, in the corner also considerably improve the energy.

Remember when you were told to sit back from the TV or you'd go blind? That's an exaggeration, but still there is a lot of concern that the glut of large and small appliances in our homes, offices, and cars might be doing more than make life easier. They might be threatening our health.

Electronic appliances emit electromagnetic fields (EMF), which have been accused of causing many problems. The fears of some scientists that EMF produced by power lines may cause cancer have been heightened by two recent studies from Sweden that show as much as a fourfold increase in leukemia among children who live near power lines. Swedish researchers at the Karolinska Institute in Stockholm have compiled extensive evidence on the extent of exposure to EMF that shows that cancer risk goes up with increasing exposure.

In 1994, researchers at the University of Southern California released the news that electromagnetic fields, already implicated in triggering leukemia, brain tumors, and breast cancer, may play a far more important role in Alzheimer's disease. Results from two new studies conducted in Finland and one in Los Angeles indicate that people with a high occupational exposure to EMFs are at least three times as likely to develop Alzheimer's disease as those without significant exposure. Dressmakers and tailors are at the greatest risk because industrial and home sewing machines produce much larger EMFs than other appliances, and people who use sewing machines regularly have the greatest exposure of any occupation—as much as three times that of electric power line and cable workers, according to the *Los Angeles Times*.

If you want your home and appliances measured for EMF, call your utility company. In most states, there are EMF home measurement programs. While waiting for the verdict on health risks of electromagnetic fields, practice prudent avoidance. Make sure devices such as clocks, radios, and air conditioners are at least three feet from the bed. Don't work with your head close to a fluorescent or halogen desk lamp. Choose a cellular phone that has the transmitter separate from the receiver. Limit the use of hand-held electric appliances such as mixers and hair dryers (as a rule, they have very strong fields). Be aware that fields are strong where the electric power enters the house and at the circuit breaker. Keep your distance. Electromagnetic fields drop off very rapidly as you move away from your appliance. Avoid prolonged exposure to high fields. Don't hover around the microwave or glue your face to the television set. But don't panic either. The risks are small and it is relatively easy for you to avoid an appliance or distance yourself from an EMF.

Another concern is carbon monoxide poisoning in homes. This colorless, odorless, cumulative poison can be produced by fuel-burning appliances such as oil or gas furnaces, water heaters, gas ranges and ovens, fireplaces, and wood-burning stoves. Exposure to high levels of CO can kill you, and there are several CO detectors on the market, some that show the CO levels in the air on a continuous digital readout. Homeowners can monitor the display for an early visual warning of even low levels of CO, so they can find the source and fix it before it becomes a danger.

It's the same with other hazardous material in your home—lead paint and asbestos to name just two. Here again, the most important thing is not to panic. Just be aware of these things. That's your first step in creating a more healthful environment.

In feng shui, there are very few problems that cannot be solved, cured, or healed with the proper antidote. First, however, you must be aware that they are there. Keep your senses alert to detect negative energy before you are affected by it. Try not to stay where the energy is bad. Either fix it or leave the room. Don't be shy. I have moved furniture in classrooms, hotels, restaurants, theaters (to the dismay of family and friends). If you are paying for the experience, why suffer because of poor placement? A word of caution: Don't change furniture in somebody else's office or home unless you are asked to. This is paramount to interfering with their destiny, and if you do it unasked, you then become responsible for that person's experiences. Remember not to give feng shui advice unless it is specifically requested.

CHAPTER 6

Applying Feng Shui

Principles to

Decorating and

Arranging Interior

Space

SPACE IS A SYMPHONY

When decorating and arranging your space, think of it as a symphony with a recurring theme or melody that threads its way through diverse values, speeds, and tones, with pauses and dramatic moments all leading to a magnificent conclusion, the creation of harmony. This will give you an idea of how different colors, sizes, patterns, weights, textures, and qualities can be used in unequal proportions to create a balanced whole.

Imagine the space empty with only the elements of design: the walls, ceilings, windows, doors, stairwells, and other features that probably cannot be changed or moved. Notice the air currents, if there are any. Observe the natural light, if there is any, and how it moves through the space to form patterns, shadows, or hot spots. Look out the windows to determine if there are any views worth borrowing. This will help you analyze the space before you paint or place a single piece of furniture.

GOOD SPACE ALWAYS SERVES A PURPOSE

A student once asked me what constitutes bad taste. What he was really asking was why some space looks odd or ugly. Usually, it's because the offending space has no purpose, or order. Its elements are combined with no coordinated scheme, too much or too little variety, and no consideration of the natural cycles of life. The first thing you notice about tasteless interior decoration is that it looks chaotic. Everything is clumped together with no definition, organization, separation, logic, or reason for being.

The first step in applying feng shui principles to decorating is to assess the function of each area in your personal space. Will it serve a single or multiple purpose? When will it be used? What time of day, week, month, or year? If a space is used only once a year when your mother comes to visit, you are wasting your space. Who will be using the space? You, your pets, friends, family, acquaintances, strangers? Where are the traffic corridors for *chi,* people, and pets? What furniture do you need to include? Beds, desk, chairs, tables, electronic equipment? Are there electrical outlets where you need them? What accessories do you plan to include? Define the purpose. Even if the space is small, divide it into separate and distinct areas that are organized. This bit of advance planning will turn chaos to order.

Next, give each space meaning by choosing a focal point, such as the view from a window, the fireplace, a dramatic piece of furniture, electronics, whatever is available. In small circles, arrange the furniture around the focal point. For example, place a sofa against a solid wall with two chairs arranged at right angles on either side and a low table in the center; or place the sofa in front of a fireplace or other focal point, with chairs arranged at right angles. The largest, most massive piece of furniture should dominate; all other pieces should act as accessories, complementing the dominating piece.

COORDINATE FURNISHING

Space looks strange when there is no coordination to the furnishings. This usually occurs when everything you like or own is included in the same place. Just because you like something is not enough reason to use it to decorate and furnish your space. When this is done tastefully, the results can be artistic, interesting, and dynamic. When done without forethought, the result is a mishmash of clashing elements. Grandma's rocker is next to the stainless steel and glass table. The acrylic-on-black-velvet picture is next to the oil painting in the heavy gold frame. The couch is covered in polished cotton and the occasional chair is upholstered in tapestry. Each piece, in itself, is fine. Put them together and you might as well use vanilla to season roast beef. It just doesn't work.

Creating a theme for the space automatically coordinates things. A theme can be anything: traditional, modern, oriental, romantic, eclectic, or let your personal interest provide the theme. Are you a film buff, gardener, astrologer? Do you adore cars, fishing, horses, dogs, birds, sewing, cooking? Maybe you don't have any special interests, but you enjoy the beach, mountains, camping, skiing; anything can provide a theme.

Maintain the theme throughout by placing all items that belong together in their own area. Place all formal, velvet, brocade, silk, traditional art in heavy gold frames in one room; all informal, cotton, canvas, organic, or wicker items in another room or part of the room.

This doesn't mean that you must eliminate variety or design a homogeneous space that excludes elements or variety. It is not natural when everything has the same size, density, intensity, and color. When one of the five elements is missing, the environment cannot establish balance, harmony will not be achieved, success is unavailable. Whenever possible, include various textures, sizes, heights, mass, colors, and intensity. Include all five elements but don't give them equal value.

PROPORTIONS CONTRIBUTE TO BEAUTIFUL SPACE

Improper proportions are the greatest factor in what we regard as ugly space. Consider the relationship of the sizes. Don't put huge furniture in small spaces or tiny furniture in big spaces, delicate tables next to a massive leather chairs, over-size tables with miniature chairs. An actress filled every inch of her tiny apartment with overstuffed couches and mirrored, angular tables. It was a nightmare with barely room to move around. She was a disturbed person who was constantly in crisis.

Once you've decided on the dominating element and color, use the three cycles (see pages 179–182) to determine the proportions of the other elements that should be included. For example, an all-white/Metal room can be enhanced by adding a black/Water coffee table displaying a crystal or decorative stone/Earth, a large green/Wood plant, and red/Fire candles. When using only one object from an element, make sure it is big enough or has enough drama to be representative of the element and in proportion to the room. Nothing looks more out of balance than an object that is too small or too large for the space.

When one of the five elements is excluded, it unconsciously feels like something is missing, which contributes to a space that feels inorganic—not alive and grow-ing. It is not natural when everything is the same. There are elements missing and when an element is absent, the life cycle is incomplete; the environment will not support life, the occupants do not progress forward.

PLACEMENT OF FURNITURE

The first consideration is the flow of *chi*. Make sure the placement of the furniture does not interfere, block, distort, angle, straighten, or force the flow. Avoid over-powering furniture that takes up too much space. It's tempting, but try not to cre-ate dense masses of objects by clumping furniture and objects too close together or so close to a wall that it leaves marks. Create "breathing room" around items so the *chi* can circulate. Raise beds, couches, and chairs at least a few inches off the floor, but no more than three feet, which provides a comfy air cushion around the furni-ture and allows free-flowing movement of the *chi*.

Basically, a minimalist approach to the design and placement of furniture is most successful because it allows for empty as well as full space in the room. Make sure the furniture doesn't obstruct the flow of *chi* between the entrance and exits, and remove obstructions from behind the doors.

Position the furniture, whether it's a bed, desk, stove, or couch, so that whoever is using it has a good view of the entry. When the entry is not visible, it tends to create a feeling of insecurity, as if things were going on behind your back. If you have to set the furniture in this way, use a mirror or any other reflective surface to

Before: Heavy, dense furniture blocks *chi* from flowing from the living room (foreground) into the sunlit kitchen (background). Notice that the stripes on the rug as well as the edges of the coffee table (a trunk) and sofa are arranged parallel to the walls, making the room seem narrow.

After: The chairs and couch have changed places and are set at an angle, as are the rug and new coffee table (a round one would have been better). The *chi* now has a wider (if not straight) path from living room to kitchen.

Notice how the rug and the numerous round images and objects encourage the *chi* to circulate, then find the door.

reflect the activities of the entry so that no one will be able to "surprise" you. Avoid placing beds, desks, or cash registers directly opposite windows or doors, particularly the main entry. There should be at least three feet of space and a small table or some type of barrier between the window and the bed, desk, or couch.

Try not to place furniture so that you face a blank wall. Computers should be placed so that the computer worker faces out into the room. This often leaves the computer wires exposed, which is not a good situation either. Try to have the computer against a side wall so that the worker can face out and the wires can be hidden.

Don't place furniture in a way that blocks the *chi* or creates angles that might be directed at the entry, bed, or desk. Place heavy furniture along the walls, using it to fill in empty corners. Just don't place it too close to the wall or, in life, you might "back yourself" into a situation that limits your options or ability to maneuver through life.

Arrange the furniture for coziness, conversation, and comfort, making sure there is empty space through which the *chi* can move. Create curves that encourage the *chi* to enter the space, meander gently through it, and finally exit from another door or window. In long, narrow rooms, use round or hexagonal patterns, round objects on counters and tables, round knobs and handles on doors, and small round carpets rather than long runners. If long runners are used, make sure the patterns are horizontal rather than vertical.

Accessories add a personal touch to any room. Organize them into groups and consider their use. In arranging shelves and mantels, place frequently used items at eye level. If you need to touch something, it should be reachable. Place accessories and hang pictures so they are not too far above eye level while viewed from a seated position. A large picture should be hung over a large piece of furniture. Two large pictures in the same room should be hung opposite each other. Place heavy items close to the ground so they act like "anchors."

Feng shui can help bring good fortune into various aspects of your life. To activate any of the following qualities, try arranging your furnishings as suggested:

Health and well-being: In the east (or where you can see the rising sun or moon), place the colors green, black, and red; images of streams, fish ponds, or trees; bright lights; heat; bubbling water; plants and organic materials such as sea shells.

Family and children: In the west (or where you can see the sunset), place the colors yellow, white, and dark blue. This is a good place for toys, family photos, reminders of ancestors, trophies, awards, special rocks, stones, crystals, square and round shapes.

Business: In the north (or near the main entry), place rocks or large trees. Use the colors dark blue, black, white, or gray; irregular shapes; metals such as gold, bronze, and copper; glass. This is a good place for the phone, desk, or computer.

Fame: In the south (or somewhere in the house or office that receives natural sunlight all day), place the colors yellow and red; pictures of yourself, your trophies, and awards; wood objects; bubbling water; electrical appliances. If you do not have a place that receives natural sunlight, create your own "sun" with lights and heat.

Money: In the southeast (or to the far left of the entry of any room, or where you can see the sunrise in the winter, or far left in the main room as you enter the house or office, or in the upper left-hand corner farthest from the entry but in the same room), place round-leaf plants and tie a red ribbon around the plant, vase, or pot. Place three coins under the plant. Do not place the following in this area: storage items, coffee pots, electrical appliances, pointed-leaf plants. Use the colors black, green, or red; round or coin-shaped objects; pictures of money or treasure; fish ponds; bubbling water.

Knowledge: In the northeast (or near the front of the house or where you can see the sunrise in the summer), place books, notebooks, computers, study and office equipment, papers, files. Use earthy materials; metals and sharp or pointed objects; and the colors brown, yellow, white, gray, and red.

Travel and friends: In the northwest (or near the entrance or exit or where you can see the setting sun in the summer), place travel posters, luggage, travel souvenirs, pictures of angels or other helpful images, rocks, crystals, bubbling or still water. Use the colors turquoise, silvery white, and light blue.

Love: In the southwest (or in the farthest right-hand corner from the entry of any room, or where you can see the sunset in the winter), place earthy colors such as yellow and brown, or Fire colors, such as red and pink, or metals and precious or semiprecious stones. You can also use crystals, wedding photos, romantic objects, and still water.

USING ILLUSION TO CREATE BALANCE AND HARMONY

When the shape, size, and placement of our space is less than ideal and we have no way to change the conditions, we must make magic and create illusions with whatever is practical. We must fool the eye into thinking it is looking at the most beautiful, perfectly proportioned, balanced, and harmonious environment possible.

Using Perspective

The rules of perspective allow us to create illusions with space. To make large space cozy and intimate, manipulate the scale and placement by using slightly oversize furniture and large, dramatic accessories—big bouquets of flowers, full-grown trees, and so on. If the entry is too large, too much *chi* enters. Reduce its size by using dark colors; bright, hot colors; bold moving patterns; contrasting floor and wall coverings. Direct the eyes to the floors by using bold, bright patterns, which make space appear smaller.

Divide a room into sections by placing furniture in groupings, using different-color carpeting or area rugs to break up the space. Add bold colors, and use red, orange, and yellow to define areas. Use large patterns, large floor tiles.

If the entry is too small, narrow, or dark, not enough *chi* can enter. No *chi,* no opportunities, no life. It's pretty simple. Enlarge and expand the space by using a unified floor and wall color, a monochromatic color scheme in light or cool colors, small still patterns, and bright lights. Add depth by placing larger, brighter, bolder, taller, heavier furniture and accessories near smaller, less dramatic pieces. Use the same colors and patterns throughout.

Small rooms can be visually enlarged beyond the property limits through the use of "borrowed landscape." To do this, use wallpaper borders or bold contrasting paint to frame a window or door that has an interesting view. This draws attention out the window to the view. Arrange furniture and accessories to create different levels, and arrange plants and accessories at different heights to give the illusion of more space. Use similar colors and patterns throughout. Add variety through inclusion of various shades, tones, and hues. Limit the number of pieces and use slightly undersize pieces, not miniatures, though. Just because the space is small doesn't mean it has to be furnished like a dollhouse.

Using Color

Color makes us believe what is not real. It appears to change the size, shape, dimensions, and quality of space, creating atmosphere and ambiance that are not really there. It can enlarge, reduce, brighten, subdue, excite, stimulate, and otherwise transform the dull and ordinary into the extraordinary. Color affects moods, sleep patterns, appetite, desire. Obviously it is important in creating balance and harmony in space.

Colors specifically associated with the five elements are primary colors: green, red, yellow, white, and black. Bold, clear, pure colors are commonly used to introduce children to color or to create a whimsical, childlike effect. However, the rainbow contains the full spectrum of light and is considered to have a healing quality. In feng shui, the five elements have correspondence with the five primary colors and include a wide range of their subsidiary blends and hues. For example, Fire is associated with red, purple, burgundy, ruby, warm pink, rose peach, and orange.

The right wall and furniture colors depend on the size, lighting, and function of a space. Basically, matching the color to the environment is appropriate. Desert colors in the Southwest look suitable; in Cape Cod, grays and blues look right; in Florida and California, pastels are apropos. In the country, barn red, beige, blue, and green blend with the landscape.

Because the color of the walls mirrors our inner feelings, sometimes we color and arrange space to facilitate a change that we are avoiding. At one of the worst times of her professional life an actress insisted on painting her bedroom a murky, dark green with black woodwork. She thought it was restful. Her friends thought she should be committed to a sanitarium. She couldn't make the payments on the house and was forced to move. What seemed to her a disaster at the time turned out all right. Her new place had a pink bedroom, which she thought was awful, but she didn't have time to do anything about it because, quite suddenly, she got a part in a movie and was very busy.

Colors aid in creating illusions. As a rule, if the space enjoys a lot of light, natural or artificial, the colors can be light or dark. If the space is small and dim, light colors make it appear larger. Color is an effective way to create atmosphere. Dark colors create cool, peaceful space. Hot, bright colors create lively environments. Blue is restful, so don't paint the office blue or everyone will want to take naps in the afternoon. A jeweler should avoid yellow because it makes the jewelry look bad. Green often makes an individual look ill, so this might be good for a doctor's office but not for a beauty salon. Red is the color of blood and life, a lucky color. Adding and changing colors in a room is one of the simplest and least expensive ways to change the vibration of space.

Do you like the colors you are currently using? If not, change them. Decide which colors will be dominant and which will play subsidiary roles in decorating your space. Go ahead, go crazy. Paint it mauve or puce or any color you want.

Green/East/Wood. Green is associated with healing, growth, psychic energy, wisdom, anger, creativity, and fertility. It represents creativity and the beginning of new projects. Green was the color of the Ming dynasty, 1368–1644, a time of creativity in the arts. Green is calming and soothes a broken heart, but too much is not good. A client was suffering from an exotic illness that he supposedly caught in the tropics. His home was completely green—walls, carpet, furniture. His skin was even a bit green because he was suffering from a jaundiced condition. He eventually went bankrupt and was forced to move out of the house, after which he experienced a complete recovery. Green is stronger than yellow.

Reds/South/Fire. Red is associated with dynamic, life-giving light, heat, laughter, good luck, and passion. It can be used to develop leadership, confidence, speed, and personal power. Red has been used as a life-giving color since prehistoric times, when cinnabar was found in tombs. Chinese restaurants tend to display an abundance of red and gold colors, believing it makes for good business. A vase tied with a red ribbon placed on a desk is said to increase business; a red door brings good luck, as do red flowers.

The Zhou dynasty, 1027–256 B.C., supposedly originated with the appearance of a mythical "red raven" and was known for its use of red clothing, hats, hair, tassels, horses, flags, and so on. Communism continued this tradition with "rule of the reds" and the formation of the Red Guard, shock troops of the Revolution.

Red is a lucky color, used for joy and happy festivals. Red lights stimulate the sensual aspects of *chi;* rose and pink blush it with health, making everybody look young and beautiful. Full-spectrum lights are pink and cast a pure white light that is very good for relieving depression. Red is stronger than white.

Yellow/Center/Earth. Originally derived from deposits of loess that blew off the Gobi onto the northern Chinese plains and subsequently turned yellow, it was the color of the Emperor Huang-di, who ruled the Middle Kingdom and was known as the Yellow Emperor. Yellow was used exclusively by the Qing dynasty, 1644–1912. Until the twentieth century, only the emperor and a few Buddhist monks were allowed to wear yellow.

The yellow chrysanthemum is still the royal flower; the path of the ecliptic, or apparent passage of the sun through the sky, is known as "the yellow way." Who can forget Dorothy traveling the yellow-brick road to find the Wizard of Oz? Yellow attracts fame, progress, advancement, sympathy, trustworthiness, stability, faithfulness, loyalty, and cheerfulness. It is the color of immortality and represents long life. Yellow dominates black.

White/West/Metal. White is used for Chinese funerals and mourning. It represents purity, death, precision, order, and ability to withdraw or let go. Surrender flags are traditionally white. White was the color favored by the Shang dynasty, 1523–1027 B.C., especially for scholars and the elderly. The White Lotus is a secret society started in the twelfth century that seeks another, better, purer world. White is a good basic color, as it contains all colors within it and is the most commonly used lightbulb color even though the light it casts is yellowish. White is stronger than green.

Black/North/Water. When Shi Huang-di of the Qin dynasty defeated the red Zhou dynasty, he choose black as his color because black represents Water, which defeats red/Fire. Black is known as the color of the devil, death, and evil as well as of honor. It represents continuity, solitude, meditation, peacefulness, and the oneness of the universe. Black is stronger than red.

Brown/Northeast/Earth. Brown was used as the dominant color of the Sung dynasty, 960–1279, and is considered to be an Earth color.

Blue/Heaven or Northwest/Metal. Represents celestial goodness. Associated with Metal and heaven, which is a nondirection as well as the intermediary direction northwest.

Purple and Mauve/Fire. Represent high office, spiritual awareness. Associated with Fire and no direction.

Using Patterns

Mixing patterns takes some forethought. You can use several patterns together if you remember that small patterns work best in small areas, large patterns in large areas. Floor patterns that run parallel to the direction of the path add a sense of speed and dynamic tension and lead you quickly to wherever you're going. Floor patterns that run horizontally to the direction of the path slow the *chi* and lend a meandering feeling to the path.

Patterns are symbols of sorts and, like colors, can be used to affect atmosphere and mood. Stripes, dots, checks, herringbone, small, closed, open, moving, bold, timid, noisy, quiet—there are as many patterns as you can imagine.

When mixing patterns, all of them should include the same two or three colors. Including more than three primary colors is dangerous to harmony. For example, in a red, white, and blue color scheme, use only these three primary colors but include all of their subsidiary colors in lighter or darker shades and tones. Use a large open pattern that contains all three colors—red and blue flowers on a white background, for example. Add one horizontal or vertical stripe pattern in two of the colors (blue and white, red and white, blue and red); add another, small, closed pattern in two of the colors, in red and white checks, or in dots. This type of combination usually works but it is not for the timid or insecure decorator. As a general rule, add a variety of colors when using similar textures; add a variety of textures when using similar colors.

Some patterns are considered lucky. Clouds represent heaven and eternity; circles, like coins, exemplify prosperity and success; bamboo symbolizes virtue; fans embody goodness and are believed to be useful in driving away evil as well in providing an instant breeze. An octagon, or *ba gua,* is considered a lucky symbol and is often seen in elements of design because it protects as well as attracts good fortune.

Using Light

A client was having trouble with his business—no sales, no clients, nothing. His office was dark and gloomy because he had all the shades drawn. Lighting can affect your mood and, subsequently, your performance at work and your potential for success. If the work space is dark, you're working in the dark. Utilize natural light as much as you can, unless it magnifies the glaring sunlight.

Lighting in the bedroom is crucial to a good night's sleep. Insomnia is sometimes caused by an ill-placed and offensive street light that awakens the sleeper during the night. If this is the case, cover the window before you go to bed. However, to sleep with the light of the moon on your face is very nurturing. The cycles of the moon correlate with the menstrual cycle, and if a woman receives the beneficent light of the moon during the night, her cycle will become more regular and predictable. In times of extreme mental stress, breathe in the light of the moon. It will calm you.

Using Artificial Light

Lamps and lights are symbolic suns and are often used as basic cures for imbalances in feng shui. Lighting can affect mood, attitude, and effectiveness, and it is essential for healthy, smooth circulation of *chi*—the brighter the light, the more active the *chi*. Ever notice how brightly lit Chinese restaurants are? Bright lights mean good business. A single bright light aimed at a small item can act like a miniature sun that brings up the *chi* and luck of the space. Sometimes, a dark atmosphere is desired, in which case low lighting enhances the mood, creating a romantic, sexy, mellow space.

Lights should be a sufficient distance from your head so that you can't feel the heat. If they are placed close to your head, use low-wattage bulbs. Fluorescent lights can cause problems when they are too close to your head. Stay as far away from them as you can or use them in hallways, stairwells, and other spaces where people don't linger. If you work under fluorescent lights, try to go outside on your coffee and lunch breaks or at least wash your hands and face. The water and the sunshine (even gentle rain or snow) will help wash or burn away the negative effects.

Using Clocks, Calendars, and Other Mechanical Equipment

A friend from Chase Manhattan's Asia branch told me he had the feng shui man in Hong Kong "do" his office, but it was no good. I asked what happened and he said he was told to put a clock on a certain wall of the office near his desk to improve business. The friend explained how he had gone to Nathan Road, purchased a very expensive antique clock, and hung it per the instructions. But nothing happened; feng shui didn't work. I asked him if the clock worked. He said no. Clocks, as well as calendars, are powerful generators of energy. If you sit under or near a clock that doesn't work, nothing will change.

A widower complained that since his wife died, time just stood still. None of the clocks in his house were working and the calendars were six months behind, still on the month his wife died. He made it a project to fix all the clocks. A neighborly widow stopped by to help him. Soon they were a couple.

Televisions, radios, stereos, blenders, fans—any kind of electrical equipment is capable of generating, activating, or stimulating *chi*. Appliances are best placed in corners, angles, or "dead" spots where they can do some good. All appliances and equipment should be kept in working condition; it's better to manage without the equipment than to have an item that doesn't work. Even the clock on the stove should be working. If it doesn't work, get it fixed or remove it from sight by applying tape over it.

A writer complained for months about his lousy telephone. Heaven only knows why he didn't just go out and buy a new one. In the meantime, his business had fallen off and he was feeling unloved and unwanted. When he finally decided to act, he bought a new, state-of-the-art phone system. As he was plugging it in, *Time* magazine called, asking if he would write a cover story.

If a desk is too close to a clock, you constantly have an eye on the time and may want to leave school or work early. If you sit under a clock, you're always "under pressure" or racing to meet deadlines, with never enough time to complete projects.

Using Wind Chimes, Bells, and Musical Instruments

Wind chimes come in all elements: I have seen them made from bamboo, animal bones, ceramic, metal, glass, and dripping water. Wind chimes and bells stimulate, activate, and balance *chi*. They call the *chi* to enter through half-doors or sliding windows, and, because they circulate *chi*, they can balance fast-moving energy.

Wind chimes, like windmills, are particularly effective in dispersing *chi* that comes from an overbearing road or a long, narrow corridor. A string of bells adds energy to the room of a sick or depressed person, and there is nothing like a loud bell to sound the alarm in case of danger. Chimes and bells are pleasant to have around the house. Like a bubbling fountain, they can help create a healthful, pleasant environment. To help you stick to your New Year's resolutions, hang a brass wind chime above your desk.

Using Money

Money is a good antidote for problems. Symbols of money, coins under plants, and pictures of money all put you in the mood to believe in the law of abundance, which ensures sufficient resources to maintain your lifestyle. There are two parts of the law of abundance: First, you get back ten times what you give freely, in secret, with no expectation to be repaid and with no strings attached; and second, if you think you are poor, you will be. The universe responds to your vibration, and if this is what your vibration is, no matter how justified, the universe will respond in kind. If you accept as a fact that you are rich right now, the universe will send you what you need to actualize the statement.

Using Mirrors

Mirrors are the panacea for many feng shui problems—so much so that they have been called the "aspirin of feng shui." Their ability to reflect supplies us with a magical tool, easy to obtain and simple to use. However, mirrors can also cause a lot of problems because they direct, move, stimulate, and activate *chi*.

In Hong Kong, certain neighborhoods have "mirror wars." One house hangs a mirror in the window to deflect a negative angle. The house opposite doesn't want the reflected angle and also hangs a mirror to deflect the image. A third house gets into the act. Pretty soon, there are mirrors hanging in the windows of all the houses. The mirrors cause the light to bounce, which confuses the cars, which then run into each other. The police periodically come in and order all the mirrors to be removed, but as soon as the police leave, the mirrors return.

The size of the mirror is not important. Larger is not necessarily better; sometimes a small one is just as effective. Sometimes you want to use the smallest mirror available, so as not to attract attention to what you are doing. An executive secretary hung a small mirror over her stove to improve her finances. Within a few days of hanging the mirror, she obtained a new job. With her first paycheck, she bought a bigger mirror, thinking that if a small mirror brought her a job, a big mirror would bring her a raise. The day she hung the large mirror she was laid off from her new job. When she looked into the mirror to see what the mirror was seeing, she realized that the larger mirror took in more of the room, including a dripping faucet from the sink. The mirror magnified the drip and she lost her job. She replaced the large mirror with the original small one and is now happily employed again.

Mirrors are made by placing silver aluminum behind glass, which is made when Fire touches Earth. Film is made by using silver nitrate behind a transparent material. A mirror can be anything that has a reflective quality, like reflective glass or water. Narcissus fell in love with himself when he saw his reflection in a pool of water. Mirrors are magic and can make us fall in love with images. Shiny pots hung behind a stove reflect the activities taking place behind the cook. Silver frames with reflective glass can reflect desired areas when a mirror is inappropriate. Tinfoil, shiny wallpaper, and glass in frames or windows all have the ability to reflect. Thus, they work well in dark spaces where you need all the light you can get. Reflections from water, glass, mirrors, film, or anything shiny have the potential to create an illusion.

Sometimes, if we have a particular image of ourselves, we gravitate to an odd or unusual mirror. A cartoonist from Atlanta said that when he took his dogs for a walk in the morning, he looked like one of his cartoon characters walking in the park. Above his sofa hung a mirror in an oval frame, but it hung at a whimsical angle, like a mirror drawn in a cartoon. An elderly woman thinks of herself as a reincarnation of Marie Antoinette. She is very vain and has many gold-framed ornate antique mirrors in her home.

When placing a mirror, remember that not all mirrors are equal and then ask yourself, "What does the mirror see?" This can help you decide where it should be placed. Does it cut off the top of your head when you look into it? Mirrors should be hung so the tallest person in the house can see the top of his or her head in it. Mirrors must be positioned with great care in an office because they reflect angles from desks, walls, and partitions. A secretary faced a wall and placed a mirror by her desk so she could see who was coming in the door. The mirror reflected the corner of a closet and magnified the sharp angle that was directed at her desk. She was always under pressure from the boss and other employees and was ready to have a nervous breakdown. When she moved the mirror so it did not reflect the corner, she felt better immediately.

Mirrors can start fires because they intensify the light. Unless you are using a magnifying glass to start a campfire, be sure the mirrors in your home do not reflect bright sunlight or interior lights because this could cause a "hot spot" in your home.

Mirrors can act as witnesses to events that have transpired. Pity the poor person who buys Dorian Gray's mirror. If you really want an antique mirror but don't want to be bothered by its history, just cleanse it thoroughly with a mixture of water and lemon juice and acknowledge that what you see may be influenced by its past.

The round mirror attracts the *chi*, then the boat and planetary photos and paintings direct the *chi* past this wall.

Mirrors in the Bedroom. Mirrors in the bedroom stimulate *chi*. Honeymoon suites sometimes have mirrors on the ceiling above the bed to encourage sexual activity. These are not restful rooms, nor were they meant to be. Too many mirrors, such as a wall of mirrored closet doors, create a very lively, active space. If you place a mirror so that you see yourself first thing in the morning, your spirit will always be a little edgy. This is not just feng shui, it's good sense, especially as you get older.

Mirrors in Business. In some businesses, mirrors are essential because they reflect light to dark areas, call the *chi* to enter, stimulate the *chi* in dead, angular corners, and are effective in maintaining security because they allow you to see everything in the store from a central position.

Mirrors help sell products. The mirrors in beauty salons are designed to make you look gorgeous and buy their shampoo; clothing stores install "skinny" mirrors that make customers look thinner than they are; ballrooms suspend a glass ball from the ceiling for aesthetic purposes but also to stimulate the dancers. Mirrors placed behind a bar multiply the bottles and glasses, encouraging the drinkers to have another.

Mirrors Can Deflect and Disperse Negative Energy. The negative energy from secret arrows, straight lines, walls and fences, poles, antennae, obnoxious neighbors, and barking dogs can by deflected by using mirrors and reflections to send the noise, angle, or problem back to its origin. Mirrors disperse overactive *chi* coming from straight lines that end at the site, from roads, T-junctions, culs-de-sac, or corridors. Place a mirror or other item, reflective side facing out, directed toward the offensive area. A small mirror, even tinfoil, will work.

Mirrors Can Make Features Disappear. Mirrors are magical and can make us believe the unbelievable. Think of the magician who cleverly uses mirrors to make objects disappear. Mirroring the angles of an obstructive square column makes the column invisible. A mirror placed on a beam "makes a hole in the beam." If there is a tree in front of the entry, a mirror hung at eye level on the tree will create an imaginary hole in the tree, thus allowing *chi* to flow through it and to your door.

Mirrors Can Move Space. Mirrors can visually move a direction or move entire rooms to more suitable directions. For example, if you want the kitchen on the other side of the room, hang a mirror where you want the kitchen to be and so it reflects the actual kitchen. Now the kitchen is where the mirror is. If you want the west wall where the east wall is, hang a mirror on the east wall, reflecting the west wall. Presto! You have moved the wall. Dangling rooms or wings of L-shaped, T-shaped, or U-shaped rooms can be made into perfect squares or rectangles by using a mirror to bring the missing area back into the space. Mirrors can visually add to the missing areas of odd-shaped rooms. Water flowing away from a property can be "brought back" with mirrors, and mirrors can "borrow" other good views into your space, like a neighbor's rose garden or Christmas decorations.

Mirrors Can Reduce Stress. Place two mirrors so that they face each other. When you walk between them, you can see yourself for infinity, which can give you a better sense of identity and keep your mind from wandering.

When Mirrors Are Not Good Feng Shui

Mirrors aren't always beneficial to our health and harmony. Observe the following cautions.

- Don't place a mirror opposite the entry of any room or opposite any door, because it will deflect the *chi* trying to come into the room and encourage negative *chi* to remain and not exit. Sometimes this causes bad temper, crankiness, or emotional problems.
- Don't hang a mirror so that it cuts off your head or any part of your body.
- Don't hang a mirror so that it splits an image, reflects an angle, or magnifies a problem.
- Don't place a mirror opposite the bed, because it will draw energy away from you and into the mirror. Likewise, don't place a mirror of any sort

(even a hand mirror or mirrored perfume tray) on the dresser opposite the door or bed.

- Don't place a mirror so you can see yourself upon awakening.
- Avoid cheap mirrors or mirrors that have a distorted surface or black spots or patches of gray on them. Don't use broken, chipped, cracked, or scratched mirrors.
- Keep all mirrors clean, remembering that dust on a mirror can bring cloudy emotions.

Animals and Feng Shui

Animals, whether they are real or represented symbolically, can have a magical effect on our environment. Pets teach us about being natural and true to our intregal nature. Animals don't suffer insecurities or try to be something they're not. They seldom do things that go against their instincts, which are keen and sharp. Animals anticipate things humans cannot, like eclipses, earthquakes, tornadoes, storms, and other natural phenomena. Animals can sense when the *chi* is about to change.

Some people have too many pets, and an excess of animals dominates what should be human space. Unless it's a barnyard, stable, or fish tank (see next section), there should be at least as many people as pets. Only domesticated animals should be kept. Snakes, tarantulas, mice, insects, monkeys, and other wild animals belong to nature. A bird in a cage, a chipmunk going round a wire ring, or a bear dancing in the circus is sad and unnatural.

Pets of all kinds are important to the emotional well-being of many because they teach us about unconditional love, loyalty, and patience. It is a mistake, however, to use a pet as a substitute for human affection or caring about others. This keeps the pet in bondage, weakens its survival instincts, and encourages you to remain isolated from humanity.

Fish. Do you desire wealth, love, abundance, regeneration? Get a few goldfish. In Cantonese, the word for "goldfish" sounds the same as "abundant gold," and therefore goldfish represent money.

In feng shui, fish are regarded as magical creatures that can increase cash flow, facilitate real estate sales, protect property, ensure fertility and safe pregnancies, and improve relationships. A picture of a child with a fish means "may you have an abundance of high-ranking sons"; goldfish in a bowl or pond mean "may gold and jewels fill your house to overflowing"; a fish with a lotus blossom means "year after year may you live in affluence." In the very oldest of Chinese literature, an abundance of fish in the waters foretold a good harvest. When fish swim upstream it is interpreted as rebellion against the social order, a harbinger of civil unrest. Fish are served at New Year to symbolize affluence for the year. They are sacrificed to the "great god of riches." Fish and water together are a metaphor for sexual intercourse or "having pleasures of fish in the water."

A computer programmer uses a screen-saver that has nine fish swimming across the screen. The fish are reflected in a mirror behind his desk and further reflected in another mirror across the room. Since he put the screen-saver on the computer, he says he receives money from orders, payments, or other resources every day. The computer generates the bubbles, the fish swim, the money rolls in.

If you are going to use fish to increase resources or as a security device, use an odd number of fish, and at least two different colors, to represent yin and yang—for example, four red fish and one black, or six black and one white. It should always be an odd combination rather than an even one because even numbers represent endings or death.

Fish act like security guards. If a fish dies, it may be an indication that negative energy has been in the room. Fish, compared to humans, are lower life forms and absorb the negativity, thus protecting you. Thank the fish for its sacrifice and replace it as soon as possible.

Dogs. Dogs have always been regarded as useful animals, symbols of loyalty and protection. They are used in hunting, for security devices, as help to the police, companionship to the lonely, and even assistance to the blind. Dogs are revered for their faithfulness.

Ferocious-looking stone foo dogs, with lionlike manes, are often seen in communities with Asian populations, where they are used as symbolic guards of the doors, protecting the entry from evil. In north China, paper dogs are used to bite evil spirits and drive them away and are buried in coffins with the dead for the same reason. In Taiwan, dead dogs are not buried for fear they will turn into dog demons. Instead they are thrown in water. In southern China, a creation myth describes the dog as bringing rice or millet to humankind. Among the Yak in south China, the dog is venerated as the forefather of the race. Pet names for dogs are rarely mentioned in Chinese texts. Foreign names may be given to dogs, or the dog may be called by its color as in "a yellow dog," but it is never given a Chinese name.

Cats. Cats, contrary to dogs, have always been considered evil because of their detached attitude. Even though they were domesticated long ago and worshipped in ancient Egypt, their independent nature and aloof manner remind us that the wild still exists within them.

Some say cats act as "fair witness," watching events on earth and reporting to an unknown secretary in the sky. Cats don't care what you think about them as long as you feed them. If you're not nice to them, they go away. In Cantonese, the word for "cat" sounds like the same as "old age," and a cat portrayed with plum and bamboo means "at all times we wish for you to reach a very old age." Cats teach us the yin/yang of life, through the contrasts in their behavior (shy/aggressive, delicate/vicious, annoying/ignoring).

Birds. It is believed that birds are messengers, carrying omens that can be good or bad depending on the viewer and the times. Frequently portrayed birds include the magpie, oriole, pheasant, quail, crow, and swallow.

Bats. Unlike in America, where they are despised and feared, in China bats are considered to be lucky. The Cantonese word for "bat" sounds like "good fortune," and five bats together is an auspicious symbol, frequently used in knot designs.

The Four Mythical Animals of the Directions.

- *Green dragon*: Dragons are lucky, good-natured, benign, benevolent, strong, and commanding. They represent male sexual prowess and female fertility. The green dragon rules Wood, the primal force of creation; the east with its rising sun; and spring, the time when life awakens. The dragon power within each spirit emerges at birth.
- *White tiger*: In China, the tiger is considered to be the king of the wild animals. In ancient villages sacrifices were made to the tiger so they would protect the village from wild pigs. Tigers represent pure yang/male energy and are symbols of bravery and courage. The tiger was very much feared in ancient times, but instead of hunting it to extinction, provincial authorities begged the tigers to go into the mountains and stay there. Legend has it that they agreed, obeying the voice of authority. A tiger on the doorpost is a guard against demons; small children are given tiger caps to protect them; tiger step is one of the thirty positions in sexual intercourse. If you want to insult a woman, call her "white tiger." The white tiger rules the direction of the setting sun, the west, and the grieving time of autumn. Middle age is the time when the tiger spirit emerges in life.
- *Red phoenix*: The red phoenix is the mythical animal of the south, Fire, and summer. When it is depicted with the dragon as emperor, it represents the empress and is a female symbol. Originally a male god of the winds, its sex was disputable. Eventually the male and female phoenix together came to represent sexual union. As a male symbol, the phoenix symbolizes the five human qualities: virtue, duty, ritually correct behavior, humanity, and reliability.
- *Black tortoise*: Turtles represent long life, endurance, patience—the slow and steady quality that wins the race. The black tortoise rules the Water, the north, and the long, seemingly endless winter. The spirit of the turtle emerges at death.

Using Symbols

Symbols are one of the oldest forms of communication. Lucky charms, amulets, religious objects, masks, and other images have been used as objects of worship since the beginning of time. Images and symbols remind us that nature is always at work; they offer us a way to connect to forces we cannot see. Some symbols offer protection from forces that would harm us. Others are used to enhance, create, inspire, control, force, or harm others. There are religious symbols like crosses, romantic symbols like hearts and flowers, and bad symbols like a skull and crossbones.

Symbols include all shapes—spirals, circles, crosses, triangles, labyrinths, and mazes. Some symbols are lucky, some are not. Symbols are associated with every area of life. Because they are personal, they are as varied as are the people in the world. A lucky charm can be a sock, jacket, rabbit's foot, coin, horseshoe—anything that you believe is lucky is a lucky charm.

Masks usually act as a kind of symbol. Before using a mask as part of your decor, find out what the mask represents. Is it the mask of a devil? Is it the mask of a fertility goddess? Is this something you want in the living room? Because symbols have power, know what the symbol means before you incorporate it into your space.

Using Flowers and Interior Gardens

For many, interior gardening is the only possibility for gardening. Filling your home with common indoor plants can actually help you stay healthier and look younger. A room full of plants can be one of the best cures for dry, wrinkled skin. Houseplants pump moisture into the air, breathe in carbon dioxide, and exhale oxygen. Houseplants clean the air of harmful pollutants by absorbing chemicals through their leaves, then transporting them to the roots, where they are broken down by ordinary microbes that eat the now harmless pollutants. This makes food for the plant and releases clean air. The following houseplants actually moisturize the skin and cleanse the air: golden pothos, lady palm, ficus alii, areca palm, peace lily, and arrowhead vine.

Before you spend money on new clothes, go buy some plants. Choose plants that are hardy, easy to care for, and inexpensive. Know which plants are poisonous and keep these away from small children and animals.

To generate life in space, place a plant inside the main entry, another inside the entry to the main room, and a third one inside the bedroom to attract, call, and direct the *chi*. As you do this, visualize growth and expansion. For emphasis, use newly purchased or freshly potted plants. If a plant dies, replace it with a more expensive one.

If you want to use more plants, place them along the path of the flow of *chi* from the inside of the front entry to the outside of the bedroom door. Use an odd number of plants to keep energy in motion. Even numbers, especially eight, will stop the flow of *chi*.

Flowers supply the Chinese with the finest designs for paintings, textiles, porcelains, carpets, furniture, architecture, and landscape. Flowers are painted according to rigid, highly conventionalized rules that designate specific flowers and animals for each season. Spring is portrayed by peacocks with cherry blossoms, peonies, iris,

Create curves for the flow of *chi* with plants, objects, furniture. Here, a *ba gua*–shaped rug greets the *chi* when it enters the room, a similarly shaped table moves it forward, and a small-leafed plant draws it farther into the room.

and magnolia. Summer is represented by ripe peaches, cherries, lotus blossoms, and ducks. Fall is represented by chrysanthemums, ornamental plum, and leaves in their various changing colors. Winter is shown with snow and bamboo or pine because both stay green all year.

Some flowers are not used. Lilac seems to coincide with family fights, willow trees represent sorrow or lust, fast-growing trees coincide with fast-growing problems. Roses have thorns and fade quickly, reminding us of our mortality.

The addition of plants is one of the easiest things you can do to improve your environment. Even if you have a "black thumb," you can buy some flowers and put them in a water jar on a table.

Part 3

FENG SHUI AND
THE WORKPLACE

CHAPTER 7

The Feng Shui

of the Workplace

To many Chinese, feng shui is essential to the art of business management. Citibank in Hong Kong would not erect their new building without the approval of a feng shui master. And Citibank is not alone. Chase Asia, PaineWebber, McKinsey and Company, the Morgan Bank, even the Asian offices of the *Wall Street Journal* use feng shui. Why? The Chinese are interested in making money and prefer to have an edge over their competitors. Feng shui gives them that edge.

People work in a thousand different types of places: medical offices, warehouses, newsrooms, police stations, factories, tollbooths, typing pools, the Oval Office. Wherever you take care of business is your workplace.

Let us assume that you are a worker, manager, or boss, and that you work at home or in an office, shop, or other place where business is conducted. Let us further assume that there is little you can do regarding the building. You can't change the orientation of the front door or remove the pillars that hold up the second floor. Your only hope is to alter your own working space.

Feng shui for commercial space is exactly like feng shui for the home, with the addition of certain information for the workplace. The same rules regarding the surrounding streets, the neighborhood, the element of the building, the *ba gua,* and all other feng shui techniques apply. The Appendix contains a section, Organizing Interior Office Space Using the *Ba Gua,* which can help you decide not only where to put your furniture but also what areas to designate for specific functions. Before you do that, however, whether you're analyzing a shop, store, office, or the kitchen corner as a possible work space, decide what type of business it is. There are basically three kinds of businesses: open, closed, and open/closed.

In this type of business, the major consideration is to entice customers into the shop, sell them the goods, collect the money, and provide an easy (but not too easy) exit. This includes such places as supermarkets, drugstores, boutiques, shoe stores, bookstores, and other types of shops. For this type of business, a southwest entry is usually preferred. If you can't have a southwest entrance, arrange the space in such a way that the customer is directed toward the southwest after entering. There should be good product visibility and accessibility. Customers won't buy if they can't see or touch the merchandise. Further, if the shop is too crowded with shelves and displays, customers will become agitated or tired or disoriented. Think of how aggressive rats becomes when confined in a tight-fitting maze. In shops where clothing, shoes, or other personal items are sold, divide the merchandise into divisions that are appropriate for the stock. Display the most valuable goods at eye level so it is easy for the customer to see the stock. Shelves can be inclined about five degrees and can follow the same dimensions as for bookshelves. Mirrors should not be placed facing the front door. In a shoe store, foot mirrors should be inclined to about twenty-five degrees. Footstools should be placed very carefully because they could block the flow of *chi* coming into the store or cause accidents. In this type of shop, the money spot is where the cash register is located or where the goods are paid for. The reception or cash counter should be placed in an area where *chi* can collect, but never directly opposite the front door. Place the cash register slightly to the side of the cashier's counter; it should be well lit and not blocked in any way.

There are some special requirements for bookstores. Categories of books should be clearly marked so that customers won't be confused and can quickly find the books they want. Ventilation also is important in a bookstore. Otherwise it gets very dusty and musty smelling. Artificial light is preferred because sunlight can damage the books.

In a beauty salon, prominent signs and advertisements are important. The reception area should be well lit and attractive, and the seats for the customers should be designed for bodily comfort. The shampoo and washing areas should be positioned so that the customers feel relaxed and do not suffer glare from sun coming from a window or an overhead light. There should be a lot of ventilation in the shampoo area because of the constant use of dyes and other chemicals.

In a drugstore or grocery store, the customer must first be enticed into the store and then the products must be available to see, touch, and smell. There should be room for traffic and circulation as well as space for stock. When the aisles are impossible to maneuver and when the exits are difficult to access, people feel trapped, tempers rise, annoyance permeates the place, thefts rise, and sales go down. Customers must know where to pay for their goods and then be able to leave the store without too much problem. The cash point ideally is between the products and the exits, as is common in most supermarkets. If the cash register is in a different location, the cashier must have good visibility to the entrance and exits;

otherwise, shoplifting is rampant. The major money in such a store should be kept in a safe in the manager's office, usually in the extreme front or back of the shop. It should be kept out of view.

In summary, the priorities for an open-type business are:

1. Entice the customer into the shop.
2. Make sure the merchandise can be seen and, if appropriate, touched.
3. Collect the money at an accessible place in the store.
4. Provide easy exit for customers, not thieves.

CLOSED-TYPE BUSINESSES

Customers seldom enter factories and workshops, which makes them closed-type businesses. Here, it is the worker, not the customer, who must be comfortable. If the workers are happy, production is timely and of good quality. If the workers are unhappy, the product could be shabby and business could be on the decline. Therefore, the first consideration here is to provide an efficient, comfortable, and safe place for the workers.

A closed shop can benefit from an entry facing northeast or northwest, but more important considerations are the size of the building compared to the size of the lot and the size of the workshop compared to the building. When the building is built to the limits of the lot, the workers are likely to have more power in the company than the management. When the building is too small for the size of the lot, management controls the workers. Consider the Detroit car factories that employ thousands of people. The factories themselves are often in the center of the lot, surrounded by a sea of cars. The power of the automobile industry is far away in some ivory tower while the workers buzz around the hive like bees.

In this type of working environment, production areas should be located where there is maximum *chi* and good ventilation. Make sure storage areas have sufficient size and are not at the end of long corridors or T-junctions. There should be sufficient space in the loading and unloading areas. If the loading beams are poorly located or if those doing the loading have insufficient space to load or to work, expect snags and delays in production and fulfillment. A place for the waste disposal and the garbage services must also be provided. Sometimes this is overlooked. Try to consider the impact on the workers of the noise that comes from the factory itself. Some factories are very noisy and the workers suffer. Make sure no harmful influences caused by external forces or exposed beams harm the workers. The choice of building materials and the placement of furnaces, chimneys, and kilns have to be functional but should be designed in such a way as to add aesthetic balance.

In a closed business, another consideration is the office of the management and the bookkeeper. These functions should be kept fairly close to each other and to the workers. Visibility of management tends to be a good influence on the work being done. When management is off in a high tower somewhere, there is a tendency to be "out of touch" with what is going on, and conflicts may develop between workers and management.

In conclusion, a closed business does not worry about attracting customers or protecting the money made from the business because seldom is any cash on the premises. Security of the factory or plant tends to be more concerned with others stealing secrets than with stealing goods or cash. It is the workers who create the life of a factory, so treating them better than what is required by law can greatly improve your business. Remember, in this type of business, even if your name is on the building or product, it is the comfort, safety, and efficiency of the workers that are important.

OPEN/CLOSED-TYPE BUSINESSES

Banks and jewelry stores are good examples of an open/closed business. Here, the security of the money and valuable stock is of prime consideration. Vaults, safes, and strongboxes should be placed in the northeast, or where the security is best. The second priority is where the goods are paid for or where the transactions take place. In banks, even these places have additional security devices. Jewelry stores have an interesting open/closed situation. Product visibility is a must, but product accessibility is not a good idea. Security is primary, and these types of stores invest many thousands of dollars to ensure the goods are protected. In both banks and jewelry stores, consider the security first, the entrances and exits last.

Other businesses that qualify as open/closed types are offices without product but with a constant stream of visitors, for example, hotels, real estate offices, medical offices. In these types of businesses, the cash is seldom seen by the customer. In a doctor's office, the prime considerations are the comfort and security of the client, who has usually made an appointment and is expected. The entrance, waiting room, or lobby should be spacious, the chairs comfortable, the lighting adequate, and reading material somewhat current. If the magazines in waiting room are five years old, question the quality of service you are about to get. When the magazines aren't current, neither is the practioner. If the waiting room is unpleasant, small, dark, cramped, or dirty, it might affect your well-being in many different ways. A chiropractor has an aquarium in the waiting room and somehow the wait is not as tedious when you can be entertained by beautiful fish. A dentist's office has a waterfall. Sometimes his patients go to his office just to relax—they aren't masochists, they just love his office.

Next consider the examination and treatment rooms, which should be large enough for comfort and, of course, private. The south or southwest are beneficial directions for examination rooms. The reception area should be large enough to contain all the office records, plus various machines, computers, telephones, and so on. The cash point is usually out of sight, near the reception area. The counselor's office, if different from the treatment room, should be well arranged for a good flow of energy, neat, and without clutter. I remember visiting a doctor's office. The waiting room was quite nice, as was the reception space. Walking down a corridor, we passed several satisfactory treatment rooms. As we continued down a long, narrow hall, more objects appeared in the path: a wooden Indian, a cow's skull, stacks of books. We kept going, and the hall kept getting more and more bizarre until we came to the end—the doctor's office. Every available space was filled with the oddest assortment of medical, anthropological, American Indian, Tibetan Buddhist, and plastic carnival artifacts. My head was swimming. The doctor, fortunately, was about to retire.

A hotel is an open/closed type business. The prime consideration is the registration desk and not the cash point (usually the office that holds the management and administration of the business). In this type of office, a northwest or southeast entry is preferred. People plan to go to a hotel. They seldom drop in just to browse. The entrance and lobby define the character of the hotel. A well-lit, spacious lobby speaks of quality and good service. There should be no staircases, sharp corners, or free-standing columns that interfere with the entrance.

The position of the registration desk is critically important. The desk should be immediately visible on entering the lobby, and it should be clearly marked.

THE FENG SHUI OF AN OFFICE'S OR A STORE'S EXTERIOR
Match the Building to the Occupation
In seeking the ideal workplace, choose a building that is best suited for the kinds of activities that are going to take place there. A carpenter would probably be happiest in a Wood-type building because he or she works in wood. Financial matters succeed in an Earth structure because they are reminiscent of vaults and other safe boxes. A jeweler would be happy in a modern steel-and-glass structure, steel being consistent with Metal (gold and silver), while glass represents the Water element, child of Metal. A company involved in communications (publishing, advertising, cable, for example) would be most prosperous in a glass building, because Water is the element of communication. Consult Chapter 1 on the five elements to determine what type of structure best suits your business.

The Address of the Building or Office
Does the building itself make a statement about what it is? Is the name or address of the building prominent and visible? Is there a building logo or identifying mark? All of these qualities affect the businesses housed within. Some office buildings hold just one company, while others may house hundreds of different kinds of businesses and offices. Each is influenced by the fortune of the owner of the building. Stores situated in malls are influenced greatly by their neighbors.

The address of the building or the number of the office can affect its destiny. Even though we've already talked about the importance of numbers in a home's address, let's take a minute and review it.

Many Chinese words, when spoken, sound alike, and Chinese numerology is based on homophonic principles. The way the numbers sound when spoken is an indication of their fortunate or unfortunate nature. Numbers can be either yin or yang. Yin numbers are even; odd numbers are yang. Zero represents nothing, but also perfection, completion, and harmony. As in other areas, consider the proportions of yin and yang. For example, an address with the numbers 44 or 111 or 2222 is not balanced, containing either all yin or all yang numbers. A better address is 123 or 651. Four is generally regarded as a bad number, but when it's combined with other numbers it is less dangerous. Review the section on numbers (pages 70–72).

Placement Within a Multibuilding Complex

If you are choosing a space within a multibuilding complex, consider that the most important buildings are located in prominent positions, in the center, or on elevated ground, or distinguished in some way to take advantage of a healthy flow of *chi*. The presence of plazas as well as landscaped, open, and semiopen courtyards gives spatial relief to a complex. Such elements act as focal points and provide yin to balance the yang of the built-up area.

There should be sufficient parking facilities and easy access to public transportation so that customers and workers can get to you.

In choosing a shop within a mall or complex of buildings, look for unifying architectural features. All windows on the same floor should be the same size, and the color should be coordinated. If one shop door is bright red and all the others are bright green, then the red door stands out, and this is not good. Uniformity creates harmony. Businesses placed within a row of buildings with completely unrelated heights, shapes, forms, and sizes do not usually succeed. It is more desirable if several blocks of commercial buildings have common heights, signs, colonnades, and roofs. For example, if one building is painted blue, all the neighboring buildings should somehow incorporate blue into their color scheme. Lincoln Center in New York and Music Center in Los Angeles are good examples of several different buildings working together in a harmonious architectural symphony.

Placement Within a Multiunit Building or Within a Mall

If your business is located in a shopping center or mall, it should be "in the flow" and close to another very popular magnet store. Usually, malls include a large department store at either end or at a different level of the mall so that customers are forced to go upstairs or from one end of the mall to the other. This stimulates the circulation. Shops in corners either are terrifically successful or they go bust. A shop in a dead corner seldom attracts walk-by customers. Look for buildings that include curves or other interesting features, avoiding buildings with sharp angles. Stay away from buildings or offices situated so that the front entry faces the intersection of a T-junction formed by two streets or two corridors. A space placed at the intersection of a T-junction may be penetrated by extreme vibrations of *chi*, causing confusing or undesirable influences. If a T-junction is present at the entry, choose another entry, keep the entry door covered, use a circular design on a picture hung on the door facing the T-junction, or hang wind chimes in the doorway, high enough not to interfere with the flow of traffic but so they move with the breeze. These antidotes can disperse the overly strong energy of a T-junction.

Avoid offices or shops at the end of a straight corridor because they can become the recipient of negative *chi*. If you are in such a space, use bright lights, colors, and tall signs to attract attention to yourself. Spaces that are close to major exits either succeed spectacularly or go in and out of business. If possible, create a barrier between your shop and the exit. Keep windows covered, use plants or fabric hangings—do what you can to keep your customers from leaving the store too quickly because they suddenly see the exit. Surround your space with plants if you can. Usually, the store or office that is closest to the front and is the most visible gets the majority of traffic.

The Ideal Building

Once you have determined the element type most suitable for your business, you are ready to examine the building itself. In an ideal situation, the most important buildings are located in prominent positions to take advantage of a flow of *chi*. In commercial centers, open and semiopen courtyards provide a contrast of yin and yang. Amenities such as covered walkways, linked passages, and overhead passages indicate that the management considers the health and well-being of the workers. In building office blocks, consider the entrance, access, circulation, and parking. In blocks of offices the floor space should be subdivided to allow for easy circulation. There should be efficient electrical and mechanical services, flexible partitioning, easy access to fire escapes and amenities areas, staff kitchens, dining and refreshment areas, bathrooms and washing facilities.

Water near a site is always good. Water that flows alongside the property or building is not as favorable as water that flows gently across the front of the building, as occurs with the Imperial Palace in Beijing. Slow, gently curving waterways are fortunate, while fast rivers rushing by take all the money and resources with them. If there are no natural waterways, try to incorporate water into the interior or exterior design scheme by installing fountains, ponds, and aquariums. Century City in Los Angeles is a good example of a successful commercial area enhanced by water fountains in the center of Avenue of the Stars, the main thoroughfare in Century City.

The Shape of the Site/Building

Buildings and sites come in all shapes and sizes. When choosing an office, note that certain shapes are considered to be luckier or more auspicious than others. The most auspicious shapes are the regular ones, either square/yin or rectangular/yin-yang shape. The rectangle is especially good when the north and south sides are longer than the east and west sides. Triangular-shaped lots and buildings can be problematic because of the lack of net usable space. Ovals, which are neither yin nor yang, are good for religious buildings. Geodesic domes tend to have missing or dangling parts. Lots, buildings, or rooms that are T-shaped, L-shaped, cross-shaped, or irregular are unfavorable. If the lot is odd-shaped, the amount of usable space is reduced and design plans are compromised. If the office is odd-shaped, it is difficult to arrange furniture comfortably. In the Appendix you will find a section on the *ba gua,* the eight-sided Chinese compass. Each of the eight sides is associated with a specific quality or area of life. We use the *ba gua* to help us arrange rooms on lots and to arrange furniture within rooms. You can skip forward and look at it now or just keep reading and think about it later. The most important thing to know is that regular, ordinary shapes are able to contain all eight sides of the *ba gua,* which ensures that all areas of life are active and vital. In an irregular shape, there are dangling or missing sections of the *ba gua.* Since each area of the *ba gua* represents a necessary part of life, if the section is missing, so is that part of life's experience.

In most cases, it is preferable for the building to be in the center of the lot. If the lot is narrow, a tall building in the center will succeed. If the lot is narrow at the front and wider at the back, good luck accumulates. An odd-shaped lot may create odd problems. People who live or work there might have odd lives or might be odd people, which is fine if you are in the circus or sideshow business (most buildings are good for something).

The visibility of the site is important because you'll do no business if people can't see you. A hotel built on a commanding point elevated above the town will enjoy prestige and admiration because the entire town is directed toward its grandeur. Further, affection is assured because the hotel provides a view for the town below, contributing to what is called "borrowed landscape." Of course, it depends on what you're trying to achieve. If your office is tucked in a tiny dark corner, no one will see you and you'll do no business.

Having an attractive sign is another way of drawing attention to your business. Signs should be pleasant, easy to see and read, and balanced in proportion to the

Sometimes you just have to call attention to yourself! That's what this car dealer is attempting to do with the gorilla.

size of the building. They should not block a window or opening. Good shapes for signs include squares, circles, and rectangles; triangular-shaped signs tend not to be as favorable. Do not make the sign out of soft wood, and make sure the sign is securely attached to the building. Signs should be painted with either three or five colors and the colors should be appropriate to the direction the sign faces. Below are listed the eight possible directions that the sign may face, along with recommendations for the height and color of the sign.

EAST: *A sign facing in this direction must be high, because the east denotes the rising sun. Best colors:* black/green/red, green/red/white.

SOUTHEAST: *A sign facing in this direction should be placed at roughly eye level. If it is too high, the flow of* chi *will be blocked. Best colors:* white/red/green *or* white/red/purple.

SOUTH: *A sign facing south should be moderately high but not higher than the building, or it will be too yang and will cause an imbalance. Best colors:* white/green/yellow, white/red/purple, red/yellow/purple, yellow/white/red, *or* white/green/red.

SOUTHWEST: *A sign facing southwest should be placed not too high—eighteen to twenty feet above ground level. Best colors:* white/red/yellow, white/green/red.

WEST: *A sign facing west should be at moderate height but not too low, or there will be friction among workers and family. Best colors:* white/black/yellow *or* yellow/white/red.

NORTHWEST: *A sign facing northwest should be fairly high but not so high that it looks out of proportion to the building. Best colors:* red/yellow/purple *or* yellow/white/red.

NORTH: *A sign facing north should be high enough to catch some sunlight during the day and to ensure harmony. Use* yellow/white/red *or* white/red/green.

NORTHEAST: *A sign facing northeast must be low to prevent disharmony. Use* yellow/white/red, red/yellow/purple, *or* white/green/red.

Entrance to the Office

To enter a public facility such as a mall or an office building, you have to find an entrance. If the parking is too distant, or the entry is confused, you may never accomplish what you set out to do. Some buildings have underground parking. In this case, the elevators or escalators should be prominently placed and visible so the path to the entrance is clear.

As you enter a building, the lobby will transmit the first impression of what will occur there. The lobby has a presence that is determined by the color, smell, temperature, lighting, and the location of the furniture. A spacious, well-lit, well-appointed lobby is the sign of a successful building. A shabby, dark, and musty lobby is reminiscent of shady businesses or has-been entrepreneurs and is depressing. The most important openings of a building are the entry and exit. Make sure the main entry door of the office/shop is not directly in line with the back door, or *chi* will come in one way and go out the exit without nurturing the space.

Examine the entrance for possible secret arrows. Check to see if there are angles from adjoining rooflines or walls or shadows from trees aimed at the main entrance. If there are, block them with drapes, plants, or other feng shui antidotes. Notice the view from the windows in the lobby. The Hyatt Hotel in Monterey, California, is situated on a golf course. One can't help wondering how many people each year are injured by golf balls flying in through the lobby windows. The Hyatt says this seldom happens, but seldom is too much for safety. Of course, someone who loves golf might have a different feeling. If there are poles, trees, or unpleasant sights outside the front entrance, use plants or a screen to block the unpleasant view upon exiting. If a tree or pole blocks the entrance, place on it a mirror at eye level, with the reflective side toward the entry.

If the entrance faces a wall or an undesirable feature such as a column, staircase, bathroom, or exit, use mirrors to draw the *chi* into the space and away from the entrance. If you can easily enter a place of business, so can the *chi.* As mentioned in the section on the home, doors ideally should open inward to allow the *chi* to enter. Fire doors should open out to let the *chi* out. If the building is in a closed space, a theater, or a club, then the entrance doors must also open outward.

The pathway from the main entrance to the elevator or stairs is the main conduit of *chi* to the upper floors. The staircases should not be placed opposite the entry because this allows *chi* to roll right out the door. Consider the flow of *chi*. If this pathway is blocked, nothing goes upstairs. If it is clear, the *chi* will flow smoothly, and businesses located on the upper floors will have a better chance for success. Make sure the entrance is accessible and that the doors open wide and completely.

Some malls do not succeed because they have too many entrances and exits. One of each is sufficient. *Decide* which doors will serve as the primary entrance and exit. Keep the other exterior doors closed, locked, and covered with a poster or picture. When there are too many interior doors, there is too much coming and going. Keep all closet doors closed, and if you can keep some of the extra interior doors closed, do so. A bookstore had five entry doors, eight interior doors, and four exits. The daily thefts almost bankrupted them. When they blocked a few doors to channel the flow of energy, and rearranged the stock to make it difficult to steal small items, the thievery stopped.

The office of an event planner was located at the top of the stairs leading up from the parking structure. The reception area contained a square conference table that took up most of the space. Further, the space itself was dark and crowded with boxes filled with personal items like skis boots, gym equipment, and sweaters. One of the problems the company was having was a lack of cash flow. Why? *Chi* entered the office and was blocked from circulating through the rest of the space by the profusion of furniture and other objects. Once they cleared this area, the energy could flow more smoothly, and cash flow increased. However, there was nothing they could do about the entrance itself. Located so close to the stairs, resources were constantly lost through mismanagement, personal luxury expenditures, and a general "party" atmosphere. The stairs reminded all the employees that it was easy to "sneak" away. All you had to do was run down the back stairs. When they moved to a much smaller space, they were able to consolidate their resources and save their business.

Another consideration involves the comparison of directions. First, compare the direction of the entrance of the building to the direction of the entrance to your office suite. Second, compare the direction of the office suite with the direction of the individual office or desk. If all three directions—the building, the suite, and the desk—are harmonious, then the building, the office, and your desk will prosper. If the directions conflict, then the building might prosper at the expense of the office, the office might prosper even though the building does not, or you might fail simply because your desk was in the wrong direction. For example: The office building faces east. The entry to your office suite faces east. The inner entry to your office and your desk itself face west. Everyone who works in the office suite gets along with the building superintendent (east/east) except you (east/west). You and he often argue. Why? East and west fight, just as Wood and Metal fight. How can you make your own office more compatible with the building and the office suite? Remember that directions can be regarded as the same as elements. Add Fire (south) to your office to reduce the influence of the Metal (west). Then add Wood/east or Water/north objects or colors to your office to emphasize their compatibility with the east directions of the other two entries.

Here's another example: A mini-mall sits with its face toward the south. The neighborhood is a Water landscape. The building faces south/Fire. To accentuate Fire, there is a large triangular-shaped sign in front of the mall. The sign is painted green (Wood), which supports Fire. However, the Water landscape puts out all the Fire. The neighborhood does not support the mall. All the shops on the ground floor face south/Fire and there is a rapid turnover in businesses. Most fail. Upstairs, there is a restaurant called Killer Shrimp, which has been phenomenally successful. The entrance to the restaurant faces east/Wood. Water supports Wood, and the neighborhood lines up nightly to eat the awful food and suffer the terrible service. No one cares. The restaurant is a success.

All these directions may seem confusing. Just remember that if there is a conflict between your office door and the entry of the building, you can add an appropriate element, color, object, or material to your front door to make it more compatable with the building. It's really pretty simple, especially if you remember that a healthful environment has all five elements. If you make sure there is one of each, and include the directions, you can't go wrong.

THE FENG SHUI OF AN OFFICE'S OR A STORE'S INTERIOR

As you analyze the interior of an office or workspace, observe the interior and exterior textures, colors, temperature, and available light. Is the room hot, stuffy, bright, dark, cold, or damp? Feel the currents and energy flow of the natural and artificial ventilation systems, the heating and cooling systems. Check the *shui*— the water lines and the way the water moves through the building, especially in the kitchen and bathrooms. Drink a glass of water from the water cooler, run the water in the kitchen sink, flush the toilets in the bathrooms. Look for leaks, wet spots, or moldy areas. Inspect the electrical connections and note from which direction they are connected. If possible, take electromagnetic readings on the power connections at the street, from the nearest power source, or from the main generators. Consider the dimensions of the interior furniture. There are other details to consider, but these are the most important because they determine which way the energy flows through the property and the building.

The Ideal Placement and Assignment of Offices

The *ba gua* can help determine the most favorable areas for each function within your office. Consult the Appendix (page 179) for the table telling you where to put each function. However, there are some generic rules regarding the placement of offices. In an office building, the offices farthest from the main entrance and major street usually have the most powerful position. However, in some buildings the office farthest from the entry is relegated to a person having little influence. It could also be the office of an employee who has been exiled. If you work in a basement office, however, don't panic. A young man who worked at a car rental company was dismayed when he was transferred to the car-parking facilities of a hotel. His new office was in the basement, removed from all the other employees. He was afraid he would become lost in the company, so he began taking his coffee and lunch breaks in the hotel. He got to know some of the hotel employees and basically made himself more visible. Now he's very happy with his job and his life. A stockbroker wanted to distinguish himself in a sea of desks and other brokers. He raised the seat on his chair, making him a head taller than all others around him. This gave him the boost he needed, and now he feels content with his job. If your office is not an ideal location, do something to attract attention to yourself and your office. Extra lights, a bigger sign, a higher chair, almost anything short of roller-skating in the main lobby can work.

The individual who regularly deals with the public or with other office workers should have a central position, easy to see and get to. If workers have to waste time looking for this person, efficiency is lost. Sometimes there are many inner doors within one office space. This can cause all kinds of problems and usually results in the employees being scattered or lacking in focus. Paint all the door jambs the same color, then emphasize each door with a colored band at the top. If the doors bang into each other, paint a red dot in the center of each door so the doors can "see" each other.

If your office has only one entrance and no windows or exits, hang pictures of pretty scenery with vistas of distance to give you the feeling of looking outside.

You can also use a mirror fashioned like a window, or any mirror for that matter, to enliven a closed-in space. Fans and other electrical appliances can activate and move energy around when there are no windows or exit doors. The addition of plants and flowers, real or artificial, does much to enliven any space.

It is important in offices to make sure there is no glare. Glaring light in the eyes of a customer or workers is irritating and makes it difficult to see computer screens and other electronic visuals. A writer complained he hadn't sold an article for over a year. While sitting at his desk, sunlight coming in through a skylight almost burned a hole in the back of his neck. When asked if the heat and light bothered him he said, "No, because I never sit there." If you can't sit at your desk, how can you ever get any work done?

If your office has a west-facing window, be sure to keep it covered during the glare time. Sitting in front of a window so that clients or other office workers have the sun in their eyes does give you the edge. This was a trick Abraham Lincoln employed when he wanted his cabinet to make up their minds quickly. You can bet they came to a decision quickly so they could leave the room! What's the solution to glaring light? Keep the window covered during the glare time or hang a crystal in it to break the light into a colored spectrum. Be careful—the glare plus glass or crystal can start a fire.

In any business, the first feng shui consideration is the office of the boss because the entire fortune of the company rests on him or her. If the boss's feng shui is bad, your job will also be bad. The boss should sit in the most commanding position to assert authority over the employees. Authority generally emanates from the corner office farthest from the entrance. The boss should have the room farthest from the entry and farthest from the main street. If the boss's office is close to the front door, there will be much coming and going and very little peace in the office. If it is too close to the street or entry, hang mirrors to draw energy into the office and away from the street or entry.

In summary, remember that the office of the person in charge determines the success or failure of the business. Who gets the best office? The boss, of course!

The Feng Shui of Your Desk

Whether you work in a typing pool surrounded by hundreds of coworkers, are the CEO with an impressive corner office, or run a successful business from your bedroom, your desk is the seat of power. Here you should have maximum control, concentration, efficiency, and authority. Its size, shape, and construction determine much about your position at work as well as in the world. Its placement determines whether you succeed or fail, rise to the pinnacle of your profession or sink miserably into obscurity.

Your desk may have a history that could influence your ability to succeed. Who owned the desk before you? Did she flourish or fail? Who sat at the desk before you occupied it? Was he promoted or fired? In what condition is the desk? Maybe it was your father's desk and just sitting at it gives you a feeling of support. Or

Are you ambiguous, bewildered, confused, doubtful, embattled, flustered, going nowhere, hating your job, irritated, or jumpy? Is your desk a mess?

maybe you're afraid you'll never succeed because your father always thought you'd grow up to be a failure.

Fancy or plain, new or used, sleek and pristine or scarred with the memories of a thousand other workers—no matter what kind of desk you have, it must be kept neat and clean. Disorganized desks mean disorganized life. Cluttered spaces can be an indication of confused or nonspecific goals, inefficient methods, or inability to complete projects.

A chiropractor's office was a mess, cluttered with all sorts of boxes and personal belongings. His desk was in a dark corner next to a floor-to-ceiling bookcase. Both desk and bookcase were overflowing with paper, files, books, magazines, children's drawings, lunch bags, and other assorted stuff. He had tried to generate new business, but nothing seemed to work. He blamed it on the recession; what could he do? New beginnings must have room to grow, so if your desk is overflowing with unfinished projects, it is difficult to begin anything new. If you and your desk are holding onto a mass of old papers and past projects, how can you "move with the times"?

The Wood Desk

A desk made of wood is a Wood-type desk. The work done there tends to be creative and artistic. A wooden desk is a gentle desk, good for those in the healing/helping professions or for those who want to be more compassionate and sympathetic in their work. When a caterer changed her metal desk for a wooden butcher-block table, she improved her business by fifty percent. Wood is symbolic of nurturing, so professionals who work with food, such as caterers or restaurateurs, do well on wooden surfaces. Carpenters, manufacturers of wooden goods, or anyone involved with plant life such as botanists and florists are also happy working on a wooden surface. Whatever the occupation, the person who sits at a wooden desk has the potential to grow tall and strong, to bend with the changing winds of the marketplace, or, less desirably, to become as rigid as a stick. At the very best, if your desk is made of wood, you'll attain the majesty of the giant sequoias, with deep roots in the business community.

To help the creative juices flow, add wood to your desk: flowers in a vase or plants; objects made of wood, such as pencils and rulers and even a toothpick, will work if you designate them as your "special" wood items. Anything with a rectangular shape or green in color can also be used to represent Wood. Since all reality begins in the mind, the force and focus of your intention are paramount. If you use something to represent an element, then in your mind be sure to designate it as such.

The Fire Desk

If your desk is triangular in shape, or is red, or is made of or covered by animal products such as leather, wool, or bones, you are sitting at a Fire-type desk (some desks are virtually covered by a leather blotter with a cotton/felt pad). It is possible that you are a teacher or librarian, or are involved in other academic occupations where intellectual excellence is the priority. In business, a Fire-type desk is ideal for high fashion, graphic design, architecture, or businesses that involve Fire or Fire products.

A Fire desk inspires intelligence and progress, but also a tendency toward flash and sparkle with no substance. You could easily burn out or dry up at such a desk, and new ideas, initially met with enthusiasm, might wither on the vine. This type of desk is best for event planning, public relations, or political affairs, such as campaigns, which require quick and timely action but then disappear when the event is over. Reason, understanding, courtesy, and ceremony are important at a Fire-type desk, and if you are dealing with someone who sits at a Fire-type desk, watch out. This diplomatic and charming person could change suddenly, becoming volatile, critical, loud, and argumentative.

When you need all your wits about you or want to be more charming at work, add Fire to your desk by draping a piece of cloth, such as a wool, silk, or cotton scarf, across the corner of your desk. If this isn't appropriate, you can use something sharp, such as a letter opener or pair of scissors, designating it as your special Fire element. Adding any item that is red or triangular also adds Fire. If it's not possible to place anything on your desk, place the representative item in the front center drawer of the desk. You can also use any animal product you choose, even (most desperate-case scenario) a chicken bone from your lunch (wash it first). Anything red, rose, or bright pink in color is also considered Fire, as are triangular shapes, such as a pyramid paperweight. If it is allowed, you could also use candlesticks with candles or burning incense.

The Earth Desk

Your desk is Earth-type if it is made of marble, concrete, bricks, stones, or other earthy material. This type of desk is excellent for banks, hospitals, financial institutions, or businesses that need to be regarded as serious and stable. If you sit at such a desk, you probably think a great deal about money or material resources. Other occupations that do well at an Earth desk are those involved in the sale or manufacture of ceramics or earth products, agriculture and farming, civil engineering, tunneling and mining, environmental agencies, and generally any business involved with earth or earthen products. An artistic person might feel blocked at such a desk, and communication businesses might have difficulties because transmissions and communications would tend to be on hold. At an Earth desk you could either be the Rock of Gibraltar or carry the weight of the world on your shoulders.

If you're having trouble settling down and getting to work, or if you just want to center your energy, add Earth to your desk by using a ceramic dish, a marble or stone pen holder, even a small pebble or rock from the external landscape. Earth tones such as yellow, tan, brown, and rust add Earth, as do square, boxy shapes.

The Metal Desk

A Metal-type desk, in feng shui terms, is made of metal. The work there tends to be precise and specific. This is not a desk where imagination is given free rein but rather a desk of disciplined, organized, and scientific work. Metal is reminiscent of coinage, so Metal desks, like Earth desks, are concerned with money matters and are suitable for banks or lending institutions. Businesses with religious or civic involvement seem to prosper with Metal, as do all occupations dealing with precious and nonprecious metals, such as jewelers or dealers of hardware, knives, swords, and other metal instruments. If you work at a metal desk, you might be worth your weight in gold or a little brassy, have a will of steel or, less desirably, come across as inflexible and stiff as an iron rod. When you pay your bills or need to be accurate and fastidious about detail, add Metal to your desk by designating a metal pen holder or other metal object as your special item. You could also use a piece of jewelry or even a chain of paper clips. Metal is associated with the colors white and silver, which can easily be found in any office. Round is the shape associated with Metal, so any coins or round, oval, or crescent paperweights add Metal to the desk.

The Water Desk

A glass-top desk is a Water desk and usually becomes the hub of communications for the office. Glass is good for all matters concerned with the transmission of ideas, such as literature, the arts, music, communications, media, advertising, word processing, computers, electrical engineering, plus all enterprises involving liquids and fluids such as oil refineries and distributors, brewing and distilling, or the manufacture of liquids. Businesses involved with the sea or with affairs that take place on the water do well at a glass desk. It is preferable to support a glass top with a Wood or Metal base rather than with a marble or concrete (Earth) base. A glass desk allows you to go with the flow, or to become as stale as a stagnant pond.

If you're having trouble making changes and want to be more flexible and adaptable, use Water in any form—a glass or cup of water, flowers in a bowl of water, or objects made of glass. Even ice cubes can be used. Anything black or with an odd, irregular shape can be used to add the Water element to a desk.

To support your efforts, your desk should be spacious, allowing room for the expansion of your ideas. If you have no room to work, you won't accomplish much. The desk is the seat of your business. How is the seat anyway? A broken desk chair gives you and your work an unstable foundation. Are you comfortable where you are sitting now? If not, don't panic and rush out to buy a new desk. Just look around and be resourceful. Right around you are probably many items that you can use to bring any element to your desk. A small object works as well as a large one; remember that your intention is as important as your action.

Placement of the Desk

Correct desk placement is an important factor in determining whether you succeed or fail at your job. The ideal placement locates the desk at an angle farthest from the entrance. This affords the maximum view of the entrance as well as the interior space and puts you in the power spot. Here it is impossible for anyone to "sneak up on you" and nothing can get past your eagle-eye perspective. If you can't see the entrance you may be surprised by anyone coming into the room and, in the same way, be unprepared for the surprises life continually offers. Never knowing what's coming tends to make an individual nervous and jumpy and affects one's potential for success. Furthermore, you'll never know what really goes on in the business, will not be privy to inside talk, and might even suffer the barbs and arrows of office gossip as coworkers whisper secrets behind your back.

A client was consistently overlooked for promotion. Her desk was placed so that she could not see the door and where others could not see her. If you can't see the entrance, others can't see you either and, as a result, you may be overlooked for advancement. Coworkers may not notice you, and you'll have little influence at work or in the world. Make sure, wherever you work, that you can see what's going on and that others can see you, too! When the client moved the desk to have a clear vision of the entrance, she could see the activity of others walking by, and, more important, others could see her. She was promoted almost immediately. If you can't see the entrance, place a mirror, or any reflective surface, so that it allows you to see the activities of the entrance. If others can't see you, place a big, bright sign on your door and place a bright lamp or light near your desk to attract attention to yourself and "put you in the spotlight." Just remember: This position makes you quite visible, so you may need to work harder than you've been accustomed to working.

If possible, place your desk on a north/south or east/west axis. However, the desk should *never* be placed in an awkward position to accommodate a direction. If it cannot be placed exactly north/south or east/west, just get as close as you can to the north or east. A view of the entrance and a comfortable placement have priority over the direction.

To find the direction of your desk, sit in your regular position, looking forward. Whatever direction your nose faces is the direction of your desk. Each direction tends to produce a different feeling. When you sit facing north, you are all business. Facing south you tend to be more relaxed and sympathetic. Facing east is inspirational, and facing west is imaginative. If the desk is not positioned suitably, you can bring the direction to you by using an element color or object related to the direction. For example, no matter where your desk actually is, if you add black, glass, an irregular shape, or water, you have added or emphasized the north at the desk.

Don't place your desk directly opposite the entrance door. If the desk can't be placed so the entrance is visible, place a mirror or other reflective surface so that it allows you to see the activities of the entrance and anyone coming into the space. Mirrors can also be used to increase the area of small offices or to draw in money-endowing views of Water. Don't place a mirror directly opposite the entrance door, however, or the energy will enter and bounce right back out the door.

A client worked at home but hadn't had any contracts in the past few months, a time period that coincided with redecorating his office. He had positioned his file cabinets too close to the door. This prevented it from opening fully and others could not "get to him." When he moved the file cabinets away from the door, allowing for a more spacious entrance, the phone started ringing and within days he had a new contract. The desk and other furniture should be placed a sufficient distance from the entry to allow the door to open fully.

A minimalist approach to the design and placement of offices and furniture is the most successful one. Avoid overpowering furniture that takes up too much space. Place heavy furniture along the walls, using it to fill in empty corners, and make sure the path between your office door and the entrance and exits of the business as a whole are cleared of all objects.

In the Oval Office, the president's desk is too close to the back wall—and the president of the United States is often "backed against the wall" with little maneuvering room. Make sure there is enough room around the desk for *chi* to flow smoothly. If you work in a cramped space, your style will be cramped, you might have feelings of claustrophobia, and, physically, you just might have chronic stomach cramps.

The first desk seen is the one that controls the office as a whole, while the desk farthest from the entrance has the most power. The desk closest to the back door is likely to belong to a worker who either always has an excuse to leave work early or gets fired first. If *you* sit too close to the door, compensate so that you're not regarded as a subordinate or someone who's always anxious to leave. You can do this by hanging a mirror on the opposite wall to draw attention away from the door.

If you sit near the kitchen or if your home office is in the kitchen, you could spend more time eating than working, but this could have more to do with your tummy than the placement of your desk. If you sit opposite the door to the bathroom, keep the bathroom door closed and hang a picture on the door facing your desk. If your desk shares a common wall with the bathroom, specifically the toilet wall, your efforts may seem to go "down the toilet." Unless you're in the plumbing business, it's best to place a mirror on the office wall with the back of the mirror to the toilet plumbing. This will symbolically move you away from the offending wall. You can use a metal tray or anything with a reflective surface. Even a piece of tinfoil will work.

No prospects for the future? Life seems empty? Reached the end of the line? Then your desk probably faces a blank wall. This is the worst placement of all because you may feel as if things are going on behind your back. A blank wall contributes to feelings of depression, resistance to work, and all kinds of frustrations and blockages. If this is the case and it is impossible to turn your desk around, then hang a mirror so that you can see what goes on behind your back. If you can't hang a mirror on the wall, place a small mirror on the desk to reflect the view behind (a small silver frame could be used); if this is not allowed, place a small mirror inside a desk drawer in the desired direction. No one will see this mirror and only you will know it is there. Many computer workers face a blank wall so that the wires from the machines can be hidden. This can lead to diminished health and vitality. Even exposed wires are better than facing a blank wall. Turn the desk so that it faces out, place a mirror to reflect what goes on behind you, put a pretty picture on the blank wall—and give yourself a little joy and happiness when you work.

If you sit too close to a window, you might spend a lot of time dreaming about life outside the office. Don't place the desk against an interior glass wall, or with a glass wall against your back, because this is very unstable and affords little protection from those who would smack you in the face or stab you in the back. If you sit too close to a window, place a Wood barrier between you and the window to help you concentrate. If you sit next to an exit, you might be the first one out of the office (irresponsible, laid off, or fired). If you sit under a clock, you'll suffer from the pressure of deadlines or other time-related stress.

A client complained that she had no business for months. Her desk was totally covered with business machines and papers. She had no place to work, so it was no wonder she had no work. To support your work you must have elbowroom. Sit at a desk that is spacious, allowing space for the expansion of your ideas. She also complained that she hated her work because she just didn't feel it was right for her personality. Her chair was broken and she was sitting on a sharp metal coil. No wonder she was uncomfortable! Sit on a chair that is comfortable, of the correct height, and properly balanced. If you're tilted while seated at your desk, your work will have a cockeyed perspective. If you hate to sit at your desk, how can you ever hope to succeed? If you love being at your desk, the possibilities for growth and success are endless.

Some offices are set up classroom style with the boss facing the employees. If this is the case, place a plant by the door to draw the boss's attention away from the employees and toward anyone entering or exiting the room.

A doctor was losing control of his life. He shared his office with a subordinate worker and, over a period of time, the worker had taken the lion's share of the room, pushing the doctor farther and farther into a corner. When he moved the subordinate out of the office and took the space for himself, he was able to regain control of his life. If the room must hold two desks, place each at an angle to the door, using the desks to make part of a *ba gua*. Make sure each worker has his or her own designated space, even if the only available space is a tiny corner of the desk or a special part of a drawer. To help master resolutions and accomplish goals, hang a brass wind chime above your desk and ring it often and loudly.

ATTRACTING AND ACCEPTING HAPPINESS

You've now read this book from cover to cover, even consulting the Appendix for a bit more advanced material. You've moved your bed, bought some houseplants, and cleaned the stove. You feel somewhat okay, more money is coming in, your friends and family are supportive—and you're still not happy. This must mean that feng shui doesn't work. Well, it's true. There are times when feng shui doesn't work. Even if your home has perfect feng shui, you still may not win the lottery or marry Prince or Princess Charming. So what's the problem?

Feng shui teaches us that an awareness of space can greatly improve our circumstances. Maybe you're not yet on top of the world, but this awareness has most likely helped you move from an airless, gloomy basement apartment to a first-floor apartment filled with plants and colors. Feng shui has helped you improve, and your life is not over yet.

Feng shui cannot fix all the problems in your life. Once you have fixed your house or office, it is up to you to accept the goodness life is offering even if that goodness doesn't live up to your expectations. Accepting happiness comes after attracting happiness. The way you do this is to create harmony within yourself. But before we offer suggestions on how to create harmony within, let's look at some of the reasons feng shui may not work.

First, feng shui may not work because the greatest skill we have as human beings is our ability to adapt. This ability allows us to survive in the worst circumstances. Your plane crashes in the Andes, yet by nightfall you have made a protective nest of the broken pieces of the plane. Survivors of the concentration camps adapted to the pain, filth, and punishment. Like King Rat, in the novel of the same name by James Clavell, we not only survive but also enterprisingly move forward. This ability to adapt requires that we ignore certain things in the environment, and this inhibits our ability to create a balanced environment.

Second, there is a natural resistance to change. We like things to stay the way they are all the time, which is irrational because Earth, in its constant revolution around the sun, is in a continual state of change. Change is natural. Feng shui is rooted in nature and the inevitable changes of the seasons. Thus, it can help you be more in touch with nature and make it easier for you to accept the changes in your life as natural occurrences.

Third, we see only what we want to see. We have selective vision and ignore what is not pleasing to us. Physically we are capable of perceiving reality only along a narrow spectrum of light. Microscopes, telescopes, X rays, and other instruments measure the things human eyes can't see. We are limited because we are human. Some things we can't see. Other things we don't want to see.

Seeing clearly is a big problem. So much of what we see was imprinted the first time we saw it. Old friends say to each other, "You haven't changed a bit in thirty years." A mother calls her fifty-year-old son "Sonny" and reminds him to wear a sweater because it's cold outside. Our impression of individuals and objects is set the first time we see them. This is why it is so difficult for family and friends to accept the changes you have made in yourself.

Fourth, you can't force a rose to bloom. Things happen in their own time. Sometimes we want something but we are not sufficiently developed to accept it. You want to win the Nobel Prize? First finish high school. If something isn't happening the way you want it to, either you're not ready for it to happen (even though you think you are), or in the long run it would not be beneficial to you. It's for your protection. If you're supposed to do something, the universe will make the way clear. If you're not supposed to do something, the universe will throw obstacles in your path to encourage you to go another way. Remember, if you don't get your own way, it may be in your best interests. Develop patience.

The fifth reason feng shui may not work is that we have all been trained to value the mental and psychological processes of life as superior to the physical. Science has taught us that what goes on in the physical world can be overcome or controlled with proper clothing and artificial heat and light. We don't need nature and so we don't value nature. Even if you live in Antarctica, where it is commonly −30°F, you are expected to go on with life as if everything were normal. Instead of working in this type of weather, we should be hibernating but, no, we continue as if nature doesn't matter. It takes an extreme expression—an earthquake, tornado, or flood—to get us to pay attention to nature.

Another reason feng shui may not work is that our desires tend to blind us to what we already have. For example, even when business improves in a slow but steady way, we complain because feng shui hasn't provided us with a million dollars in profits. Desire occurs when we want something we don't have. If we could just release the desire for whatever it is that we think we want, we could avoid a lot of suffering.

Remember the story of the old man who caught a magical fish? The fish had the power to grant him any wish. His wife wanted a house. The fish gave them a house. Then she needed a palace. The fish built them a palace. Then she demanded the fish crown her empress of the world. The fish crowned her empress of the world. Then she insisted the fish make the sun go backward in the sky. The fish dove deep within the ocean, never to return. Our expectations blind us to the blessings we already have. Life is a gift. Count your blessings now.

To release a desire is to be free. When we focus on what we don't have, we miss the goodness in our lives. Just say to yourself, "I release the desire for———." Say it as many times as you have desires. Stop when you have run out of desire. Then take a deep breath. If you're still not happy, think about this: Happiness can exist only along with its polar opposite, unhappiness. This is the yin-yang of life. When you seek happiness, you automatically find unhappiness. So why desire something that can only bring you pain? Better to desire and seek your own true nature. Nature is essentially harmonious; you and nature are one: The moment that you accept yourself, you have a better chance to be in harmony with life.

How can we create internal harmony when the world and all its temptations and desires interfere? Aristotle knew the answer, calling it the Golden Mean, which is the result of the balance of body, mind, and spirit. When you strive for balance in your thoughts, words, and deeds, you reflect the perfection and essential harmony of the universe. Without this balance, life manifests the negative things of this world. Developing a balanced life doesn't come easily when all around is chaos and mixed messages. Here are a few thoughts to contemplate.

People have *chi,* too. Body movement, facial expression, posture, clearness of eyes and skin, and other physical clues indicate the amount and type of *chi* each person has. This individual *chi,* along with an individual's heritage, environment, horoscope, karma, and so on, determines the quality of a person's life.

When *chi* is strong and balanced, the individual is robust and lively and takes life's problems in stride. Too much *chi* is like a balloon ready to explode; too little *chi* makes a weak, unhealthy individual who has no strength to handle life's problems. Among the interactions of people, both good and bad *chi* can be expressed. Even when an individual is destined (for whatever reason) to have a troublesome life, he or she can improve the quality of life by cultivating subtle energy or *chi* in its yang/positive phase.

Chinese doctors believe that cultivating subtle *chi* prolongs and extends life. Lao-tzu, an ancient Chinese philosopher, supposedly lived to be 280 years old. Many practitioners of Chinese arts are in their eighties yet look about thirty-five. With smooth, unlined skin and bright, clear eyes, they float lightly above the ground, skipping and dancing through life. Taoists maintain the enthusiasm and joy of a child because they lead a balanced and healthy life. In this time, when youth is revered and plastic surgery readily available, other natural methods provide the same results.

There are several ways to cultivate subtle energy. The first is breathing—focused, conscious breathing. Since this is an automatic reflexive action in the body, we don't think much about it unless it goes haywire. Notice how a sleeping breath is smooth, regular, and deep. Notice how you are breathing now. If you're excited, angry, or too intense, your breathing will be shallow and irregular. During an emotional crisis, we tend to hold our breath, as if this would stop the flow of life. Deep, regular breathing puts you in touch with the natural yin-yang of breath, which connects to your integral self faster than anything else. You become one with the flow of nature and are immediately more centered. Yoga, tai chi chuan, and other popular disciplines or techniques offer directions and guidance for proper breathing.

The second way to cultivate subtle energy is through proper movement. Walking is good exercise, and you don't have to join a gym or buy another book to learn how to do it. Competitive games and some aerobic exercises can be detrimental to the health. Internal martial arts, such as tai chi and chi gong, afford the practitioner opportunity to learn another way of building health and strength without damaging the body.

Meditation is the third way to cultivate energy. Again, there are many systems that teach the individual how to do this. Unfortunately, many people mistakenly feel that meditation is the goal. It is not; it is simply a way to relax, calm down, and return to who you are. One of the best meditations is to focus on your breathing and then let go. When things get really bad, force yourself to have a good belly laugh, saying loudly, "Ha, ha, ha." Life will change momentarily. Count on it.

The fourth way of cultivating positive *chi* is diet. Since this book is not a book about nutrition, let's simply acknowledge the saying "You are (or you become) what you eat." There are as many theories on food and diet as there are stars in the sky. For those who are interested in the Eastern approach to eating and food, there are some simple guidelines to follow. Eat food that is as natural as you can get it. This means stay away from highly refined or processed food. Eat the freshest, least-altered products you can find. Try to eat only foods that are in season and, preferably, locally grown. Eat simply and try to eat only one or two things at a time. Stay away from combining foods. The typical American dinner of steak, potatoes, vegetables, salad, and dessert causes many problems in the digestive system. Eat steak, if you want, but by itself. Next meal, eat potatoes and vegetables. Next meal, eat a big salad. Eat dessert by itself. Eat earlier in the day rather than late at night.

The fifth method of cultivating *chi* is through acupuncture. Acupuncture is based on the idea that the entire body works as a whole system. Each part is regulated by one or more of the organs. Each organ is associated with one of the five elements. The goal in acupuncture, as in feng shui, is to activate, stimulate, harness, or channel the body *chi*. Unlike Western medicine, acupuncture is primarily preventative, not curative. You pay your acupuncturist to keep you healthy.

Remember, you have *chi,* too. When your *chi* is strong and balanced, you feel vibrant and healthy. Life's challenges can be met with a smile and laugh. When your *chi* is weak or out of balance, you'll cry when you break a nail. Healthy *chi* is available and accessible to you all the time. And you don't need a prescription to get it.

The presence of positive, abundant *chi* promotes a healthful environment and a harmonious and happy atmosphere, which contribute to success and long life. Abundant *chi* also brings prosperity and love. Who could ask for more?

IN A CRISIS? FENG SHUI CAN HELP YOU FEEL GOOD ABOUT LIFE

When you are spiritually challenged, in crisis, or just feeling bothered by the world, follow this plan, based on feng shui, guaranteed to make you feel better and designed to help you live in a gentle world.

1. **Relax.** Most problems stem from tension in the body, mind, or spirit. When you relax, tension goes away. Breathing in a slow and steady manner helps you relax. Now you are able to reach the center of your being where it is calm. Here is where the questions are answered and the problems solved. If you feel uptight, scared, nervous, anxious, or just out of sorts, give yourself permission to take a deep breath and relax.

2. **Don't do anything you don't want to do.** When you do things you don't want to do, you go against your true self, your basic nature. This is not an excuse for not going to work or school, or for not taking responsibility for your life. It's encouragement to listen to yourself. Your gut feeling and your instincts are always true for you. Do what you feel is right for you regardless of what others say or think. When you are true to yourself, you are never wrong.

3. **Live in current time.** The past is dead, the future is unborn. If you live in the past or future, you live nowhere. Life happens only in the present. Monitor your thoughts; when you start drifting into the past or future or when you are comparing, criticizing, and judging yourself and others, yell "Stop!" Then check the position of your feet. Where are you right now?

4. **Accept all life and experiences as equal. Hold no preference.** Imagine the transition from day to night. Dawn to sunset, the change in light is gradual and gentle, like the flow of a curve. Life imitates this curve. When you hold preferences and manifest extreme desire, you turn this gentle curve into a sharp angle. Now you're on a seesaw. Preferring one moment of reality to another is a waste of time, like trying to catch a bird. Nothing stays the same. If you prefer something other than this moment, wait. Everything changes sooner or later. Everything.

5. **Use nature as a model.** When you are in crisis or spiritually troubled, don't complain, because you can't change the world. The world is what

it is. Problems never cease. Don't expect them to. Instead, change yourself. Use nature for your teacher:

- *Wood*: Like a seed sprouting through the earth, make every moment a new one. Life is always beginning anew. Hug a tree for strength.
- *Fire*: You have a mind. Use it to control yourself so you can choose how you respond at any moment. Turn on the lights. Sit in the sun.
- *Earth*: In a crisis, slow down. Give yourself time to return to the center of your being where it is calm. Walk barefoot in the park. Keep a stone in your pocket and touch it often.
- *Metal*: Let go. Endings are as important as beginnings. When the time for change comes, the best thing to do is change. Wear your favorite jewelry.
- *Water*: Remain profound and quiet as the deep ocean; fit yourself into any circumstance. Assume any form required. Go swimming or take a bath.

Just as the goal in feng shui is to establish harmony through nature, the goal in life is to establish harmony through acknowledgment, acceptance, and appreciation of our true nature. Remember this: You are unique. What you do, how you live, and the choices you make will always be right for you as long as you listen to your inner self.

Let this idea give you confidence to invite feng shui into your space, knowing that Mother Nature's helper will bring you the gifts of long life, health, success, and peace of mind.

I hope this book has helped you see yourself and your space differently. It will never be able to substitute for a good and healthy attitude toward your own life or the benefit of seeking advice from a proper feng shui expert, but it will open the doors of perception to the relationship between yourself and your environment in a way you never dreamed possible.

No book could ever consider the infinite number of details that exist in a home or workplace. But that's the fun of this book. It will help you start seeing it all for yourself—the funny little correspondences that exist between, say, a leaking faucet and a high Visa bill. But that's just one. You'll find a million more on your own. And you'll slap your forehead, amazed, at the accuracy of it all. Enjoy.

THE *BA GUA*

To determine the influence of the directions, in feng shui we use the *ba gua*. It is an eight-sided figure, with each side symbolizing a direction and an area of life such as family, health, children, love, friendship, travel, business, and money.

Whether you are analyzing an entire shopping center, a lot with a building on it, or a single room in the building, just imagine there are eight different sections within each space, each with its own energy field. Each energy field represents a distinct and separate activity of life. The eight sections of the *ba gua* are:

East	Health	Wood
Southeast	Money	Wood
South	Fame	Fire
Southwest	Love	Earth
West	Family	Metal
Northwest	Travel	Metal
North	Business	Water
Northeast	Knowledge	Earth

The practice/philosophy of using the *ba gua* is based on the idea that when the space is a regular shape, the eight sides of the *ba gua* are easily contained within the space. The eight sides of the *ba gua* cannot all fit into an odd or irregular shape, like a triangle or an L-shape. If the space is not perfectly square or rectangular (and most places are not), there might be some parts of the *ba gua* that are missing entirely, while other parts of the building or room may dangle outside the *ba gua* shape. Since each area of the *ba gua* represents one of eight areas of life, the occupants living in such a space would be apt to live an unbalanced life. They might, for example, spend all their energy on business and have no family life, or spend so much time with family that health suffered.

To study a specific location using the *ba gua,* draw a plan of your house, room, or office. Superimpose the *ba gua* on the map, and turn the *ba gua* until it aligns with the wall holding the door of the house or room. For example, if the door faces east, arrange the *ba gua* so that its east side is parallel to the wall with the door. If the door faces north, arrange the *ba gua* so that its north side is parallel to the wall with the door.

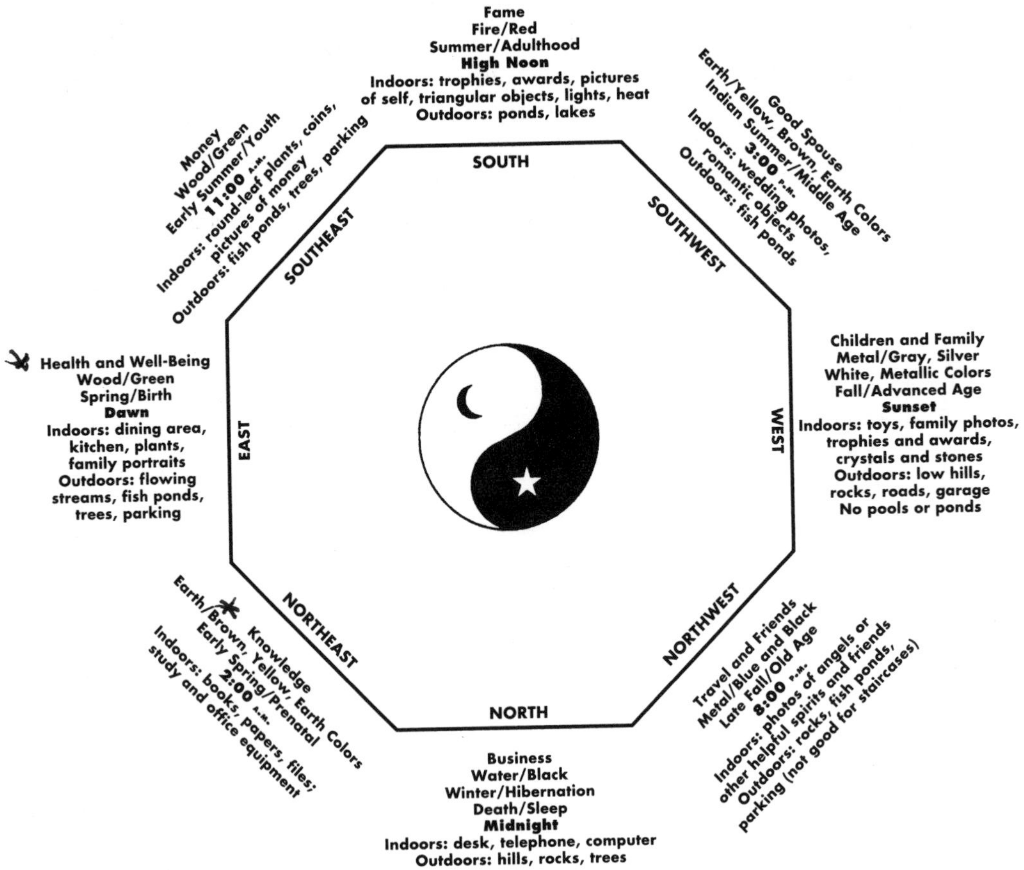
Fame
Fire/Red
Summer/Adulthood
High Noon
Indoors: trophies, awards, pictures of self, triangular objects, lights, heat
Outdoors: ponds, lakes
SOUTH
Good Spouse
Earth/Yellow, Brown, Earth Colors
Indian Summer/Middle Age
3:00 P.M.
Indoors: wedding photos, romantic objects
Outdoors: fish ponds
SOUTHWEST
Children and Family
Metal/Gray, Silver
White, Metallic Colors
Fall/Advanced Age
Sunset
Indoors: toys, family photos, trophies and awards, crystals and stones
Outdoors: low hills, rocks, roads, garage
No pools or ponds
WEST
Travel and Friends
Metal/Blue and Black
Late Fall/Old Age
8:00 P.M.
Indoors: photos of angels or other helpful spirits and friends
Outdoors: rocks, fish ponds, parking (not good for staircases)
NORTHWEST
Business
Water/Black
Winter/Hibernation
Death/Sleep
Midnight
Indoors: desk, telephone, computer
Outdoors: hills, rocks, trees
NORTH
Knowledge
Earth/Brown, Yellow, Earth Colors
Early Spring/Prenatal
2:00 A.M.
Indoors: books, papers, files; study and office equipment
NORTHEAST
Health and Well-Being
Wood/Green
Spring/Birth
Dawn
Indoors: dining area, kitchen, plants, family portraits
Outdoors: flowing streams, fish ponds, trees, parking
EAST
Money
Wood/Green
Early Summer/Youth
11:00 A.M.
Indoors: round-leaf plants, coins, pictures of money
Outdoors: fish ponds, trees, parking
SOUTHEAST

The *Ba Gua* and Its Correspondences

The ideal space is square or rectangular because it is able to include all eight sides of the *ba gua*. If the room is L-shaped, U-shaped, T-shaped, or odd shaped, some areas of the *ba gua* may not be able to fit in the space. Each side of the *ba gua* represents a particular part of life, and when areas of the *ba gua* extend beyond the space, or are missing from the space, it is an indication that the corresponding parts of life might also be dangling or missing. You will have to use mirrors or add elemental qualities to symbolically "bring into the *ba gua*" whatever is lacking.

Each direction corresponds with one of the five elements. To encourage activity in any area of life, determine the direction that suits your need and use accessories from the element that rules that direction. For example, if you want to achieve prominence, place Fire objects in your home or office, preferably in the south part of the space. You can also use objects similar to the quality you want to attract. In this case, a picture of yourself, diplomas, awards, or other trophies could enhance the fame sector.

Place furniture in the direction that best corresponds to the purpose of the space. For example, the west rules family. Place family mementos, family pictures, or other objects related to family in the west. If you need more cash, activate the southeast (the direction of wealth) by placing money objects, plants with coin-shaped leaves, red ribbons, or bubbling water in the southeast.

Have fun with this and see how creative you can be in placing your furniture, artwork, office equipment, and so on, using the five elements and the *ba gua*. Use your ingenuity. Don't run to the store. Use what you have to activate the directions that will help you get what you want.

Working with the *Ba Gua*

A magnetic compass has only one fixed direction, north, and for use must be turned so its arrow points north. From this set point all other directions are derived.

The *ba gua* is similar in that the directions on the *ba gua* are set, fixed, and cannot be altered. North is always north on the *ba gua*. However, the *ba gua* can be turned so that any direction aligns with the direction of the entry door.

The orientation of the *ba gua* depends on the location of the entry. The *ba gua* is placed within the house or room and turned so the direction of the *ba gua* is aligned to the direction of the entry door. This allows us to see which areas of the *ba gua* have been included in the space and which areas are missing or stretch beyond the *ba gua*'s eight sides.

Directions are relative to the location of the viewer. When determining the direction of any door, whether to the building, a room, or an exit, stand in the doorway and look forward. Always look forward and out of the room using your nose to point the way. Directions are never determined by looking into the space, only by looking out from the entry. The *ba gua* will be placed within the space being considered.

IF I STAND HERE, I LOOK TOWARD THE SOUTH

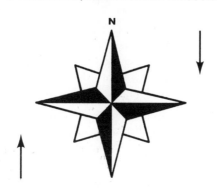

IF I STAND HERE, I LOOK TOWARD THE NORTH

When using the *ba gua* over the entire building, it is possible to see how each room within the building corresponds to a specific area of the *ba gua*. Some directions are favorable to specific functions. For example, west is associated with rest, relaxing, and children's fame. If the president of the company occupies an office located in the western part of the building, he or she will be thinking of rest and relaxation when at work and might take time off to play golf or go to the movies instead of working.

When the *ba gua* is placed over a single room, align the *ba gua* to the door to the room. Now it will be possible to see which areas are included, missing, or dangling from the room and which directions are emphasized by furniture or other items. For example, if the bed in the bedroom is placed in the north, a person lying in the bed will have thoughts of business and career rather than relaxation or sleep. If the desk in the office is placed in the southwest, the direction of love and marriage, the occupant of the desk may spend more time on office romance intrigues than on work.

For an irregularly shaped room, antidotes and illusions with mirrors can transform the irregular shape to one that includes all parts of the *ba gua*. When the entire structure is irregular, landscape or other constructed features like fences and light poles will have to be used to transform the irregular shape to a square or rectangle.

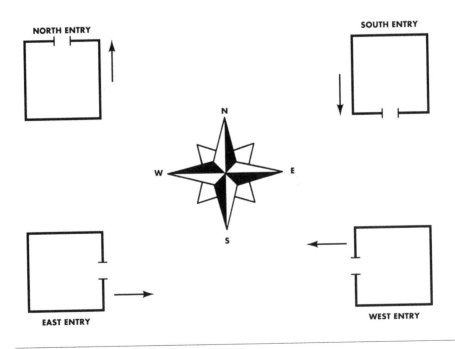

Any room or building can have any direction as its entry.

Steps in Using the *Ba Gua*

1. Draw a floor plan of the space you are analyzing.

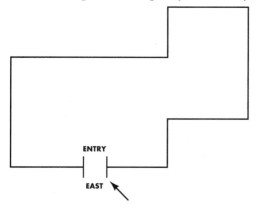

2. Use a standard compass to determine what direction you are facing when you look straight out the entry door, using your nose as the pointer.

3. Draw a *ba gua* using the same scale as your floor plan. The *ba gua* does not have to have all of its sides equal in length. Only parallel lines, such as east/west or north/south must be exactly the same length. The *ba gua* can be stretched or shrunk to almost any size.

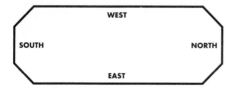

4. Place the *ba gua* on your plan so it fits as much as possible inside the room, with its direction matching the wall that holds the entry door. The *ba gua* must align with the entry door.

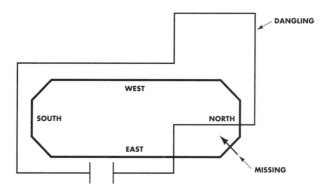

5. If the space is not exactly square or rectangular, some areas of the space and the *ba gua* will not overlap. These will need to be "pulled in" to the space with mirrors or by adding accessories from the direction/element that is dangling or missing. The *ba gua* easily fits within rooms or buildings that are square or rectangular. Odd shapes, L-shapes, U-shapes, T-shapes, or other variations cannot include all eight sides of the *ba gua* within the space.

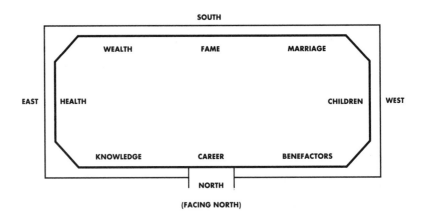

SOUTH

WEALTH   FAME   MARRIAGE

EAST   HEALTH   CHILDREN   WEST

KNOWLEDGE   CAREER   BENEFACTORS

NORTH

(FACING NORTH)

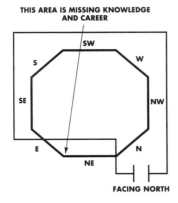

THIS AREA IS MISSING KNOWLEDGE AND CAREER

SW
S   W
SE   NW
E   N
NE

FACING NORTH

THIS AREA IS MISSING MARRIAGE

SE   S   SW
E   W
NE   N   NW

FACING NORTH

THIS AREA IS MISSING CAREER AND BENEFACTORS

6. Refer to the table on page 181 to determine which elements you can add to include all eight aspects of the *ba gua* in your room or home or office.

Organizing Interior Office Space Using the *Ba Gua*

Use the *ba gua* to determine where to place the furniture, office machines, cash register, the offices of management, the typing pool, the secretary, the employees' kitchen, the bathrooms, the storage, and all of the areas required for a particular building.

East: Suitable for depots; transport and distribution of goods; mail room; dining rooms; founder's office; company photographs, mementos, awards; the receptionist, greeter, or host/hostess.

Southeast: Suitable for routine work; assembly lines; typing pools; money box, cash register, and financial records or other items that require security.

South: Suitable for processes using heat, electrical engineering, computers or laboratories; counseling, personnel departments, training departments.

Southwest: Medical centers, rest and eating areas, dining rooms.

West: Recreation, rest, entertainment, children's areas, stages, kitchen and dining areas, parking.

Northwest: Suitable for management, sales, leasing, travel, convention planning, marketing, advertising, public relations departments.

North: Suitable for workshops, race tracks, mechanical communications, management offices, computers, faxes, telephones.

Northeast: Suitable for entrances, security systems, storage, warehousing, parking, archives, library, training centers, books, files, important papers. If a bathroom is in northeast, put mirrors on all four sides of the room.

THE THREE CYCLES OF THE ELEMENTS

Nature maintains balance through order and structure, combining the five elements in three predetermined sequences, designed to continue life and create new forms.

In the Cycle of Creation, elements give birth to each other in order, producing a growth-oriented, flowing relationship, like a mother to a child.

In the Cycle of Reduction, elements reduce the strength of each other in order, producing a slow but harmonious growth, like a child to its mother.

In the Cycle of Control, elements compete for power. When elements are combined in this sequence, the results are dynamic tension producing high energy, like a father and a child.

The three cycles work together as a system of checks and balances, keeping the environment ever balanced. Understanding the sequences of the three cycles is essential in determining which elements to add and which to subtract from any space.

Cycle of Creation: Cycle of the Mother

The Cycle of Creation is one of harmony. Elements give birth to, create, or generate the next element in a forward, clockwise motion, like a mother gives birth to a child. Mother's rules are soft, yielding, noncompetitive, encouraging, and loving. If the natural order is adhered to, the mother gives unconditionally to the child. If the mother gives too much, she smothers the child and depletes her essence; if she gives too little, she suffers from excess and the child fails to gain autonomy and independence.

In the Cycle of Creation, Wood is the mother of Fire. To make a fire requires fuel; to keep the body fires going requires food/wood. Fire is the mother of Earth. Nowhere is this more dramatically displayed than in a volcano. Volcanoes are nature's contractors, building sheer volume and mass of earth surface from their fiery interiors. As molten lava hits sea and land, it lays the foundation of continents and ocean basins just as it did four billion years ago when volcanic gases formed our planet's primitive atmosphere and seas.

Earth is mother to Metal. Earth particles, under extreme pressure, reduce single-atom minerals to precious metals (gold, silver, copper, tin), which are mined and made into coins and jewelry.

Metal is mother to Water, creating it out of thin air, attracting moisture through condensation, like dewdrops on a mirror. When metal is melted, it has the same properties of water and can be stretched, twisted, curved, straightened, and shaped into various forms.

Water is mother to Wood. Water flows, nurturing all life. If mother Water does not nurture the child Wood, the wood will not grow and will die.

Cycle of Reduction: Cycle of the Child

The Cycle of Reduction is the reverse of the Cycle of Creation. In a counterclockwise motion, the child takes from the mother, which reduces the mother's power but doesn't destroy it. The child obeys the mother by taking enough of her essence to nourish itself and counterbalance any excess that might remain from what was required to create the child.

Mother Wood is reduced by child Fire as in a fireplace or oven. Fire touches a lump of dough, transforming it into bread, food for life. Mother Fire is reduced by the addition of child Earth, which is why fireplaces and campfires are encircled with stone, tile, or other Earth materials, and why miners wear lights on their helmets to pierce the blackness of subterranean earth. Earth is reduced by pressure, which turns minerals into gold, silver, and precious diamonds. Child Earth can also be reduced once metal is extracted and shaped into a shovel or plow, reducing the earth to fertile fallows and rows. Child Metal takes from mother Water: Minerals dissolve in water and, when evaporated, turn into crystals. Metal, when added to water, reduces its level just as salt will aid in the evaporation of water. The child Wood takes from mother Water, as if it were sucking up sweet, warm milk.

ELEMENT	WOOD	FIRE	EARTH	METAL	WATER
Creates	Fire	Earth	Metal	Water	Wood
Controls	Earth	Metal	Water	Wood	Fire
Reduces	Water	Wood	Fire	Earth	Metal
Shape	Rectangle	Triangle	Square	Round	Wavy
Direction	East	South	Center	West	North
Season	Spring	Summer	Pause	Autumn	Winter
Color	Green	Red	Yellow	White	Black
Climate	Wind	Heat	Humid	Dry	Cold
Taste	Sour	Bitter	Sweet	Hot	Salty
Emotion	Anger	Joy	Sympathy	Grief	Fear
Sound	Shouting	Laughing	Singing	Weeping	Groaning
Sense	Sight	Taste	Touch	Smell	Hearing
Energy	Psychic	Directing	Primal	Physical	Creative
Virtue	Kindness	Humility	Trust	Integrity	Wisdom

Child is naive and innocent and must be cared for physically by the mother while the father teaches the child the natural laws. Eventually, the child will seek an opposition and, unknowingly, will try it out on the parents. If the child fails to oppose the parents, it never becomes independent. If the child's opposition is too great, its rebellion kills the parent. Life is interrupted.

Cycle of Domination: Cycle of the Father

In the Cycle of Domination, also referred to as the Cycle of Control or Destruction, the elements have the power to destroy or control one another. Elements in this cycle behave like father and compete to produce dynamic tension.

It is the father's responsibility to exemplify impeccable behavior and obedience to nature's immutable laws. Father's rules are strict and unbending. He teaches, instructs, directs, guides, disciplines, punishes, restrains, controls, and ultimately dominates the unruly, rebellious child, the methods increasing in strength until the lesson has been learned. The father assumes the power because he is older and more experienced than the child, and nature allows it if it has been earned through adherence to the law.

If the father fails in his role, the laws are not upheld and life disintegrates into chaos. If the father is too strict, if the punishment is too great, or if the father demands too much, the child is irreparably damaged and cannot continue the cycle.

Father Wood controls child Earth by absorbing and consuming it, just as plants take nourishment from the soil. Over a period of time, nutrients must be replenished to restore balance that might be diminished. When the violet breaks through the rock, father Wood has intruded on the domain of the child Earth. Father Metal cuts, chops, removes, inhibits, or reduces child Wood. Father Earth absorbs child water as mountains, rocks, and tiny grains of sand stop the enormous ocean. Father Fire melts the child Metal, transforming it into liquid, which can be shaped in any form. Father Water destroys the fire just as rain clouds darken the sun.

THREE CYCLES

The Cycle of Creation

Wood burns and creates or sustains Fire.
Fire burns and leaves ash, which creates Earth.
Earth applies pressure to particles, which creates Metal.
Metal attracts moisture, which creates Water.
Water feeds and nourishes Wood.

The Cycle of Reduction

Fire reduces Wood by burning it.
Wood reduces Water by absorbing it.
Water reduces Metal by dissolving it.
Metal reduces Earth by condensing it.
Earth reduces Fire by smothering it.

The Cycle of Control/Domination

Wood consumes Earth.
Earth stops Water.
Water puts out Fire.
Fire melts Metal.
Metal, when shaped into an ax or saw, chops down Wood.

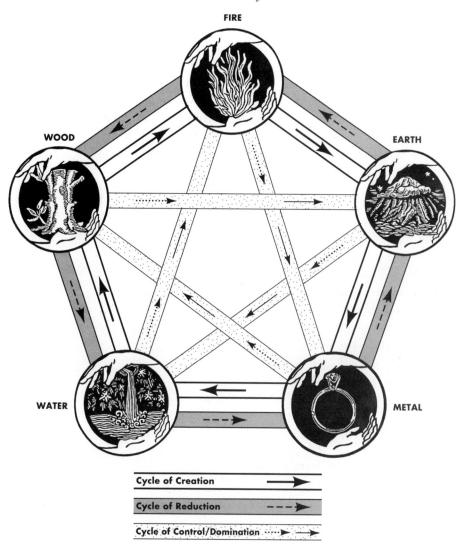

FIRE

WOOD

EARTH

WATER

METAL

Cycle of Creation

Cycle of Reduction

Cycle of Control/Domination

Beinfield, Harriet, and Efrem Korngold. *Between Heaven and Earth*. New York: Ballantine Books, 1991.

Blofield, P. P. *I Ching*. New York: E. P. Dutton, 1963.

Caruso, Paul. *Chinese Astrology*. London: Open Court, 1974.

Chang, Stephen T. *The Integral Management of Tao*. San Francisco: Tao Publishing, 1988.

Chu, W. K., and W. A. Sherril. *The Astrology of the I Ching*. New York: Samuel Weiser, 1976.

Cleary, Thomas. *I Ching Mandalas*. Boston: Shambhala, 1989.

Cozzi, Steven. *Planets in Locality*. St. Paul, Minn.: Llewellyn Publications, 1988.

Eberhard, Woilfram. *Dictionary of Chinese Symbols*. New York: Routledge, 1986.

Eitel, Ernest. *Feng Shui*. Hong Kong, 1983.

Fields, Rich. *Chop Wood, Carry Water*. Los Angeles; Jeremy Tarcher, 1984.

Furlong, Monica. *Zen Effects*. Boston: Houghton Mifflin, 1986.

Gallagher, Winifred. *The Power of Place*. New York: Poseidon Press, 1993.

Graves, Tom. *The Diviner's Handbook*. Rochester, Vt.: Inner Traditions, 1986.

Groves, Derham, *Feng Shui and Western Building Ceremonies*. Singapore: Graham Brash, 1991.

Jayne, Charles. *Introduction to Locality Astrology*. New York: Charles Jayne, 1970.

Jenner, W. J. F., trans. *Journey to the West*. Beijing: Foreign Languages Press, 1988.

Kaptchuk, Ted J. *The Web That Has No Weaver*. New York: Congdon and Weed, 1983.

Lau, Theodora. *The Handbook of Chinese Horoscopes*. New York: HarperCollins, 1979.

Lawson, Joyce, and Denise Lawson-Wood. *The Five Elements of Acupuncture and Chinese Massage*. Devon, England: Health Science Press, 1973.

Legge, James, trans. *The Four Books: The Great Learning; The Doctrine of the Mean; Confucian Dialects; The Works of Mencius*. Culture Book Company.

Lip, Evelyn. *Chinese Geomancy*. Singapore: Times Books, 1979.

———. *Chinese Numbers*. Union City, Calif.: Heian Publishers, 1992.

———. *Feng Shui in the Home*. Union City, Calif.: Heian Publishers, 1991.

———. *Feng Shui for Business*. Union City, Calif.: Heian Publishers, 1991.

Mann, A. T. *Sacred Architecture*. Element Books, 1993.

Ni, Hua Ching. *The Unchanging Truth and the Book of Changes*. Los Angeles: College of Tao, 1979.

O'Brien, Joanne, and Kwok Man Ho. *The Elements of Feng Shui*. London: Element Books, 1991

Pennick, Nigel. *The Ancient Science of Geomancy*. London: CRCS Publications, 1979.

Rabten, Geshe, and Geshe Dhargyey. *Advice from a Spiritual Friend*. London: Wisdom Publications, 1984.

Rossbach, Sarah. *Feng Shui*. New York: Dutton, 1983.

Schonberger, Martin. *The I Ching and the Genetic Code*. New York: ASI, 1979.

Senzaki, Nyogen, trans. *The Iron Flute*. Tokyo: Charles Tuttle, 1961.

Skinner, Stephen. *The Living Manual of Feng Shui*. London: Routledge & Kegan Paul, 1984.

———. *The Oracle of Geomancy*. San Leandro, Calif.: Prism Press, 1977.

Taylor, Norman. *Taylor's Encyclopedia of Gardening*. New York: Chanticleer Press, 1961.

Walters, Derek. *The Chinese Art of Designing a Harmonious Environment*. New York: Simon & Schuster, 1988.

———. *Feng Shui Handbook*. New York: HarperCollins, 1991.

———. *Ming Shu*. New York: Simon & Schuster, 1987.

Wilhelm, Hellmut. *Heaven, Earth and Man*. Seattle: University of Washington Press, 1978.

———. *Lectures on the I Ching*. Princeton: Princeton University Press, 1979.

Williams, C. A. S. *Chinese Symbolism and Art Motifs*. Boston: Charles E. Tuttle, 1974.

Wintle, Justin. *The Dragon's Almanac*. Singapore: Graham Brash, 1983.

red flowers, *xiii*
red phoenix
 as one of the four mythical animals, 141
 as symbol corresponding to Fire, 10
reduction, cycle of, 180–81, 182
reflective glass, special considerations concerning, 59–60
regions (assessing feng shui of), 43–49
 dominant features, 45–49, 45, 49
 Earth landscapes, 44–45
 Fire landscapes, 44
 Metal landscapes, 45
 special considerations, 51–60
 Water landscapes, 45
 Wood landscapes, 44
reinforced (ferro-) concrete as material corresponding to Metal, 16
reliability as virtue corresponding to Earth, 13
reversal as quality corresponding to Metal, 16
righteousness as virtue corresponding to Metal, 16
rings (placement of)
 for creativity, 14
 for love, 14
 for personal power, 14
 for scholarly success, 14
 for stability, 14
rivers as dominant features, 48–49
roof, 111–13
roofline, 82
rounded shapes corresponding to Metal, 16

sand as material corresponding to Earth, 13
Saturn as planet corresponding to Earth, 13
scholarly success, placement of rings for, 14
School of the Compass, *xv*
schools, special considerations concerning, 59
screen savers with fish, feng shui of, 140
seasons
 corresponding to Earth, 13
 corresponding to Fire, 10
 corresponding to Metal, 16
 corresponding to Water, 18
 corresponding to Wood, 6
semicircles as shapes corresponding to Metal, 16
sha (negative *chi*), 34–35
 beams, 36–37
 secret arrows, 35–36, 82–83, 83, 92, 94
shapes and types
 corresponding to Earth, 11, 12, 13

 corresponding to Fire, 7–8, 8, 9, 10
 corresponding to Metal, 15, 16
 corresponding to Water, 17, 19, 19
 corresponding to Wood, 5, 6, 7, 7
 mountains, 46–47, 46
 used to imitate nature, 3–4
shiny fabric as material corresponding to Fire, 10
signs
 direction facing, 155
 drawing attention, 154–55, 154
silver as color corresponding to Metal, 16
skyscrapers as dominant features, 45–48, 46
sloping roofs as shapes corresponding to Fire, 10
social activity as virtue corresponding to Water, 18
socialization as quality corresponding to Water, 18
South
 as direction corresponding to Fire, 10
 direction you approach home, 62
spas as interior corresponding to Water, 19
spirit life as quality corresponding to Fire, 10
splits in the road, 64, 64
spring
 and the element Wood, 5–8
 as season corresponding to Wood, 6
stability, placement of rings for, 14
staircases, special considerations concerning, 59
stairs, 119–20
 broken or too steep, 119–20
 dark and narrow, 120
 double, 120
 ending at front door, 120
 floating (space between risers), 120
 spiral, 120
steel as material corresponding to Metal, 16
storage areas as interiors corresponding to Earth, 13
stores. *See* workplace
stoves and Fire, 10
streets (feng shui of), 61–67
 condition of, 62–63
 direction of your approach, 62
 final approach street, 62–63
 name, 61
streets (problem)
 culs-de-sac and dead-ends, 65–66, 66
 in disrepair, 63
 as dominant feature, 49
 flat and featureless, 63
 located at the corner, 66–67, 67

 sharp turns and twists, 63
 splits or forks, 64, 64
 T-intersections, 64–65, 64
 too narrow, 63
 too straight, 65
study, 111
subways, special considerations concerning, 59
summer
 and the element Fire, 7–10
 season corresponding to Fire, 10
sunset as time corresponding to Metal, 16
swamps, special considerations concerning, 55
swimming pools as interior corresponding to Water, 19
symbols
 corresponding to Earth, 13
 corresponding to Fire, 10
 corresponding to Metal, 16
 corresponding to Water, 18
 corresponding to Wood, 6
 using, 141–42
sympathy as quality corresponding to Earth, 13

T-intersections, 64–65, 64
Tantric Buddhist Black Sect, *xv*
thinking (flexible) as virtue corresponding to Wood, 6
tiger. *See* white tiger
time
 corresponding to Earth, 13
 corresponding to Fire, 10
 corresponding to Metal, 16
 corresponding to Water, 18
 corresponding to Wood, 6
tile as material corresponding to Earth, 13
tin as material corresponding to Metal, 16
tortoise. *See* black tortoise
train stations, special considerations concerning, 59
travel
 and arrangement of furniture, 129
 and the influence of direction, 27–28
TV room, 110
types and shapes
 corresponding to Earth, 11, 12, 13
 corresponding to Fire, 7–8, 8, 9, 10
 corresponding to Metal, 15, 16
 corresponding to Water, 17, 19, 19
 corresponding to Wood, 5, 6, 7, 7
 used to imitate nature, 3–4

underpasses (highway) as shapes corresponding to Metal, 16